S0-AKZ-178

love, west hollywood

other titles of interest from alyson books

Love, Castro Street: Reflections of San Francisco
Edited by Katherine V. Forrest & Jim Van Buskirk

Love, Bourbon Street: Reflections of New Orleans
Edited by Greg Herren & Paul J. Willis

love, west hollywood

reflections of los angeles

edited by

Chris Freeman

and James J. Berg

New York

© 2008 by Chris Freeman and James J. Berg.
All rights reserved

Manufactured in the United States of America

Published by Alyson Books
245 West 17th Street, New York, NY 10011

Distribution in the United Kingdom by Turnaround Publisher Services Ltd.
Unit 3, Olympia Trading Estate, Coburg Road, Wood Green
London N22 6TZ England

First Edition: May 2008

08 09 10 11 12 13 14 15 16 17 a 10 9 8 7 6 5 4 3 2 1

ISBN: 1-59350-055-6
ISBN-13: 978-1-59350-055-9

Library of Congress Cataloging-in-Publication data are on file.

Cover design by Victor Mingovits

In Memory of Jim Weatherford, 1918–2007

table of contents

foreword

torie osborn

Los Angeles is a city of dreams, a city of immigrants from everywhere, including, in my case, San Francisco. Driving down Route 1, September 1978, in my battered, old, white Honda Civic, heading for Santa Monica's Civic Auditorium to road-manage Holly Near and Meg Christian on their sold-out California concert tour rallying lesbians against the Briggs initiative, I felt suddenly seduced. I think it was the sunlight. The ocean, the mountains, even zinging along the freeways, made my spirit soar—but most of all . . . it was that light. That glorious, glaring light that suffuses everything and seems to signal limitless possibility. A few years later, I arrived for good, escaping San Francisco's lesbian-feminist community that, for me, had become chokingly ingrown. When I needed a place to be free to reinvent myself, I headed here, along with so many others, gay and straight, over the decades.

As the following stories attest, L.A.'s key words are *imagination* and *diversity*. Both seem imprinted in the city's DNA. Remember that L.A. was founded in 1781 by a motley group of forty-four Native Americans, Latinos, and African Americans called the "Pobladores," who were inspired by the beauty of this place to found the "City of the Queen of the Angels." I have no doubt that some of those folks were two spirited because glbt people have been part of L.A.'s vibrancy forever. Over time, of course, this place has become a city of wild contrasts and multiplicities: of multicolored ethnic neighborhoods and infinite suburban sprawl; of constantly changing demographics and extremes of wealth and poverty; of dashed as well as deeply fulfilled dreams. L.A. often seems at once utopic and dystopic. Hollywood is home to unmatched glamour *and* those thousands of homeless gay and trans street kids. And you'll find all of it in this book.

Yes, throughout L.A.'s history, we have been there, but, until recently, we have flourished outside the limelight, illuminating New York and San Francisco for the broader world. Finally, our collective voice is shouting out, and it is nothing short of astonishing, as you will glimpse in the following stories. Who could not believe in the glory of a place that gave us two Latina lesbian semi-pro football teams with fabulous names: the Dandy Lions and the Pussy Willows?

One uniquely Los Angeles contribution to the broader, national LGBT community has been the amazing array of organizational "firsts." I attribute it to queer Angelenos's intense need to connect, to create community across the wide geography, to find permanence in this city of transience. Our collective inventiveness has generated organization-building unmatched in the nation. Los Angeles spawned the Mattachine Society of the homophile 1950s, and the Woman's Building of the feminist 1970s, and VIVA!, the great Latino/a performance art group of the 1980s, among a thousand examples. Other LGBT Los Angeles "firsts" became permanent fixtures on our national social-movement map, transforming social, spiritual, and political possibility forever: the One Institute, *The Advocate*, the Metropolitan Community Church, the L.A. Gay and Lesbian Center, to name a few. During the intense years of AIDS activism, L.A.—not San Francisco—featured the largest ever civil disobedience action in California history when, in October 1989, eighty-eight of us were arrested with ACT UP for blocking the Westwood Federal Building demanding AIDS drugs. In the pages that follow you'll meet some of the characters who populated this extraordinary work of catapulting LGBT community-building to an unimagined scale—and lots more.

Gay L.A.'s startlingly diverse and imaginative narrative is just beginning to be told. This book is an important contribution. You'll be transfixed by the range of people you'll meet and by their experiences in this City of Angels. I don't think it's a coincidence that LGBT L.A. is at last proclaiming its legacy just as Los Angeles in general is experiencing a renaissance, a surge of energetic innovation and national acclaim in every field of the arts and culture, in politics, and in social reform. Some of us even say that L.A. is to this new century what New York City was to the last century: a city of immigrants, a city of dreams serving as a vibrant laboratory for the nation on racial and economic justice and finding common purpose in a fragmented, globalized world. America is working out her future in Los Angeles, and the LGBT community here, thriving after the agony of AIDS like a flower after winter, is a huge part of that. You'll see why as you read on.

introduction

EVERYONE TALKS ABOUT THE TRAFFIC—how they hate driving in L.A. But if you live here, you learn the secrets of driving, of parking, of idling. You know you can drive up to Mulholland on a full-moon night, park on the side of the road, and sneak into the scenic overlooks (closed after sunset, as the posted signs warn you). If you don't overstay your welcome, or meet the indigenous coyotes or rattlesnakes, you'll get a glimpse of the most expansive, beautiful city in the world. If you don't believe us, you haven't done it.

The main title of this book is perhaps a bit misleading. "West Hollywood" is shorthand. Los Angeles is a conglomeration of villages that have grown up, grown together and apart. These villages are now either neighborhoods or independent cities we know as West Hollywood, Santa Monica, Koreatown, the Valley, Silver Lake, Los Feliz, Beverly Hills, Boyle Heights, Brentwood.

The through-line in *Love, West Hollywood* is revealed in its subtitle, "Reflections of Los Angeles." We think of this book as a mosaic of our city and its people. One of the inevitable complications of "gay Los Angeles" is how to have community in such an expansive place and with such a range of people and identities. Many of the essays collected here acknowledge and address the tensions between and among these various identities and geographies.

We wouldn't pretend to tell the whole story, in three hundred pages or three thousand. But we are confident that what we've assembled reflects the multifaceted reality of L.A. in the last seventy-five or so years.

Gay Los Angeles is finally beginning to share its secrets. We've learned the Hollywood stories from William Mann and David Ehrenstein. Recently, an exceptionally complete history emerged in the award-winning *Gay L.A.* by Lillian Faderman and contributor Stuart Timmons. We intend this volume to tell some of the personal stories of GLBTQ Los Angeles. Our thought going into this project was that anything worth a mention in *Gay L.A.* was worth telling here.

By turns gritty and glamorous, personal and historical, *Love, West Hollywood* need not be read from beginning to end. We trust you to make your own way through this city's tales: eighty-four-year-old Malcolm Boyd describes swimming naked at Pickfair; fifteen-year-old Eva S. tells about a job offer she got from a pimp on her walk home from Hollywood High. In between, we have stories of movies made, hearts broken, friends and lovers buried, political fights won or lost, lesbian football injuries, bathhouses, bar raids, pride parades, and wildfires.

Reading some of these stories, you may wonder how they connect, what makes them important or interesting, what makes them Los Angeles, or West Hollywood, stories. What unites them may only be the fact that they take place in a part of L.A., whether that part is Boystown or the barrio in East L.A. or in some remote corner of an author's past. The mortar of the L.A. mosaic is its famous boulevards and avenues—Santa Monica, Sunset, Hollywood, Ventura, Venice, Highland, Hyperion.

•

EACH OF US has worked and lived, short- and long-term, in Los Angeles for the past ten years. Our writing partnership began with a trip to L.A. in 1998, researching a book on Christopher Isherwood. That visit led us, through contributor Dan Luckenbill, to our shared gay grandfather, the late Jim Weatherford. In many ways, Jim's life typifies the gay immigrant's story in Southern California. Raised in West Virginia, Jim spent World War II in Aruba (not exactly Normandy). He fell in love with the warmth and the beaches, which led him here after the war. Jim's first long-term partner was English character actor Rex Evans, a fixture in George Cukor films. Jim and Rex lived together on the periphery of the film industry for over twenty years. They owned James Rex, a custom shirt shop on Sunset near Doheny, and the Rex Evans Gallery, on La Cienega, where the artist Don Bachardy, longtime companion of Isherwood, had one of his earliest shows. Jim's tales of old Hollywood could fill volumes, and, in fact, Jim served as a source for *Gay L.A.* His warmth and hospitality welcomed us to his home on Genesee above Sunset every time we came to town. We both now live and work in Southern California, at least in part because of witnessing the beautiful life Jim made for himself here, so it is to Jim Weatherford's memory that we dedicate this book.

•

ENJOY THE STORIES; relish them. Relive the past, get a little nostalgic, and get a glimpse of the present as you may not have seen it before. Meet Lucille Ball and Mary Pickford; get to know some men from the WH2O swim club and some women from the Dandy Lions football squad. Visit 8709, the most notorious bathhouse in L.A. (if you're hot enough to get in, and, if you're not white, have three picture ID's handy). Walk the beach (and slip under the pier when no one's looking). Beware of that alley. Wear curlers to the Brown Derby. Have a martini at The Abbey (if you can find parking). See a naked performance artist at Highways (don't sit in the front row). Find out about one of California's first openly gay judges.

We hope you learn as much as we did along the way. If you don't find your L.A. story here, get busy writing. Part of the point of a book like this is to get these stories told, and you can always post them on MySpace. If they aren't written down, they won't survive. They won't become part of history, part of the mosaic of our queer lives.

Love, Chris & Jim
West Hollywood, December 2007

remembering forgotten los angeles

daniel hurewitz

SEVERAL YEARS AGO, a friend e-mailed me to ask if I could help out a documentary filmmaker who was traveling to major American cities—New York, Los Angeles, San Francisco, Chicago—to explore their gay history: could I help get him started in L.A.? At the time I was living in Mid-Wilshire, going to graduate school, and researching some of the city's early gay history. Sure, I said, and shot off an e-mail to the filmmaker. But by the time I'd sent back my "Yes," L.A. had been dropped from the project: it wasn't necessary, they said.

Last year I published *Bohemian Los Angeles*, a book exploring how and why Los Angeles gave birth to the national gay rights movement in the 1950s. Regularly, when I mention the book in casual conversation, people look at me with funny expressions—

some mix of concern and doubt. "In L.A.?" they ask. "Gay politics started in L.A.? Don't you mean New York or San Francisco?"

It's always an odd moment for me. I've come to accept people's misperceptions about what's important in the gay past and their overlooking L.A. But the centrality of Los Angeles's gay history to the country as a whole is hard to overstate: both of the nation's first long-lasting gay rights organizations—the Mattachine Society and ONE—were founded here in the 1950s; the first lesbian periodical was produced here in the 1940s; there were sizable protests against police harassment here in the mid-1960s, well before Stonewall; and the nation's first gay church (1968), first gay community center (1971), first gay temple (1972), and first gay political action committee (1977) were all founded here as well. Los Angeles has been a vital place for the development of a national gay consciousness, community, and civil rights movement. And yet, ask anyone about where gay history occurred, and they'll mumble something to you about Greenwich Village or the Castro.

Even with the exciting historical work done by scholars like Lillian Faderman, Stuart Timmons, and William Mann, it is a battle to convince people that Los Angeles has a history that matters for gay men and lesbians. As the late Yolanda Retter, a lesbian activist, archivist, and scholar, said to me several years ago, "San Francisco and New York *appear* to be more historically visible." In fact, Los Angeles is a historical treasure trove of the gay past.

•

THE TALES OF EARLY gay and lesbian Los Angeles are riveting. While court records make clear that at least since the early 1900s local men had been committing the "infamous crime against nature," by the 1920s, Harry Hay and his high school friends swapped knowing comments about Pershing Square. There among the crisscrossing paths, dense foliage, and underground bathrooms, men dropped propositions and inhibitions in pursuit of sexual intimacy. During Prohibition, Angelenos with money and know-how found their way to speakeasies scattered across the city for some well-lubricated sociability. Hay told me about returning from Stanford during winter break, 1931, and being invited to a party at a Hollywood speakeasy called Jimmy's Backyard. "That was an enormous gathering. There must have been at least four hundred." The guests were done up in gowns and tuxedos, "and not only that, but they were dancing together"—the men with the men, the women with the women. Once liquor consumption was legal again, nightclubs like Club 808 on Figueroa offered not only drinks and dancing, but a fully staged drag revue along with beer and wine. In fact, Club 808 was so successful it had to move from a small bar to a full theater to accommodate its growing clientele.

Not all the stories are so delightful: local officials responded to this emerging social world with increasing hostility. The choreographer for Club 808 reported that when that club opened in the mid-1930s, the original permits mentioning the "female impersonators" were all readily granted. Only later in the thirties did the authorities begin to intrude and harass. One night the cops closed the place down, insisting that the front curtain wasn't fireproof, even though its tags made clear that it was. With growing frequency, plainclothes detectives arrived on Saturday nights, walking slowly down the aisles and eyeballing the customers. People became so scared of being arrested and having their private lives made public that eventually business died off. By 1940, cross-dressing performances were officially deemed illegal, and police, psychiatrists, and the military all began to crack down with ferocity on "the homosexual."

And yet, in spite of the crackdowns—or perhaps because of them—the elements of a gay and lesbian "community" began to take form. Lisa Ben (a pseudonym) moved to L.A. at the end of World War II. A group of women in her apartment building introduced her to the growing world of bars, beginning with the If Club on La Brea. "When we all walked in there, someone was bringing a birthday cake to one of the booths. There were some girls sitting there, and they were all singing 'Happy Birthday.' I looked around me, and tears came to my eyes—partly because of the cigarette smoke—and I thought, 'How wonderful that all these girls can be together.'"

•

THESE EARLY TALES of gay life are fascinating: they reveal the way that ideas about gay identity came into sharper focus in the early twentieth century and how a gay community started to form. To a degree, though, similar stories can be told about other cities. More striking and more significant is the central role that Los Angeles played in the last sixty years, launching and sustaining a national gay rights movement.

In 1950, Harry Hay and a group of friends gathered on a Silver Lake hillside to initiate what would become the first wave of the political battle for gay equality. The idea behind the Mattachine Society was to start a series of discussion groups—hosted in people's dens and living rooms—to talk about homosexuality. Officially, the discussions were a chance to analyze Alfred Kinsey's 1948 report on male sexuality—the one that said one in three men had had homosexual encounters. Unofficially, the discussions focused on developing a consciousness of what it meant to be gay: what were the shared features of that identity and what kind of community could be built around that? The discussion groups spread across the city—and around the country—and soon evolved into dialogues with religious, medical, and legal experts about the oppression of homosexuals in American society. When one of the founders was arrested for "lewd" conduct, Mattachine funded one of the first successful efforts to combat police entrapment. By the mid-1960s, Mattachine members joined other so-called "homophile" activists in picketing the White House and Pentagon. While the work of homophiles was overshadowed in later years by the more visible tactics of "gay liberation" activists, Mattachine served as the nation's first gay rights organization, and through it and the other organizations it inspired, it laid the foundation for a national gay political community.

When younger activists in the 1970s built on that foundation to form the more confrontational gay liberation groups, their impetus (according to gay mythology) is said to have come from New York bar patrons' aggressive resistance to police efforts to close the Stonewall Inn in June 1969. In truth, Angelenos had already embraced those tactics. On New Year's Eve, 1967, the L.A. police led violent raids of two Silver Lake bars: the Black Cat and New Faces. Both bars were vandalized and customers assaulted: one man's spleen was ruptured and his skull fractured. In reaction, picketers took to the streets with signs like BLUE FASCISTS MUST GO! and POLICE LAWLESSNESS MUST BE STOPPED! And a legal challenge that went as high as the Supreme Court was launched to dispute the constitutionality of police raids.

Angelenos fought back with an unprecedented militancy. The Black Cat and New Faces protests were followed by a march down Hollywood Boulevard. Activists invaded psychology conferences to discuss homosexuals, and picketers and boycotts challenged businesses that fired gay employees or refused gay advertising. Perhaps most famously, Morris Kight helped coordinate an ongoing battle with Barney's Beanery. Since at least the 1950s, the West Hollywood dive had a misspelled sign demanding FAGOTS STAY OUT. Kight and others continually pushed and picketed until the sign was finally taken down.

•

THESE ARE TALES of important, path-breaking political action. They are not, though, the first stories in the national pantheon of gay history and myth. For some reason, even Angelenos tend to look east or north to where they imagine gay political history occurred. In fact, as Eric Rofes, director of the Gay and Lesbian Center from 1985 to 1988, pointed out to me years ago, "The gay pride celebration in L.A. is called 'Christopher Street West.' To me, this says it all." Christopher Street is the New York street where the Stonewall Inn stands. Angelenos have treated their own gay community celebration as an echo of the somehow more significant event across the country even though L.A. saw gay liberation actions well before Stonewall.

Several years ago, I asked community leaders why the history of gay and lesbian Los Angeles has slipped out of our shared memory. Some of them suggested that we suffer from East Coast bias. To Torie Osborn, the East Coast has a tradition "of taking itself seriously. Certainly there is an illusion that politics pretty much happened on the East Coast." Los Angeles is imagined as a place whose only serious developments came out of the entertainment world.

That illusion is sustained, activist Jeanne Cordova claimed, "because most of the brainy historical writerly types are in New York. They're the ones who are writing the gay history books." That lack of scholarship has, thank goodness, begun to change. A handful of exciting books about gay L.A. have recently appeared. But it may well be that there are further reasons that the historic centrality of Los Angeles has been so steadily overlooked.

Los Angeles gay activism over the last several decades has principally been about organizations, not street actions and public displays. Despite the gay liberation "zaps" of the late sixties and early seventies, in Los Angeles, where the people and the streets are much more geographically dispersed than in New York or San Francisco, the action has often been much less visible. While gay New Yorkers took to the streets again and again in the seventies, people in Los Angeles were more often working the phones or in offices coordinating meetings. Some of the most important achievements in Los Angeles were far less photogenic. The Gay and Lesbian Center was founded here in 1971: it was the first such in the nation, and it remains the richest and largest. Perhaps its greatest strength has been in addressing the health and social service needs of the community. None of that makes for dramatic copy or flashy headlines, but it has proven essential to the vitality of our city.

Los Angeles tends to lack street life, and so the post-sixties gay community increasingly opted to pursue their gay rights agenda within the framework of mainstream politics. That choice, while perhaps less glamorous than other political styles, proved tremendously successful. For instance, in 1978, when state senator John Briggs proposed an initiative to forbid gays from teaching in the public schools, the response from activists altered the profile of the activist community. Torie Osborn recalled that coming out publicly in the early 1970s was like jumping "into the counterculture. You were not connected to mainstream society." But the threat of Briggs struck a chord with more than the usual activists. In the movement, said Jeanne Cordova, "the atmosphere changed from being kind of radical and influenced by black civil rights and the left, to being very middle class. Now we were having luncheons at the Beverly Hilton to defeat Briggs." And by a margin of 58 percent—much larger than anticipated—they did.

The success against Briggs proved the willingness and capacity of gay men and women to function as a traditional political bloc. Many had the political courage to come out in the public record and an impressive number had the financial resources to make significant contributions. The campaign demonstrated that gays and lesbians possessed genuine political power.

That new style of gay politics was also linked to the emergence of the Metropolitan Elections Committee of Los Angeles (MECLA), the first-ever gay political action committee. Formed in 1977 largely under David Mixner's stewardship, MECLA represented a determination by these newly active middle-class gay men and lesbians "to play the game as everyone else played it." That decision to operate within the mainstream again proved powerful. Before MECLA, many politicians simply wouldn't accept contributions from openly gay contributors—Mixner had more than one check returned to him. It was rare to find openly gay people working on campaigns, let alone appointed to office. And it was equally rare for a political candidate or official to attend a gay event. After MECLA and the Briggs defeat, all of that changed as gays and lesbians were wooed by local politicians, and gay issues increasingly showed up on their agendas.

Perhaps the ultimate expression of the "mainstream power" cultivated by the Los Angeles gay community was the 1984 incorporation of the City of West Hollywood. Long a haven for gay recreation and residences, the area had never been annexed into Los Angeles proper and so had escaped the surveillance of the LAPD. By the early 1980s, local gay residents joined with seniors in the area to vote for independent incorporation and elected two gay men and a lesbian (who became mayor) to the new city council. According to Mixner, "West Hollywood was one of the first places in the country where we took a majority on the city council and then showed that we could not only organize well, but govern. West Hollywood has become a showcase for a well-run, extremely livable, exciting city."

•

ON THE ONE HAND, the incorporation of West Hollywood—like so much of L.A.'s gay political past—is unique and does not fit easily with the gay histories of New York or San Francisco. On the other hand, the birth of West Hollywood, like so many of these other events, marks a high-water mark for gay men and women across the country. We need to appreciate the dramatic significance of our local history and shout about it. And we need to recognize that if we neglect that history, we lose a powerful tool for understanding how the future might unfold.

Yolanda Retter insisted to me that, "People try to hide our history. They change it. They dump it. They certainly don't want it brought into the schools. In that context," she said, "tracing our history is a political act." Remembering our past functions as a form of resistance against a homophobic culture.

It is a potent form of resistance because it sharpens our perspective and strengthens our vision. The history of the gay and lesbian civil rights movement in Los Angeles offers clear lessons about campaign tactics, institution-building, and co-gender coalitions—all of which can guide how we pursue our goals in the future.

Certainly the contours of that future are far from definite. We live in a moment where politicians who promise principled, if incomplete, expansions of gay rights are met head on by powerful movements who oppose any such advances. It is a moment where only the blink of an eye separates the much-celebrated embrace of gay characters on TV from the continued violence of antigay hate crimes. It is a moment of uncertain potential.

What is clear in all that ambiguity, though, is that where we've come from and what we've fashioned in Los Angeles is unlike anything our community has done elsewhere in the country. And the lessons of this city may well be the crucial lessons for a national movement still struggling to achieve the kind of institutional power that has been achieved here locally. What is more, as Yolanda Retter reminded me, "If I were young and coming out and I heard about our past, I would take heart. I would know I wasn't alone. People were there before me and are pushing for me." And that push from the past may be just what we need.

power play:
lesbian lovers, artists,
feminists, witches
in the 1970s

terry wolverton

THERE ARE PROBABLY NOT many lesbians in Los Angeles who could boast of having eaten lunch at the original Brown Derby with their hair in curlers (or, to be precise, in Spoolies). In its heyday in the 1920s and 30s, this dining establishment—shaped like the chapeau for which it was named—was frequented by Hollywood's elite. They displayed their power in the gowns and furs they wore, the limousines that dropped them at the door, being seated at the best table, and admiring their photos in the tabloids the next day, having been spotted at the Brown Derby. By 1977, the place had lost some of its luster, as had Hollywood's elite who now wore ripped jeans and tie-dyed shirts, who might be found riding Harleys or partying with rock stars in Laurel Canyon. Still, the Brown Derby retained its reputation as a fine restaurant—a place one might dress up to go to—certainly not a venue in which one committed the big fashion "don't" of wearing hair curlers.

I grew up in Detroit, daughter of a gas station manager and a secretary. I had never pictured myself at a place like the Brown Derby. I'd moved to Los Angeles just a year earlier, drawn not by the lure of celebrity but by the feminist art movement, centered here at the Woman's Building, "a public center for women's culture." When my new girlfriend called one morning and suggested we go to lunch there, I said, "OK, but I have to wear my hair in Spoolies."

For me this excursion was yet another in a long list of "What I Did for Art." I was performing in a play at the time, and I had been cast in the role of the French author, Colette, known from her most famous photographs to have had a mop of curly hair. To achieve her look for the evening's performance, I had to spend the day torturing my own decidedly unwavy tresses into ringlets. This constituted another kind of fashion transgression—lesbian feminists in 1977 did not "do" their hair; lesbian feminists in 1977 claimed their power by renouncing all trappings of traditional female beautification.

Somehow, committing this sin of coiffure under the cover of "Art" elevated the act. I wasn't just some white trash chick from the Midwest who didn't know any better, or some retrograde femme dressing up for her butch. One kind of power "Art" has claimed for itself in the Western world is the prerogative to hold itself outside ordinary social customs and conventions.

There was a certain orthodoxy to lesbian feminism of the late 1970s. A lesbian was expected to cast off the accoutrements of femininity—hairspray and eye makeup, bras and pantyhose and skirts among them—but should she appear too masculine, she might be accused of mimicking the values of our sworn enemy: the Patriarchy. She also wasn't supposed to have too much money; downward mobility was seen as the appropriate stance from which to express solidarity with the oppressed. Nor should she be too ambitious to glean the rewards of the corrupt capitalist system— a good job, a new car. Needless to say, the lesbian feminist community had an uneasy relationship to "Art." With its rule-bending proclivities, its claim of exceptionalism, "Art" and those who practiced it were viewed as slightly suspect. I'd once had a lover in the Midwest tell me, "When the revolution comes, you'll only be fit to entertain the troops." That culture could be a powerful tool of this revolution was not apparent to all.

Although it was easy to feel frustrated by such attitudes then, and even easier to parody them now, they grew out of a sincere effort on the part of "wimmin-loving wimmin" to claim the power of self-definition, to construct authentic identities independent of the heterosexual view of women as passive receptacles or the homophobic distortion of lesbians as depraved sinners. There was a determination to dismantle the society that had confined us too long, and we understood that we had to begin with how we saw ourselves.

Life in those days was full of contradictions between our political ideals and the lives we actually lived.

•

THE WOMAN'S BUILDING was a place where women studied, created, and exhibited Art; it also hosted an ambitious array of events—from lectures to film screenings to dances—that allowed the women's community to gather. I'd come there from the Midwest, hungry for a feminist context in which "Art" was celebrated. I was cheered to find that that community wholly encouraged bending the rules when it came to expressions of personal style. At a performance-art "fashion show" held at the Woman's Building that fall, one woman wore a Suzy Wong dress with a plastic parrot glued to her shoulder; another ported top hat and tails; and a third wore her pajamas and a flannel bathrobe. I strolled the catwalk in a vintage 1940s evening gown. It was all part of the "Art."

In preparing to play the part of Collette, I thought it was a stroke of luck that I had saved, inexplicably and through numerous moves, a lunch sack full of the spongy Spoolies, on which my grandmother had set her own hair and mine when I was a child in the late 1950s. These were pliable pink plastic rollers, shaped like a three-dimensional Y. You wound a lock of hair around the skinny end, then folded the top over to cover the whole curl as with a cap, holding the hair in place without leaving a seam, as clips or hairpins would do.

Far from being embarrassed, I found it perversely satisfying to walk with my girlfriend into a high-class restaurant—me, a working-class lesbian with radical politics, whose status was only somewhat skewed by my participation in "Art"—with my hair in Spoolies. My girlfriend, whom I adored, was from a prominent northern California family from whom she had inherited wealth. She'd gone to prep schools and cotillions, and it was she who'd suggested the Brown Derby in the first place. She was slightly scandalized by my appearance at lunch, and at the same time seemed to be slightly awed by my audacious lack of concern about it.

Many feminists of the 1970s—in revolt against a lifelong pressure to be "good girls"—placed a high value on breaking the rules. "Bad girls" had power. We believed that to be transgressive—to flout convention, not be nice, not worry for once about making others comfortable—was to be revolutionary; this is how such individual and symbolic gestures as not wearing a bra or wearing rollers in a public place could be considered radical. Such strategies derived from a core principle of the feminism of that time—*the personal is political.* I considered my appearance at the Derby with my head a sculpture of sponge pink to be a performative act, an artful way to *épater le bourgeois*—both the restaurant patrons and my girlfriend.

Given the times, class couldn't help but be an issue between my girlfriend and me. Had we not both been active at the Woman's Building, it's doubtful that we ever would have met. Although I was thrilled to be with her, we also engaged in subtle and not-so-subtle power plays. Some of her power derived from money and privilege, which had allowed her access to experiences that I didn't even know existed. Some of my power came from the fact that having money was slightly scandalous in our sector of the women's movement, and, I'm not proud to say, from the fact that she felt bad about herself for having it. This, despite the fact that I benefited from her resources; she did, after all, pay for lunch.

•

THE PRODUCTION IN WHICH I portrayed Colette was a world premiere, *The Rise of the Fates* by Zsuzsanna Budapest. Z., as she was known to her many acolytes, had escaped Hungary in 1956 and immigrated to the United States. She studied theater at Second City in Chicago before moving to Los Angeles to become active in the women's movement. It was here that Z. founded the first feminist coven, the Susan B. Anthony Coven #1. In 1975, Z. had been arrested after reading the tarot cards of an undercover cop, who busted her because Los Angeles had a law against fortune-telling, and this had increased her celebrity in the women's community.

To some feminists of this era, witchcraft became an arena for exploring women's power. Theorists forged links to the witch burnings in Europe from 1400s to the 1800s, positing the Witch as the ultimate symbol of threat to patriarchal authority. Many feminists replaced obeisance to an oppressive God the Father with celebration of the Goddess, a deity in their own likeness. Feminist witches celebrated the cycles of the earth, the solstices, equinoxes, and lunar phases. Some, but not all, practiced the art of casting spells as a way of cultivating power.

My girlfriend had been raised to believe in Freud. Though she had a poetic soul and a philosophical mind, she was not a seeker of alternate realities. While she loved the natural world, especially the forest landscape of northern California, she was not the kind of woman to be found dancing in a circle under the full moon.

She didn't believe that power was necessarily more benevolent in the hands of women than when wielded by men. Besides, she had a certain amount of power within the dominant culture—economic freedom and family status; she had no need to resort to burning candles or scrawling her wishes in dove's-blood ink. It's possible she would have privately disdained Z. Budapest and her followers, but these were the first few months of our relationship, and she claimed to find my involvement in this theater project both charming and crackpot.

•

THE RISE OF THE FATES celebrated the triple Goddess, the Three Fates—Alecto, Tisiphone, and Magera, who govern the cycles of birth, life, and death. In the play, these Goddesses engage in the Battle of Thought Forms with parodic representations of male religions—Judeo-Christianity, Hinduism, and Islam—and ultimately prevail. A number of heroic foremothers—Susan B. Anthony, Amelia Earhart, Emmaline Pankhurst, Elizabeth Cady Stanton, and of course, Colette—represent aspects of female power, such as courage, intelligence, and, in the case of Colette, the power of seduction. Rounding out the cast was the Nymph, who represents a dawning new age of post-Patriarchy, and the Virgin-in-Chains, the woman brainwashed by male oppression. As Colette, it was my job to seduce the Virgin-in-Chains, to present her with the option of freedom of choice.

Freedom—a popular word in the 1960s and seventies. Popular

and ambiguous: Freedom from . . . ? Freedom to . . . ? A whole generation romanticized the word, but failed to grapple with its responsibilities.

Another aspect of the power play between my girlfriend and me was the issue of nonmonogamy. Many lesbian feminists, rebelling against the property relations within heterosexual marriage, considered monogamy to be a patriarchal value. In practice, this gave license to a lot of acting out; women might intellectually embrace the premise of free love, but not all of us were prepared emotionally to watch our lovers leave to spend the night with someone else.

I'd told my girlfriend at the beginning that I wasn't monogamous. That this was a masquerade for my own malnourished ego and terror of intimacy was something of which I wouldn't be conscious for another decade. My girlfriend, on the other hand, was still deeply in love with her former lover, who'd moved away to marry a man. They continued to have courtship throughout our relationship. Somehow we believed our respective positions could constitute a viable basis for love and romance between us while allowing us both "freedom." Now that seems like magical thinking.

·

WITHIN THE SPECTRUM of feminisms that were espoused in the 1970s, there were disagreements about power: how much to have, how much to want, how to go about attaining it, and for what it might be used. Some women aspired to what men—or at least straight, white, upper-class men—already seemed to possess: financial means, status, opportunities in proportion with one's ambitions, and women to do our bidding. Other women wanted to dismantle this system of power altogether, to constitute a different kind of society. Even these women couldn't agree on whether the goal was a system of total equality (e.g., no one had more power than anyone else) or whether some structures or hierarchies made sense. Still others insisted there were forms of power that were uniquely female—forms such as healing, psychic ability, witchcraft.

At our first rehearsal, Z. told us she considered her play to also be a spell, an act of witchcraft, one that would have a positive impact on those who performed it, those in the audience, and indeed on the entire planet. Our roles, she purred in her rich accent, were our destinies. Had I been a little older—I was twenty-three—I might have questioned the choice of "goddess of seduction" as my destiny; looking back, I find it curious that Z. chose to focus on this aspect of Colette's life rather than her artistic accomplishments, which is the spell I truly wanted.

My upbringing had been a confusing assortment of worship, abuse, and neglect that left me in no way prepared to cope with sexual power. But this didn't stop me from exhibiting sexuality, dangerous to myself and others as a loaded gun in the hands of someone who never learned to shoot. I hadn't come to lesbianism with the sense of being attractive. As a child, I was always told what a great beauty my mother was, and how I must take after my father's side of the family. I was big, I was smart, and I was brooding—three strikes against prettiness; I believed this mode of female power eluded me. Even after I came out, women seemed wary of me.

But suddenly, this seemed to be changing. I'd managed to attract my girlfriend. And the spell of playing Colette seemed to cause others to take notice as well. There was the saxophone player in the band, a motorcycle-riding butch who wore a leather aviator cap over her short Afro. On opening night I went home with her on the back of her bike. There was a flight attendant with a sweet smile who came to the play one night and ended up in my bed afterward. There was a friend I'd met back East who came to visit and stayed. As time progressed, there was a songwriter, and a filmmaker, and an artist. My ego was high on flirtation and seduction. It felt like power.

But then there was my girlfriend, whom I considered the most magnificent blessing in my life. Incredibly, it somehow eluded me that my affairs would undermine the solidity of our bond. She practiced the power of denial as long as she could. We did persist for six years, even lived together for some of them. Even as we wove the mythology of our relationship—the songs, the rituals, the secret codes—it was unraveling.

•

WHAT IS A SPELL? Z. Budapest used to describe it as "thought form become material." It's projecting an intention so that it will manifest. With no disrespect to Christians intended, I would say it's not so different in concept from offering a prayer for something to occur. If one lacks the power or resources to make things happen on the material plane, why not try to exert one's influence in the supernatural realm?

A couple of years after the play, I went to have a consultation with Z. I asked her advice about casting a spell, so my girlfriend would fall in love with me again. Z. could have just taken my money, sold me a candle, some purple incense, given me a few words to say. Instead, she looked deep into my eyes and said, "When you cast a spell, you bind yourself. You can't make someone else feel or do something; you can only commit yourself wholly to that intention. Is that what you want to do?" She held my gaze and would not let me look away.

I thought about my girlfriend—her talent, her intelligence, her humor, her love of nature, all the things I treasured about her. I thought about the world of privilege she came from that I would never know. I thought about the thick letters from her former lover that still arrived at the house where we lived together. What we each wanted, what we could not find in each other, was a genuine love, driven not by power plays and ideology but by compassion, surrender, devotion. I lowered my eyes from Z.'s and sadly shook my head.

•

AS LESBIAN FEMINISTS, we spelled for and bound ourselves to the intention of power for women. Not (for most of us) the power of currency or weaponry or hierarchy or intimidation, but the power that comes from being authentically ourselves. We couldn't begin to know how deep a commitment this would entail, how ill prepared most of us were to live the change we so desperately invoked. And while this spell didn't revolutionize the world in the way we imagined, the transformations that resulted were no less profound.

The original Brown Derby closed its doors in 1980. The Los Angeles Conservancy fought to preserve the derby-shaped façade. Hollywood celebrities are currently famous for their distinctly unglamorous stints in rehab, their willingness to display the power of self-destruction.

In 1984, the City of Los Angeles finally struck down its law against fortune-telling. The same year my girlfriend and I finally parted ways.

The Woman's Building closed its doors in 1991. Now women artists compete in the same arenas as men. The notion of a "women's culture" has largely faded from consciousness.

Now lesbians are on television, in bras and hairspray, lipstick and eye makeup. Selling yogurt and American Express and lifestyle.

It's been thirty years since I blew kisses at my then-girlfriend across the table at the Brown Derby, thirty years since I stepped onto the stage at the Woman's Building, purring in a bad French accent and tossing my Spoolies-rendered curls. I was spelling seduction, ego gratification, transgression, freedom. It would take me years to learn that none of these can approach the power or reward of genuine love.

tuesdays with lucy

brad taylor negron

LUCILLE BALL was my acting teacher every Tuesday night at 7:00 for eight weeks in the fall of 1977. She taught me that I'd better know my lines, be prepared, and show up early. Lucy taught us how to play drunk: "Say every word slowly and clearly. Drunks don't want people to think they are slurring." And: "Know your props! Everything you've seen me do on *I Love Lucy* was practiced and rehearsed for days!" Her tone was serious.

When I'm channel surfing and see America's favorite redhead, she connects me to a world more black than white. I was a witness to her wounds. Lucille Ball altered me.

It was the year of *Saturday Night Fever*, before AIDS and cell phones, when there were only thirteen channels on TV and afternoons were meant for hitchhiking and taking naps. Hollywood Boulevard was an old-fashioned street then. Japanese gift shops were tucked between musty bookstores; old ladies with Andrews

Sisters' hairdos walked down the street in ancient silk dresses; male hustlers clogged the ice cream store at the corner of Las Palmas Avenue, where rail-thin girls in paper hats sold peppermint candy ice cream in big, sweet waffle cones.

I had a job at the Sherwood Oaks Experiential Film School on the corner of Hollywood Boulevard and Ivar, upstairs from a Thom McAn's that sold only platform shoes. Working at Sherwood Oaks was my first job after high school. I was paid to run errands for the school's director, Gary Shusett, and to help him track down celebrities to come and lecture for a nominal fee. The school's yellow linoleum floors were sprinkled with the discreet remains of well-smoked joints. A signed poster of *Taxi Driver* was taped to the wall just above two well-worn Danish Modern sofas on which student groupies and visiting professors often made love in the wee hours.

One of my daily tasks was to read *Celebrity Service* and let Gary know who was in town. "Louis Malle is at the Beverly Wilshire," I would tell him, not looking up from the paper. Gary would then call the Beverly Wilshire, ask for Louis Malle, get connected to Louis Malle, and launch into a pitch-plea for Louis to "come down to our tattered, makeshift campus on Hollywood Boulevard and share your insights into the craft with the next generation of artists." Louis Malle came.

These days, it is hard to believe that people (much less celebrities) would show up and share of themselves practically for free. But, we are talking about the late seventies, a rare time when Hollywood's excesses were eclipsed by hippie décor; a time when Sunset Boulevard was considered a shortcut, and the worst thing you could ever do to someone was "bum them out" or bring in "bad vibes."

Back then, these successful people came to our school seeking to impress by a lack of display, an absence of possession—except for Warren Beatty's crocodile cowboy boots and turquoise.

One stiflingly hot afternoon, Leslie, a pleasantly overweight girl who also worked at the school, ran into our cluttered office shouting, "Lucille Ball just walked into the optometrist's on Ivar!"

"What?" Gary stood up and then disappeared out the door. Leslie followed, leaving me alone to read the *Hollywood Reporter* in peace.

Gary reappeared after a few minutes. He was smiling and confident, looking like the cat that swallowed the canary. "Lucy is going to teach a course here," he stated.

"He's right. I was there," Leslie said. "Lucy said she would do eight Tuesdays." My mind reeled. Lucy Ricardo was going to teach here! At this school! I asked Leslie if Lucy was nice. "Well, I don't know if nice is the way to put it . . . She seems stern," Leslie said.

A few months later, Lucy's sold-out class began. Over a hundred eager wannabes who had paid their one hundred twenty-five dollars were packed into the studio half an hour before Lucy was scheduled to arrive. I could barely contain my excitement.

Gary was matter of fact as he handed me a list of items to pick up and place in her greenroom. Lucy had requested a pack of Pall Mall nonfiltered cigarettes, a bag of chocolate Pogen cookies, and a bottle of scotch.

"I can't get alcohol, Gary. I'm not twenty-one."

"Oh. I'll get that and you get the rest." With urgency, I ran the two blocks to and from the Hollywood Ranch Market. Gary handed me a bottle of Chivas discreetly wrapped in a brown paper bag, and I dutifully placed the three items on a Formica table off to one side of the stage, hidden behind musty brown drapes.

Then Gary asked me to wait in the alley behind the school for her car so that I could welcome her and escort her upstairs. I was shocked that I was given such a task. At 6:45, a green Country Squire station wagon with wooden-paneled doors, appeared and parked.

The driver, a portly, serious man, got out of the car. This was Howard, who ran Lucille Ball Productions. He shook my hand,

and there was a moment of hesitation when I felt that something was about to be revealed to me. From where I stood, I could see Lucille Ball, still sitting on the passenger side, attempting to apply her lipstick. Her hair was pink. Pink like the inside of a flamingo's hairbrush. I have never seen hair that color again, and it distracted me for a moment from the shocking fact that Lucille Ball was crying. She was wiping tears from her eyes. I watched her struggle to fill in the large stencil of a mouth that had been drawn around her own for countless close-ups and magazine covers with a pinky-orange lipstick that obliterated her very thin lips. Protectively, Howard moved around the car to open her door.

I spied her take a jar of Vaseline out of her purse, open it, take a dab of the stuff, and rub it all over her teeth. She did this quickly, then dabbed her eyes again. Then Lucille Ball got out of the car. She was taller than I had expected. She wore an orange polyester pants suit that flared at the foot. I had imagined her in black-and-white polka dots or smart cocktail pajamas. I wasn't prepared for this Lucy with no makeup, no false eyelashes on her swollen blue eyes, this human, sad Lucy standing before me in the hazy, fading, Hollywood twilight.

Lucy walked in front of me as if she knew where she was going. Howard and I followed her up the back stairs, through the throngs. She walked over to the tall director's chair and the audience stood on its feet. They cheered for Lucy and for themselves. This collective ovation was a celebration of something beyond their comprehension. In that room, like bees deliriously sucking up pollen from an abnormally bright, giant sunflower, they cheered for Lucy's offerings of undistracted happiness.

Lucy seemed slightly disturbed by this adoration, and her face looked like a snake that had come out of its curl, an ancient creature suddenly woken by a coming parade. Then she sat down, looked out at the crowd, and began to cry again.

A hush came over the room. Some people thought it was a gag

and laughed nervously. Howard shifted the weight on his foot and looked on. I felt a knot in my stomach.

Lucy spoke. "The kindest, most lovely woman in the world died an hour ago. Lela Rogers, Ginger's mother."

The class was flabbergasted to witness such an unexpected show of raw emotion. We hung on Lucy's every word. There was rage in her voice. She gestured as she continued: "In the early thirties, women came to Hollywood, and when they got off the train, they were met by men impersonating agents and studio executives who offered them rides. The men *raped* these women." This ugly word unleashed more fat, wet tears.

"Lela Rogers created the Hollywood Studio Club, a place where young actresses could live and be safe from these rapist men. In those days, when a girl was raped, she never mentioned it." Lucy was disoriented by her own lack of control and embarrassed by this very public display of emotion. Howard stood at attention with his hands in his pockets. Her face was a contorted mask of pain and suffering. Her intelligence was keen, and after a few moments she stopped crying and looked out at the crowd like an old pink gorilla.

This class was not going to be a class about Vita-meat-a-vegemin.

Candid, frank, and rough voiced, Lucy pointed at the students who dared put their hands up. "Girl in the black sweater." "Boy in the paisley shirt."

Every twenty minutes or so, she would put more Vaseline on her teeth. We soon learned that this was an old studio trick that kept her teeth moist so her lips would work.

"Most of you are not going to make it in show business." The crowd hushed. "Most of you aren't that good." She inhaled, picked a bit of tobacco out of her teeth, and flicked it into space.

The older members of the crowd laughed uncomfortably, the younger members became sullen. America's favorite clown had become a strict governess, a wicked Mrs. Danvers.

Shirley Hemphill, a rotund girl with a sloppy Afro who had yet to make a name for herself as the waitress on the sitcom *What's Happening!!*, was one of the students. Shirley was working at a fast-food restaurant on La Brea. When she stood up she meant business. "I want to be on a TV show! Now! I am ready. Where do I go?" she announced, with her hands placed firmly on her considerable hips.

From her perch, Lucy gave the girl a withering stare.

Undeterred, Shirley continued petulantly, "I want to know where to go. You can get me on TV."

Lucy pointed at Shirley with her cigarette, then slowly turned her body and stabbed the Pall Mall out in the ashtray, speaking the whole time. "You're not ready, and you will never make it with this attitude of yours. Terrible. Awful." Lucy rubbed more Vaseline on her teeth. You could hear a pin drop. "Hollywood does not stand for that."

Shirley said, "Oh, shit," gathered her things into a mucky backpack, stomped out of the big room, and asked for her money back.

Lucy continued: "There isn't enough room for all of you. You have to be honest with your chances in this business. I didn't do the pilot for *I Love Lucy* until I was forty years old." She lit another Pall Mall.

I remember thinking that forty sounded very old.

"Desi and I knew it was our last chance." She inhaled deeply, smiling when she said Desi.

"We got a sponsor, but the network balked at the idea of me having a spic husband and refused to put up money for the insurance policy we needed in order for the show to be filmed. To pay for that insurance policy, Desi and I had to take out a second mortgage on our house in Chatsworth. Our house was all we had. If the show failed, we would have lost everything. I would have had to move back to Jamestown, New York. Hollywood would have been over for us."

There was something cold and brutal in her tone, as though she never had gotten over the injustices.

"For days, Desi and I stewed over the decision to put up our house as collateral. One night, I fell asleep, completely exhausted, and in the middle of the night, Carole Lombard walked into my room and sat down on my bed! I knew it was a dream, because Carole had been dead for six years." Lucy spoke with urgency. "Carole was someone I'd looked up to a great deal when we were at MGM. She was married to Clark Gable and died when her plane went down in an ice storm over Nevada during the war. Carole Lombard was selling war bonds." Her voice softened.

"In my dream, she looked *wunndaful*." Lucy was taught by studio dialect coaches to speak in a clean, r-less, mid-Atlantic accent. Lucy did not say *wonderful*. She said wunnd-a-ful. The sound of it gave me a sense of hope for all of the things in life that are *wunndaful*.

Again, Lucy started to cry. "Carole looked at me and said, 'Mortgage this house, Lucy. Sign the papers! This is what you wanted. Sign the papers and you will be free.' Then Carole walked out of the room."

•

LUCY SIGNED THE DEAL, and in return for paying the insurance policy, CBS gave her and Desi ownership of the footage. Because they owned the actual film, they became richer than either of them could have ever imagined.

Years later, I remember watching a TV biography of Lucy where a colleague of theirs remembers Lucy and Desi having a fight. "Lucy was standing over Desi with her red nails inches from his face saying, 'I wish you were dead.'" I could see her doing that.

•

WHEN SOMEONE in our class asked her what it was like to be the most famous woman of the 1950s, Lucy took a long time to reply. "I didn't know it until the sixties. I was too busy driving over Laurel Canyon twice a day to notice."

I remember being flabbergasted to learn that Lucille Ball drove herself to work. I imagined Lucille Ball walking out of the soundstage, finding her car, fumbling in her purse for the keys, shifting into reverse, and disappearing into the traffic, far away from the APPLAUSE signs and the key lights, her mind pummeled by the hard, black rain of the past, her heart filled with sorrow and rage for midnight spectral visitations and raped starlets.

Lucy only wanted a home with a white picket fence and kids and a husband who stayed close by. What she got was a white mansion where buses filled with fans holding cameras were always parked and phones rang twenty-four hours a day. Lucy paid a heavy price for fame; she knew its depthless, lonely suspension.

•

THERE IS A LARGE, old craftsman house on the corner of Laurel Canyon and Lookout Mountain Road. Thick, dusty leaves of ancient ivy cover the house like a fisherman's sweater. Whenever I drive through that haunted canyon and stop at the traffic light there, I think, *Lucy stopped here.* Sometimes stoplights provide necessary punctuation, a period, a few minutes to pause and connect the past to your spot in the present.

Lucy was from that generation of women who saw terrible things at a time when women had no rights, no recourse, no place in a world where lecherous men were free to take advantage of them in rooms with only one lightbulb.

•

WHEN WORLD WAR II CAME, they saw their fathers, husbands, and sons leave only to return and require those women to have babies and make the world normal again after all the bombs.

Lucy was in the middle of it and never grasped the cost or the price. She just connected the dots and the days, creating hilarity from darkness. Lucy Ricardo hit a key; Lucille Ball hit a chord, and that's why we love Lucy.

She told us her favorite episode of *I Love Lucy* was when the Ricardos went to Hollywood and met William Holden. Nearly fifty years after its first airing, I am still transported to a state of gleeful anticipation as I wait for Lucy to light her plastic nose on fire, then rearrange the putty with her fingertips and declare, deadpan, "This California sun sure makes your skin soft."

I imagine that when she was doing this, immersing herself in her work, she forgot her pain. When we watch her, we are distracted from our own.

This is *wunndaful*.

streetwork: l.a./hollywood

1982: one night

karen marie christa minns

IT'S NINE-THIRTY. On the corner of Highland Avenue and Santa Monica Boulevard.

Dark and muggy, more like Miami than L.A. I keep the motorcycle jacket on. It's leather: my black armor, my second skin. *My own skin's never been enough.*

I check in at the reception desk of the Gay and Lesbian Community Services Center, the oldest of its kind. I scrawl my autograph, letting them know where I'll be for the next eight hours.

"Don't forget to come back." The new receptionist is my age, slightly older than the clients. He's volunteering for the night shift because he thinks it's an adventure—the "real deal"—suicide prevention lines; lonely queer teens; lonelier queer adults. Then, there's me: the one street counselor, out there, solo, between Sunset and Santa Monica Boulevards, east of Highland, to however far west I can cover by morning.

The three men who've been hired to work with me have all quit. The first one looked like a narc. Kids would scatter like roaches when they caught sight of him.

"It's your shoes, man. They think you're VICE!" I pointed to the black lace-ups.

"I have to have support if we're going to be walking around all night," he complained. He lasted less than a week.

The next partner was straight. Really straight. An ex-carnie/recovering alcoholic, reinventing himself via social services. For him, the job counted as a training program, and he got credit for it through Antioch University. But he hated "fairies." He had fists like hams; the kids took off when he turned the corner.

"I don't trust those kids. They been out here too long," he'd rasp between roll-his-own cigarettes and cups of black coffee.

To pass the time on "quiet nights," he'd clean his fingernails with a pocket knife as we sat in the dark of Plummer Park. He didn't know how to take me. Twenty years younger than him, I was the first lesbian he really ever knew.

"So, let me get this straight. You're the man, right? I mean, when you go out, you open the doors, pull out the chair at restaurants, right?" He would squint at me real hard and move away.

Sometimes he'd brag about his "hobo days" hitching rides on the trains, downtown, in a full alcoholic blackout, then coming to without shoes or booze. He'd watch for my reaction as he talked about his "hot sociologist girlfriend from USC," who was dating him because he was "a real man," not some "academic wuss."

One night we both showed up wearing Levi 501s and jean jackets. He never recovered. But the final straw was when he discovered we shared the same birthday.

He left to "finish his master's at Antioch." I stayed, avoiding mine.

The last guy that applied for the job was OK, for a little while. My age, out of college in the Midwest. On the third night out, he confessed that he had met a group of guys who sold dope on the boardwalk and were living in Venice. He was beginning to question "his options." I didn't see him again for six months.

I finally ran into him, buying porno up on Hollywood Boulevard. He gave me two kisses on the cheek and introduced me to his boyfriend.

"Minns, I don't see how you do it! Frankly, it just scared the piss out of me!"

His new lover gave me one of those straight-girl-asses-out-arms-about-the-shoulders hugs, and they were gone.

•

"MINNS, YOU HAVE TO COME, QUICK!" Stoney is sixteen but looks forty. His bleached blond spikes match my own. But his leather jacket has ripped-out sleeves, and his jeans haven't been washed in weeks.

I am forced to change direction.

"Angel got into a fight with this drag queen," Stoney blurts out. His voice is slurred. He's high. Still, he keeps his grip and pulls me by the elbow.

I don't have a choice. I have to keep up with his longer strides. As my carnie ex-partner found out, fairies or not, these kids are full grown and they're plenty strong.

"Come on, girlfriend! He'll listen to you!"

The motorcycle-booted punk ushers me to the first cheap motel on the corner of Sunset. If the tourists only knew! We pass a dozen kids in various stages of undress, all lounging around the murky pool. A few wave as we pass—whether for me or Stoney, it's hard to tell. Stoney's rapping his bony knuckles on one of the motel windows.

The turquoise door slams open, and I'm pushed in.

As my eyes adjust, I see seven boys crammed inside, most yelling. Stoney puts two fingers between his chapped lips; his whistling pierces the screams.

"Shut up, you queens!"

Everyone stops. A skinny kid in a torn Dead Kennedys T-shirt and skintight jeans moves forward. He shakes his bangs out of his eyes. It's Angel himself.

"What's up, Angel?"

The room smells of amyl nitrate, male sweat, and too many used condoms. It's hard to keep from gagging.

"I was there. I was there!" A smaller boy I don't know claps like a five-year-old seeing his first Christmas present.

"Somebody tell me what's going on," I say, frustrated.

I don't want to sit on the bed. I don't want to sit anywhere in the room. I lean against the door jamb.

"This dumb-ass blonde," Angel begins, earnestly. His face is why he earned his name. His perfect, bow-shaped lips and pale blue eyes compound the innocence in his voice.

Stoney moves over and puts an arm around the hustler. I am surprisingly moved, again, at how easily these kids slip into each other's arms. It's about human comfort. It's about connection. It's about anything but sex.

Angel calms down enough to tell me the story.

"She started a rumor out on Santa Monica that I had the crabs," he sputters.

I stifle a laugh. But, it's not funny. It's about "making rent" and putting food on the table—for all of them. When one kid "scores," all his friends eat—or get a safe place to stay for the night.

I'm a white girl from New England, with a snooty college education that prepared me to teach English classes to other uptight Boston kids. To be discussing rumors of pubic lice, in a dingy Sunset Boulevard motel, is not where I expected my life to take me.

"So, where is he?" I try to soften my voice. I'm trying to avoid a bigger confrontation which might result in all the kids being tossed. I say, "Angel, just cool it for tonight. Tomorrow, I have you scheduled to come in and talk to Tony about the rehab program. He thinks he can get you in. You still want to go, right?" I squeeze Angel's bony arm.

He sniffs, coughs, shakes his head yes.

Stoney grabs my arm, again, before I can slip away.

"Thanks!" He reaches inside my pocket. He isn't looking for money. He withdraws his palm.

"OK. Later, man. I'll see Angel in the morning," I answer. Then I'm back on the street. In my pocket: a handful of pills, along with a doobie and a little brown vial of low-grade coke. Hustler thank-you notes. Like everything else they have, they share. I sigh. I laugh. If I don't, I'll cry.

•

THE SCENTS OF GREASE, gas, and night-blooming jasmine flood the street. Okie Dog is raging, selling its fast food. I stand in line and get a long, split bun, upholstered with sauerkraut. I let the Freudian imagery go. There is a smell of weed and hairspray mixing with cigarette smoke. I sit at one of the empty picnic benches and nibble "dinner." I'm alone for about five seconds.

"You holding?" the fishnet-swathed Goth wannabe whispers into my ear. His breath is all onions and menthol.

"No." I finger the "gifts" the kids placed in my jacket. Got to turn them in next time I pass the Center.

I finish dinner and pop a Chiclet from Tijuana and hope it covers the Okie Dog smell. The pills in my pocket make a clickity sound against the vial of coke. I wonder if anyone else notices.

Cars move along Santa Monica Boulevard as if they are running out of gas. Chicken hawks cruise the meat rack, eyeing kids of all colors, sizes, degrees of desolation. Queer runaways afraid to stay at home; straight-boy runaways finding no shelter amid the city of bad dreams; gay youth trying to survive "The Life," or what they believe is "The Life," swallowing stereotypes, existing over the top, without benefit of role models. Kids hoping to be discovered and make it as actors, as singers, as real-life lovers.

The boys frame this street. The younger, fresher runaways are further west; it gets raunchier as you move east. East runs into the trannies—some so gorgeous you are almost willing to bet a year's salary that they are really women. Others barely covering chin hairs beneath the pancake base. In the alleys around Benito's Taco Stand, they do business. Or take a break.

Every bus stop is packed. Every streetlight a spotlight on a BoyShow. The cars understand. Everything.

"The trick is looking inside, before you say anything," Stoney told me my first night out. "If the car's too clean, it's a cop. Also, check the shoes. If they look like they just been polished—or like, they're business shoes—it's a cop. Vice don't wear no loafers, baby!"

•

"HEY, MINNS!" Two short, red-headed boys in cutoffs and wifebeaters wave. They could be taken for brothers. They are brothers. They hang at the bus bench by the Formosa Café.

"A bus stops and a cop drives by, we get on," the shorter one laughs. (Old trick, but it works.)

I wave and keep walking. I put one hand in my jacket. Like a bee sting, the presence of the drugs gets my attention. I understand the honor in the gesture, of slipping it into my pocket. These kids have nothing. What they manage to scrounge, they share. Nights like this, I feel I give them nothing, but they remain generous. I understand, but I need to get rid of these drugs. All I can do is turn them over at the Center and hope they get flushed. I keep a record. I cover my ass. But it gets harder and harder. So much happening, all the time. No let up. No ease. This is real life. For these kids, this is how it is.

No stars on the Boulevard, or over it, as I look up. I smell goulash cooking—like the scents in someone's grandmother's house, on a weeknight. Makes me homesick for a minute.

Plummer Park, again, the Russian neighborhood. In the day-time, the park is full of chess- and checker-playing seniors, or mothers with foreign accents pushing strollers.

"They ain't foreign to them," Precious, the Cherokee boy with the killer cheekbones, says. I bump into him and José as they emerge from the edge of the park. They need a place to crash. Nobody's made enough on the street to get a room. Precious doesn't look well.

"Just a cold," he tells me. I watch him shake. I don't believe him. José promises that he can hook Precious up, but it's a little complicated.

José promises the guy with the apartment will meet them. They just have to wait.

"He won't stop if he sees you." José kicks at a cigarette butt on the curb. He can't meet my eyes. I get it. Their minds are already made up. For tonight, I don't have a better offer. I'm not easy about this.

Precious looks twenty-five, but he's closer to fifteen. Hitch-hiked to San Francisco, looking for an Anglo father who split when his mother got pregnant. Got turned out on the street—gang-raped by some straight boys, coming home from a soccer game.

"Didn't change anything—I knew who I was," he stammered when we first met.

That was months ago. He's aged a decade since. Strung out, dirty, he takes it up the ass faster than any of the other boys I know. Nothing is off limits. He never uses protection.

"More money like that," he grins, as if this is a big secret.

"Hey, don't worry about me. I'm an Indian. I'm magic," he explains. Maybe he believes this. For a magic man, he's alone a lot.

I spent weeks trying to get him into one of twelve city beds designated for runaways. Just two centers for teens, and over a thousand kids flooding Hollywood every day. When they found out how he was spending his time, the "openings" dried up.

In disgust, in desperation, he went back out. What good could I do? "Least nobody's lying to me out there," he whispered.

I wake up crying, some nights, his whispers still in my ear.

•

THE VICE SQUAD KNOWS ME. Had to go through a special Street Training, with the carnie-boy partner. On the inside of my jacket, my photo ID. They know who I am. They know we are a legit pilot program. They know we are part of the Gay and Lesbian Community Services Center. Didn't stop them from patting me down. Didn't stop the ride to the station and the call to my director. I got street cred with the kids after that. Tonight, I don't need any more credibility.

Outside the Center's locked front door, a dark figure is slumped. Another figure runs away, in a clear panic, down the street.

I rush up.

It's PrettyBoy.

I kneel down.

"She cut me!" he spits, his voice a spray of blood. I begin to yell. I kick at the front door. Two kids come running, hearing me over the traffic of Highland.

No cars even bother to stop. They just drive by, watching us, windows up tight. There are no pedestrians this time of night, just the hustlers and me. One white kid about fourteen, clean smelling, obviously a runaway, grabs PrettyBoy under one arm.

"I just was talking to him!" the kid says, shocked at the sight of the blood.

I hold my hand against the cut. It's above a rib. I feel Pretty-Boy's heart beating. I feel his breath rattling between the bones of his chest. I start screaming for the receptionist to open the damn door!

The third boy, a black kid I don't recognize, grabs PrettyBoy under the other arm and begins kicking at the door. Finally, we get the attention we need. The door swings wide. The kids help drag PrettyBoy inside.

"Call 911!" I scream at the receptionist.

He jumps the counter. He's on the phone. All I can do is to keep talking to PrettyBoy to keep him from going into shock. His blood is all over us. It's still pumping over my hand. The two guardian-angel boys from the street have gone to the bathroom. When they get back, I'm still on the floor with PrettyBoy.

"Look, I don't want no trouble. I gotta go," the white runaway explains, and then is off into the night.

His buddy hesitates, then blurts out, "I got a warrant. Sorry. I didn't see anything anyway. You be cool, my brutha." He taps PrettyBoy on the head and follows fast, behind the white shadow.

The receptionist brings a towel to blot at the blood. Also a Salvation Army blanket to keep the kid warm. Where is the Salvation Army, now?

I keep talking to PrettyBoy. The receptionist begins singing "Amazing Grace" in a soprano voice which annoys me, but I can't think of anything better.

It's over an hour before the ambulance arrives.

They put on gloves.

They put on masks.

They put on coveralls.

They don't even want to carry PrettyBoy to the vehicle. They make me and the receptionist help him to the curb and climb inside.

These are the plague's first days. We are inside the Gay and Lesbian Community Services Center. I am an obvious leather-wearing lesbian, covered in faggot blood. The receptionist has limp wrists and a too-lovely face. We are as suspect as PrettyBoy. Finally, the ambulance whisks away from the curb.

I go into the restroom and retch. I wash the blood off from everywhere, including my jacket. PrettyBoy will end up at County. He'll test positive and then be released.

In a year, he'll be dead. It won't be from a stabbing.

"Please don't tell me you're going back out there." The receptionist pulls a little Chivas nip from his briefcase.

"Got to. I won't be able to sleep if I don't." I try to shrug it off.

I hit the door. It's going on 2 A.M. I'm wired now.

At home, my three middle-class, twenty-something roomies will be dreaming about the weekend.

On Santa Monica Boulevard, it's getting rowdy. Cops are swarming. One of them recognizes me: "Your name is Minns, right? You work with these kids out here? Social worker?" She's about forty, a vice cop. I've met her only once.

"What's up, officer?" I keep my fist around the contents of my pocket. I completely forgot to empty it out because of PrettyBoy.

"One of your kids?" She moves and I see Precious, in cuffs, spread-eagled across the hood of a cruiser. Suddenly, the street is eerie; too quiet. Even the hiss of the streetlamps is clear. I think I can hear my own heartbeat. They won't let me get close enough to talk.

I call out, "Hey, Precious," just to let him know he's not alone.

"Don't you say a word, boy," one of the male officers orders. I hear Precious sob.

"He's in real trouble. You better contact his lawyer and his social worker." The female officer pulls me aside. "I don't know the whole story, but he got into a violent altercation back in the alley, there, with an older man. The older man just got taken to the hospital. Looks like he's going to lose an eye because of your kid."

I give the cops my card, my director's phone number. I yell to Precious that somebody will meet him down at booking. I watch the cops pull away from the curb. I watch Precious, with the killer cheekbones and proud Cherokee profile, disappear. I get all the paperwork I need to take back to the Center.

I head back up to Sunset. Halfway to Angel's room, I see Stoney stumble out of an alley. He stinks of whiskey and cum. He pulls me into the alley with him.

"I was there. I saw it go down," he growls.

"What?" I stop short. I pull him closer, my fists wrapped around his reeking T-shirt.

"Precious was waiting for a date. José set him up. The guy drove by. They went into the parking lot behind the car place. The guy got rough. He tried to do something Precious didn't want to do. Precious just went off!"

I tried to think what Precious wouldn't do.

"He put his thumbs into the guy's eyes! He popped one of the eyes *out*, man! Just popped it out! I couldn't believe I was seeing it, but the guy was screaming and blood was shooting everywhere. The cops were driving by. They heard him. They picked the guy up and came right after Precious. José took off. I took off! I was looking for you, but I didn't want to go around Highland and be in front of the Center with all them cops around!" Stoney was grinning and growling and high.

"Angel's sleeping. He'll be at the Center, in the morning. Wants that rehab." Stoney moves into the shadows.

"Yeah?" I watch him shuffle off.

"Yeah."

I am wrung out.

I am done in.

I am the alley.

I am the night.

This is my life.

This is all of our lives.

Behind me, the loud purr of an expensive engine. I turn. It's a Jaguar. The window slips down, silently. There is someone in dark glasses, hunting, behind the wheel. My jacket is close around me. My Levi's are faded and frayed. My boots speak the language of "butch" as I continue down the walk. Short-haired, young: the driver can't tell whether I'm a boy or not. For a split second, I stop. My hand curls in my pocket. The brown vial clicks against my ring. I feel the pills slip through my fingers.

It's been such a long, sad night.

For a split second, I get it.

The hunger moves across my skin.

glass kids in hollywood

karen marie christa minns, glass, inc.

IN THE EARLY 1980s, a social worker in Hollywood noticed how foster youth in the System were being treated. She especially noticed that the gay, lesbian, and then-called "questioning" youth were being given short shrift by the Department of Social Services and Probation. Misunderstood, misread, or simply feared, these kids were discriminated against in the most basic ways. So, Teresa DeCrescenzo mortgaged her home, borrowed from and badgered her friends, and opened the Gay and Lesbian Adolescent Social Services (GLASS) agency, which was the first of its kind in the country. Focusing on GLBT youth, GLASS grew in leaps and bounds and became the first licensed group facility for HIV-positive youth in the nation. Today, GLASS is a twelve-million-dollar operation with six foster group homes in the L.A. area. Two new homes have opened in Long Beach and one in Oakland.

GLASS now operates foster family agencies and is in the process of becoming a fully licensed adoptive services program.

The following two accounts of "Life in Hollywood as a Queer Teen" have come out of a workshop I ran, for GLASS, along with Joyce Lee, from the Los Angeles Women's Theatre Festival. The workshop was made possible through a grant from the City of West Hollywood. Seven foster teens, all in the GLASS group homes, participated. In addition to working on autobiographical material in the workshop, the kids also put together a perform-ance for the city, which debuted in West Hollywood's Plummer Park, in the summer of 2007.

Dalton is eighteen and has chosen to use his full name, which is his right to do. Eva is still underage, so she can only use her partial name. Look for her in the future as a writer to contend with. Both GLASS residents hope their stories will not only en-tertain and enlighten you about life in the twenty-first century for queer youth, but will also offer hope to other disenfranchised kids. Their stories are true and uncensored, in their own words.

love kills the small amount
of emotions you have left

dalton fronterhouse

LIFE AS A TWENTY-FIRST-CENTURY TEENAGER who is out of the closet and living in "the System"—as a foster kid—can be kind of hectic. No one really gets you. They think you are just a teenager—or just a child who can't make his own decisions. But the real truth is that I'm very much aware of my surroundings—and my lifestyle.

I live in a group home with six other foster kids who make my life a living hell, every day. The Princess (not her real name) is always in our faces about how *her parents still love her and are still there for her and she has a house she can still go home to*—but, she's in foster care . . . hmm. Angel Child (not her real name) recently was taken to a mental hospital because she had another episode about her murdered mother. KnockOff Jackson (not his real name) picks at me, constantly; every little thing I do. Ciara's Clone (not his real name) carves words into his skin, meanwhile criticizing staff and kids who aren't living up to his standards. And then there's PyroSkeptic, who recently tried to burn the house down. He failed. These are my "siblings." Like I said, things get a little hectic.

On top of this, I am gay and totally out of the closet. What does that mean, in the twenty-first century? In parts of L.A., it's actually pretty easy being gay. In other parts, you can get shot, on sight. I spend most of my time in West Hollywood. In West Hollywood, you can be open and odd, and people just accept you for who you are. You can walk around with pink hair, black leather high heels, and a red miniskirt and still be accepted (not that I do that!). There are a lot of older people—people over twenty-one—who hang out there. Lots of clubs, shops, restaurants, gyms, and things to see. There is a gay boy vibe everywhere! I look forward to being older so I can get into these places—I can't wait!

There is a problem with gangs, though, even in WeHo. There are gangs everywhere. But they pretty much leave me alone. We have even had kids in the house who are active gang members. We don't bang on each other, but I can't say a lot of words and phrases in the house anymore without stopping to think if they will send someone off.

I was twelve when I came out of the closet. I hadn't planned on actually coming out, but my cousin and I decided to run away from home. We stole my father's (my sperm donor) car and got about three miles before the cops pulled us over because we didn't have the headlights on.

I told the police I was seventeen and that I was teaching my cousin how to drive. The cops bought the story, but they called my house anyway. They got my "sperm donor" on the phone. They sent a car to pick him up. He arrived, drunk off his ass, in his underwear. They allowed him to drive me home while they drove my cousin back.

I was very pissed off. He asked me why I stole the car and I told him the truth. I said, "I'm gay—and you're homophobic—and I can't live with you anymore." He denied it, almost running into another car, and then took me home and proceeded to beat the crap out of me. I went to bed around four o'clock, then got up in the morning and went to church the next day. We were Jehovah's Witnesses.

He made me tell about all the "sexual activities" I had done, in great detail, to the Elders and other people in charge at the church. They got off on it. Then they told me that I "needed to pray"—then, they sent me home. My father beat me up, again.

We were living in Barstow at this time. Then, we moved to Rialto, where I got involved in major use of alcohol—just like Dad! I was back in the closet, just to survive, so daily drinking helped me push down those feelings. My father attempted suicide, just to get attention for himself. We kids were taken out of the house and went to live with our grandparents. My sister, who is two years older and also lesbian, was with me, but she had not come out of the closet, yet.

We moved back to Barstow, and they began to give me what they called "affectionate discipline"—including such things as "pray out the gay." My sister was running wild, but because she was in the closet, they let her be. She tried to commit suicide at this time, too. It was too much for the grandparents, so we packed up and went back to Dad.

I told my father that I was definitely gay and that I was going to go back to my mom's. He tried to strip me naked, saying everything I was wearing belonged to him, and I couldn't take it with me. Then, he beat the shit out of me again. I got away and moved to Florida with my mother.

In Florida, things were not OK. I began to cut, just to feel relief from pressure. I began to smoke weed, continued to drink heavily, and sleep with people I hardly knew. I tried to commit suicide in the middle of this horrible setup. I finally got arrested and wound up in juvenile detention. They sent me back to my father in Barstow.

By this time, my sister had been kicked out of school and was being home-schooled. She had also come out of the closet. The double standard from straight guys about women on women being somewhat OK held for my father, for a while at least. But one night, he was drunk and began beating on her, too. He gave her a black eye and bruised her chest pretty badly. She ran away to her girlfriend's house. He called the girlfriend's mother and outed both of them. The mother drove the girlfriend and my sister back and had a big talk with them, with my father there. My sister had to move back home.

At this time, I was living at home, but I was spending as little time as possible there. One evening, Dad was extremely drunk and began beating my sister and me. He pulled a knife and threw it at us. He ripped the phone out of the wall and began hitting us with it. I got hold of the cell phone and called the police. At first, they didn't believe me, but when we called a second time, they came. They took us into foster care and they put him in jail—but only for two days.

I bounced around in the System from Barstow to Victorville and back and finally arrived in Los Angeles. My sister was in foster care until she emancipated and got out. I landed in L.A., and here was where I could finally be who I really am. Kind of.

I came to a program called GLASS and got into a group home where most of the other kids—though not all—are queer. This is where I am writing from, right now.

While GLASS is safe and allows me to be gay, openly, I'm still a foster kid and in placement, which means living with strangers and under rules and regulations which are not my own. I've got to be in the house by six in the evening; I have to write down every single step I take—every place I go or think I might be going. I have to be in therapy groups every day. I have to talk with a shrink every two weeks. I can't get any more piercings or tattoos until I leave placement; I can't dress completely the way I wish—no chains, no studs, no leather. But, I have to admit, in the middle of Los Angeles, and in WeHo, life is pretty good. Actually, it's better than it's ever been.

I'm in touch with my sister—who is currently living with her girlfriend. I have new friends. I'm clean and sober. I'm being responsible and safe when I get together with my friends. I'm thinking that I want to go into law enforcement when I get older, but I'm not sure.

What advice I would give to the world about treating people in general, is this: just be open and accepting of the differences everyone has. I leave you with these words of wisdom: Life is hard; we all make mistakes; but the hardest thing you will ever have to do is love and live with yourself. So yeah, peace.

eva in west hollywood

a true life adventure

eva s.

I'VE BEEN SEVERAL PLACES around the city of Los Angeles, but nowhere have I experienced things like in West Hollywood. From seeing my first tranny prostitute on Santa Monica Boulevard to becoming addicted to crystal meth at age fourteen—all that took place in West Hollywood.

I was first offered crystal meth by my fifteen-year-old, super-skinny friend. I was twelve. She said the crystal made her feel really good. Being young minded as I was, I decided to try it. We smoked from the pookie—which is the glass pipe used to smoke crystal. After puking my guts out, I decided I wanted more. I enjoyed the fact that it kept me restless and not hungry. It made my eyes appear even more beautiful than what people usually tell me they look like. Although this wasn't reality, I enjoyed it. It was my own world. I felt nothing. I found I could express myself in writing and talking at tremendous speed and people could still understand me. I went from smoking it to snorting it in a week's time. But snorting it burned like hell—also you could taste the crystal dripping down your throat and it made you gag—so, I went back to the most addictive method: smoking it.

My friend had a supply from her homey who would give her as much as she wanted as long as she kicked it with him. This went on until I got moved to Lancaster, as a foster kid, and I lost my connection.

Man! Being a foster kid has no true definition: it depends on who you get placed with. Since I've been enrolled in the System—which was from age twelve to now—I have been in five different placements: Lynnwood, Lancaster, Inglewood, Long Beach, and now, Hollywood.

When I was eleven, I was raped by my mother's boyfriend. This put me into foster care. Not only that, my mother was abusive, though she denied it.

Now, I want to put something out here and make it clear: just because women who are born lesbian are raped by men, it doesn't determine their sexuality. I knew I was lesbian, even then, and being raped didn't affect that.

So, at twelve, when I finally told my mom, I was beaten by her and told I was a liar. Later on, I became depressed because I wasn't being protected by or believed by the adults around me. I ended up in a psych hospital and attempted suicide. Twice. I had been back and forth with both sides of my family, trying to find someplace I felt safe. Every time it just got worse. Finally, I was put into foster care, full time.

In each foster placement I dealt with average teenager issues: jealousy, hatred, fighting, bullying, drama, stealing, lying—only thing is, I had no mother or father to comfort me. I was basically alone. I felt empty inside. Frankly, I also felt that maybe I didn't deserve a real family—I was the one who had turned my own mother in, after all.

These are all, and more, feelings that we foster children share.

My ways of dealing with these emotions were drugs, cutting on myself, crying, sometimes praying, talking with other kids and adults, crying some more, breaking down, building up, opening my eyes to my reality. That's when I finally learned that NOTHING WAS MY FAULT!

From the time I was eight I had always been attracted to lovely women. Older female relatives would change their clothes around me, and I found I couldn't take my eyes off of their bodies. I had realized that I had a dangerous interest in women! I say "dangerous" because it was always the older women I would be attracted to. Years later, I found that I was actually searching for my mother through these women.

Around age twelve-and-a-half, I met "Cynda." She was the most freakin' gorgeous, beautiful baby doll woman I had ever seen. Just my type. Until she broke my heart—with a DUDE! This made me have a rage toward men! I became a "straight lesbian"—a lesbian's lesbian, hard core. Then, I was on a rampage, seeking to find "that special woman."

Let's just say I was in a lot of relationships—some were good, some were bad; some were VERY good and some were VERY bad. I was accused, misused, abused, and mostly confused. But, finally, I met my real baby doll; my butterfly. My peanut butter.

We met through a friend who knew "my type."

We didn't actually meet in Hollywood, but it should have happened here.

Now, we went through some cow dookey together. Oh the drama! Cheating, lying, trust issues, all those wonderful teenage scenes. We had to learn how to communicate because we both got irritated with lying to each other. We would be sitting right next to each other and have to write a letter to get across our messages. I began to get mad about the letter writing and demanded she start to talk out our issues. Damn, it wasn't like she was deaf!

At first she didn't want to, but, eventually, she broke down. This was her first committed relationship—mine, too. I told her that cheating was when a person doesn't get everything she needs from her partner, and she goes out looking—physically, emotionally, mentally, every way. We didn't have a need to go out looking. We are still together—so our plan of helping each other must really work.

During this time with Peanut Butter, I went through a lot of placements: from Lancaster to Inglewood; from Inglewood to Long Beach; from Long Beach to Hollywood. Through all this time, Peanut Butter stuck by my side.

Since I've been to Hollywood, my life has been adventurous. I've seen some famous people. I've seen a few other people too. Prostitutes: all different colors, sizes, shapes, and sexes. I've even been hit on by a few pimps.

Let me tell you that story: On Hollywood and Vine, I was standing at the light, coming from Hollywood High, when some black, nicely dressed freak got up in my face. He walked me all the way to Hollywood and Wilton, telling me that if I went into business with him I wouldn't have to be a prostitute; I could just dance a few days and then become a cyber-sex girl. He told me I could become so rich just on my beauty. He started asking me about my sexuality. I told him I was gay and that blew him away. He answered by saying, "Well, OK, so, you just wouldn't get turned on, so what's the problem?"

I tried to get away but he kept following me, all the way to the group home.

I told him to get lost. He was going to give me his number in case I changed my mind. I gave him my pen to write it down because it was better for me to take his number than for him to have mine. I could always throw his away. I was looking and sounding strong when this happened, but I was really scared.

In Hollywood, I've learned that by staying focused, you can get far—if you don't allow things like drugs, sex, and prostitutes to get in the way. I've also had a change in my fashion life. My hair keeps changing, too: it wasn't that long ago that I was a blonde! My friends were blonde, too! Blonde must be going around . . . I've seen a few junkies, punkies, and even a few skunkies living in my backyard. I don't know what they eat, but whatever it is, it doesn't agree with them.

I've learned how to socialize in a positive way, too, like asking for help.

My life at the GLASS group home and their Day Program (for after-school groups) has helped me learn to trust people again. If I am having a bad time, I can talk with people my age, or even adults, and be really listened to. People care about who I am—and who I want to become. They take me seriously, even if some of the kids drive me crazy. Sometimes there is just too much drama with these high school kids. But, if they stick around and work on themselves, they'll eventually figure it out and get more mature. Just like what happened to me.

People always ask me what I want to be when I grow up. I think they mean what do I want to DO when I get older. Well, I already consider myself a dancer and a writer and I want to keep doing those things. I also would like to go on to college. I want to help other kids in the System. Maybe be a probation officer or a social worker or even a psychologist. Whatever I become, I want to work with kids. Lots of foster youth feel like that. You would be surprised. It's probably because we will never forget how hard and alone it was growing up, and we don't want other kids to have to feel like that.

My life is turning around. I am getting adopted into a family who really wants me exactly the way I am. My mother has apologized for what happened in our past. I can forgive her, but I can't forget—at least not just yet. My school is going fine. I am still in love and I am working with the Los Angeles Women's Theatre

Festival as one of their youngest interns. Adilah Barnes, their executive director, saw me perform my poetry and prose in a workshop I did through GLASS, at Plummer Park, in Hollywood, this past summer. She invited me to come work with her and I took her up on the invitation. So, I guess Hollywood is always going to be a place where lots of my real-life adventures and dreams come true.

black opera gloves

stuart timmons

IN BOYSTOWN, S & M meant "stand and model." That joke, in the 1970s in West Hollywood, wasn't far from truth. The Boulevard seemed paved with guys who knew how cute they were. The scene at the Blue Parrot, the Rusty Nail, and the brand new Mother Lode had the feel of a photo shoot: carefully lit and staged, warm as pancake makeup and almost as deep. Every other boy on the Boulevard knew he was a latter-day Lana Turner, destined for stardom.

"This twisted strip is just a roll of seamless paper," snapped a drunk I met in a Boystown bar one uneventful night. "Someday WeHo is gonna get crumpled and trashed." He sipped his White Russian. "You'll see disoriented queens stampede. Grabbing for their bronzer."

Snipes like that were flavored by the sour grapes of those not invited to the orgy—the one that went on every night via whispered invitations, behind an automatic gate guarding a hilltop view, a pile of cocaine, and picture-perfect guests who snubbed anyone failing to measure up.

For others, the turnoff cut deeper than attitude. It was the beat, disco, saturated with synthesizers and drum machines. Disco, as addictive as liquor to a junior high schooler, eventually was as nauseating. I'd adored it for years, but disco had finally driven me (along with many others) from the clubs. The music embodied a social problem: If you weren't structured and amplified just so, you didn't get to the floor. You had to be pumped upstairs and trimmed downstairs, clad in the Levi's-and-Izod uniform. The same barfly who cracked wise about crumpling up Boystown also insisted there should be a "Beauty Board" at the boundaries of WeHo, screening those who didn't measure up. Even the excluded wanted more exclusion.

There had to be a better beat.

I found it in a dark bar on the east side of town, on a street crammed with narrow storefronts hosting launderettes, liquor stores, evangelical churches; peopled with tired mothers by day and speedy gangsters by night. The interior repelled with shadow, but attracted with a music I hadn't heard before, flowing around a central bar. Aimless as angelfish, spot-lit men drifted and rested against beer-case benches and a chain-link mesh that wrapped the bar. The mood at the One Way countered any West Hollywood nightspot. No sonic bursts set men prancing; rather, imperceptible parades countered the unspooling tunes. An immediate regular, I ambled with the others, Kraftwerk washing through me like the beer and the weed in my blood.

Over the island of a bar that dispensed only Budweiser and Calistoga hung the blowup of an advertisement from one of the butch fag mags: DOMINANT MUSCLE TOTAL TOP SEEKS PIG SLAVE FOR RELENTLESS RAUNCH SESSIONS WITH PISS, SCAT, TIT TORTURE, WHIPS, FISTS, MOTOR OIL, SWAMP WATER, HEAVY CHAIN LINK, AND

BIG CHUNKS OF CONCRETE. The place that called itself "L.A.'s Most Notorious Leather Bar" was entwined with camp.

The flat-black walls offset glints from leather clothes; along with T-shirts and jeans, black leather jackets were omnipresent there. Conversation was not. Sometimes the only word uttered for an entire evening was "Hey"—or "No." Men left sometimes in pairs; often alone. The consolation of the One Way was that if you didn't pick up, you could say that you went for the music: Europop, New Wave, New Romantic, and Punk. At least the deejay, his face illuminated from below as he studied his twin turntables, smiled occasionally. His awkward handsomeness would have disappeared in any Boystown bar. Here, his face lit a corner of the void.

One night the deejay, Bobby, slipped me a postcard bearing a stark graphic. It advertised a party the following Sunday afternoon. Like a ragged logo, a word appeared, parsed as in a dictionary: SPEC·U·LA·TIVE: A RANDOM SUNDAY HAPPENING, followed by a list of performers, a certain date, and a familiar place. The One Way.

"Is it going to be a concert? A party?" My confusion amused him. "We think so." Bobby shrugged. "All we can do is *speculate*, right?" He turned to fade in the next cut.

Something new, and possibly scarier than Dominant Muscle Total Tops, was heading for the One Way. These bands would bring a music crowd, mostly Punk Rock. Punk style—aggressive hair, makeup, and facial expressions—aimed to horrify polite society, and did. The average punker looked like a wild animal cornered and struck by lightning. Punk's shock troops were performers who snarled into microphones, scowled at cameras, and otherwise vomited their alienation everywhere. Their infestation of L.A.'s most notorious leather bar was not to be missed.

The day of the Speculative Party could not come soon enough. I donned jeans too torn for Boystown, a black short-sleeve T-shirt, and something I'd never taken from my dresser drawer: a pair of matte-black, stretchy-cotton opera gloves. I pulled them all the way up; my bare, skinny bicep peeked between them and my shirtsleeves. It was a discordant getup; formal but trashy, a bit femme, a little raunchy.

The bar was so packed that one had to push against bodies clothed black as the walls, creating a sea of floating, chattering heads, most belonging to cute guys. Leathermen mixed with boys from Cal Arts, and young actor-types drunkenly soul-kissed girls; genuine heterosexuals had joined the invasion. Suddenly one could not take much for granted. This was no longer just a leather bar, though the punk aesthetic seemed like a perfect complement. Bright dyes and stiffeners took the place of blow-driers. T-shirts revealed blue-toned tattoos, which I'd never seen on young skin, only on the blurred arms of World War II vets.

"Uh, hello? Please?" The chattering crowd focused on a small stage of planks set over beer cases. Like a schoolteacher, a guy waited until every eye was on him. Without a word of welcome or thank-you, he said, "Ladies and leathermen, Miss Edith Massey." He handed the microphone to a mountain of a woman, spilling like lumpy vanilla fudge from a black catsuit she had been lashed into, with leather thongs binding her exposed arms, legs, and middle. She whined, "Big Girls Don't Cry." The crowd howled. Next, three white rappers called Age of Consent charged through "Missionary Position," a song mocking the Religious Right's imposed version of heterosexuality. They followed it with "Schizo Gay," mocking homosexuals who came out only to party on weekends. Louder howls. Red Wedding, a contemporary rock band with a queer twist, finished by throwing a wall of live electric sound, absorbed by the dark, warmed-up bodies. The afternoon melted into beer and meeting lots of new people and going home with someone whose name, face, and dick now escape me.

What I do remember, over that summer, is finding a crowd. In my mid-twenties, it felt like some social teenage summer I'd never gotten. At the One Way or in barely furnished lofts east of

Alameda Avenue, oddballs and artists converged, refugees equally from suburbia and the gay ghetto. Many of them, though striking, would never have passed the La Brea Beauty Board. I learned names. Bobby worked as relief for the announcer. Tom, who had conceived the Speculative party, was regarded as a prickly genius. Utah Jack, boyish and craggy, was making up queer time since realizing at thirty-five that he wasn't interested in women. Mack, with the silver buzz cut, worked at a bank; Frank, with the retro pompadour, for the phone company.

The One Way became transformed by those parties. I began to wander into the bar and find Bobby, or Jack or Frank, just to have a beer and be somewhere I fit. We laughed about everything, even the new disease, determined it would not crash our party. One midnight, Utah Jack and Mack linked arms to toast, honeymoon style, with each other's Budweiser. Immediately they did spit takes, yelled "Ewww! AIDS!", wiped their mouths furiously, and cracked up.

•

ONE SUNDAY, as the second or third of the Speculative parties was waning, a ragged edge of the party crowd held a strip of sidewalk in front of the bar. Bobby lit a joint. The ratio was switching between the hip partiers and the cruisers, and we wanted away from the creak of old chaps. Unready to retire, we joked and coughed as the joint passed through twice.

A car slowed and a leather-capped face stared. "What you lookin' at, Lady-Man?" The rude demand came from Matthew, a sneering, self-styled rock star of zero accomplishment. He was gayer than anyone but liked to call you it first. "Hey Lady-Man!" He lunged. The car accelerated.

"Let's go," Bobby whispered. "I think the party's moving to the Pound."

I'd already been to the abandoned Craftsman-style bungalow,

on a cul-de-sac near the Hollywood freeway and a short walk from the One Way. The crash pad of punk squatters, tattered banana trees flanked the Pound. Its front window screens were torn; inside, the chairs and sofas had been dragged in from the street. Built-in hutches and niches overflowed with beer cans and bottles abandoned by glamorous partiers crowding in.

"What the fuck are *you* doing here?" demanded a shrimpy boy with a chipped tooth and an uneven crew cut. His dark eyes dared me to say a word.

"Cool it, Jackie. He's my friend." Bobby grabbed my wrist and led me farther into the house.

"This place is hard core," I said nervously. A trio of pit bulls sniffed guests. "No one owns it? How are there lights?" Bobby just smiled and pulled me farther in. I didn't know if it meant anything that he'd grabbed my hand. Lights burned and toilets flushed, though some guys peed on the unkempt grounds, which included a free-standing garage and another small building behind the house. "Jackie lives there. Those are her dogs." I stared at Bobby.

"*Her*? That—boy?"

Bobby nodded. "Her girlfriend lives here too. She kinda takes care of the place. Jackie breeds pits." More than Jackie's dogs, it was human strays that gave the Pound its name. No one knew who would flop there, how long they would stay, and what trouble they might bring. Crabs, heroin, cops—the Pound had seen everything. Luckily, across the street was a halfway house for ex-offenders. Neither place complained about the other.

While absorbing the scene, I'd lost Bobby. I saw him in the open garage, slipping on headphones. An older bald guy approached behind him. Bobby snuggled into his embrace, then shrugged out of it to concentrate on his records. Bobby had a lover; I felt a little sad.

A short woman and a tall man approached the house. The woman resembled a drunk canary: a fluff of blonde hair, vintage sequins hugging her curves, warbling nonstop chatter. Her companion, broad in the jaw with dark hair and eyes, swigged a flask. Toward them ran Jackie, shoving the man out of the way and hugging the petite sexpot. "Now that Celia's *married* she'll be all the sweeter."

"Fuck you, Jackie," the tall husband smiled.

"No man ever will, Gino," Jackie cackled. She pulled Celia's arm and led her toward beer. Catching my stare, Gino walked in my direction. I ducked out, certain that no matter how ambiguous the crowd, I could still find a way to get punched out if I looked at the wrong guy the wrong way.

"Big Gino," said Utah Jack, amused contempt curling his voice. "New York Italian. Rich. Hates his family. He just got married to Celia—who used to be Jackie's girlfriend." Jack paused, a smirk spreading over his face like syrup on a waffle. "You just might be *his* next girlfriend. I kinda thought that was why he avoids New York." I blushed and scowled.

There was dancing, and I jumped in with straight couples and guys who seemed indifferent to the guys they would be glued to in a few more hours and after a lot more beers. The music caught us up, Exene and X wailing "Sex and Dying in High Society," which turned to Lee Ving of FEAR screaming, which reverted to Exene moaning about leaving Los Angeles. A Mohawked guy laughed as he pushed a girl who then knocked into me. Shoving erupted, and some laughing idiot stomped on my foot with his big, heavy boot. It really hurt and, like always, I ran away.

Right into Gino, glowing alcohol and heat. Despite his overcoat, he was built like an athlete. "Sorry, man," I blurted, but he laughed and looked through red slits. My foot throbbed. "Sorry," I repeated, and must have looked upset, because he rubbed his hand through my hair. "Forget it." He handed me the beer he was holding and I took a sip. He reached out to tug my head back, and put his hand at the back of my head as I swallowed and wondered what the hell was going on. His big palm rested on my neck.

I chugged the beer and broke away, saying, "I'll get us more beer." This time he grabbed the top of my gloves. He stuck two fingers in each and pulled me toward him. "You come back here," he said, a little slurry. "It's a bad neighborhood, y'know. Very bad." Then he reached in his coat and pulled out something. The dark obscured it until streetlight outlined its metal form. I couldn't quite believe what I was seeing, and only as he held it up close to me and grinned did I realize that this drunk had a gun.

You first see a gun with shock and fascination, like it's not real, like it's a parallel world, not the one you're in, because you're already leaping to the possibility of not being part of it. Instantly, innocent night romping turned deadly serious. I didn't know what Gino wanted, or if he knew. Or if he got loose when he got loaded. That was how it was for a lot of guys in that crowd. I slipped away quietly to my car.

I kept my distance from those parties for a while, wondering if I'd ever again meet anyone as hot as Gino. Months had passed when I heard that Gino and Celia had gone back to New York. Then one night at the One Way, Utah Jack told me that Celia was in New York City and Gino was in an upstate cemetery. He had died of AIDS, and Celia, the little sex canary, was sick. "Heroin," people shrugged. As I wondered, a noise raced in my head, the sound of a near bullet. I heard that noise every time I learned about one more person who died. A score of questions formed and collapsed as I thought about the invisible bullets; about what made me not turn my head and never see it coming, about whether I'd already taken a bullet that was working, silent and steady, toward a vital organ. It became less fun to wear black; life became funereal.

Not long afterward, I heard that Bobby had died. AIDS: a shock. He had slipped out of the scene for most of that winter, but so had I. I learned he'd gone to his lover's, then to his mother's, then to a hospital. Folks gathered at the Pound, where beer and tequila and jar candles crowded tables. In the rear garage, remaining deejays spun Bobby's records.

On the slab between the garage and the house, a bonfire devoured scrap wood from the yard. A crowd already danced around it. The Sisters of Mercy groaned out their distorted chorus of "Gimme Shelter," unleashing memories. That segued to Bonnie Pointer's "Ring My Bell." It was odd but somehow perfect that this crowd of disco haters was jumping to disco; the irony doubled when the beat melted into "Born to be Alive." The mix evoked other songs, other crowds, and memories of someone that would now be only a memory. The records blended into a trail we climbed in our dance, tiring, unable to stop, the deejay pushing us on.

The beat trail suddenly veered into folk, and the New Christy Minstrels crooned "We'll Sing in the Sunshine," a ballad about loving warily, just for a while, laughing every day, and being on your way. Each sappy lyric brought me closer to Bobby, a man everyone wanted to sleep with, and now no one ever would again, and there was his boyfriend trying not to look sad.

I turned to see a chair in the fire. It was a classic, armless side chair, from an expensive set, carved cherry. Its back support formed a shield, curved for comfort. I searched for a broken leg or a cracked support that justified its burning but found no flaw. It was perfect. Some bad-boy punk had thrown it on the bonfire, just to destroy something beautiful with time and purpose ahead of it. The fire looked like a halo that had not yet grabbed the wood; I lurched forward hoping to save it, but varnish bubbled on its flared legs. The chair poised, apparent but already gone, ashes in minutes.

The New Christy Minstrels number is the last song I remember from that night. I wasn't sure I would laugh every day ever again or be on my way in any direction. I just floated in whatever music spun through the speakers. The chair, a bright outline, glowed orange. It collapsed. We danced.

wh2O, i love you!

terry allison

MY FIRST IMPRESSIONS of West Hollywood: the corner of Santa Monica and Robertson, an intersection of cars, bars, clubs, restaurants, and the strange social interactions that erupt when the celebrated car culture of Southern California collides with a rare flourish of pedestrian activity. This was the early 1980s, before traffic calming methods—islands of plants and flowers or wider sidewalks—had been overlaid onto busy Route 66, also known as Santa Monica Boulevard. At the time a Bay Area bicyclist and not-so-gentle derider of La La Land, I stood fascinated, hair windblown by the passing speedway, at my own sudden interest in cruising only the hottest cars. Short of removing one's shirt, what was a boy to do to get a little street action? I usually just straggled into the Mother Lode, elbowing my way to a desirable spotlit position, cocked my head, and tossed my chlorinated Farrah-like wings. Since I could do the same in San Francisco, or usually better—blonds are less common there—I gained little special attachment to West Hollywood.

Did I say chlorinated?

This is the very point of my brief memoir: the permeation of chlorine into the follicles and the pores, the elaborate circles of precedence, the goggle-visioned grind, and the crack of the starting gun that comprise the pleasure, ache, introspection, and focused repetition of competitive swimming. I have a limited sense of West Hollywood as a physical space, not like upper Market and Castro Streets, where ghosts of dead friends flirt and tango with my rambling memories, where I still search faces for fellow survivors. Not like Berkeley, where I recklessly rose and descended hillsides, helmetless, earning my scars. And not like Hell's Kitchen in the mid-eighties, when frozen sidewalk spit followed rank piss to mark the passing seasons. My memory of West Hollywood includes swatches of asphalt along low-profiled buildings, dense ficus splitting sidewalks, waxy magnolia leaves littering lawns, and occasionally a hint of rose or angel's trumpet wafting through the crazy quilt of trapezoidal blocks covering the hill that leads from Santa Monica Boulevard to Sunset. Although I can't exactly name West Hollywood's perfume, I'm still nostalgic for it and for the gay and lesbian swimmers of West Hollywood Aquatics (WH2O) who represented this odd panhandle of a city, for the Whitmanesque ideal of gay camerados that my relationship with WH2O evokes. West Hollywood Aquatics, I recall your generosity, your life, and your spirit.

I love the memory of WH2O, from the mid-eighties to nineties, when I was a master's level swimmer, coach, and gay athletics organizer. Rivals, friends, colleagues in organizing International Gay and Lesbian Aquatics (IGLA), coaches, role models, but never teammates, WH20 members were supposed to be the archenemy, the fiercest rivals of my swim team, Different Strokes San Diego (DSSD), the center of my athletic and social life for nearly a decade. But my memory is anchored in the things we did together: swimming, drinking, playing games, planning an aquatics association, and putting on the famed Pink Flamingo Relay. I remember sometimes who won and who lost, and most particularly when I believe I could have swum better than I did. Still, there's none of the tribal rancor that I strangely feel, having graduated from UC Berkeley, for our greatest sports rivals, UCLA and USC. I never displayed, as with my FCULA T-shirt or my waving dollar bills at visiting USC fans, any open contempt for my alleged opponents, WH2O. Instead, I remember knowing individuals' best times in an event and urging my pals to swim faster—and they did the same for me.

My first association with lesbian and gay swimmers began while preparing for the first Gay Games, held in San Francisco in 1982, but I have no strong memory of Los Angeles swimmers from that time. Photographs and newspaper accounts now tell me that some of the swimmers whom I recall fondly and even one, Frank, who later became my San Diego swimmate, competed for the Los Angeles team. Because of space and time limitations in '82, each city could only have one swimmer from each age group and sex. In other words, only one 26–35 year-old male butterfly swimmer could compete while representing Los Angeles. As athletes from cities with large potential populations of swimmers found themselves excluded from Gay Games I, they formed multiple-city teams so that in '82 there were teams from Los Angeles but also from Santa Monica and Beverly Hills. While the one-swimmer-per-team rule no longer held sway, by Gay Games II teams had only begun to coalesce. There was only one gay swimming event between 1982 and 1986 that I can recall, a meet held at Beverly Hills High School in 1983, so civic solidarity had not quite gelled. West Hollywood had a considerable number of swimmers in Gay Games II, but a separate Los Angeles team was equally prominent.

My association with DSST began in 1987. Soon after I moved to San Diego I became a team stalwart, a member of the board, chairman, team captain, and then one of the coaches. After Gay Games II, a group of leaders including Mark Wussler from San Diego, Rick Peterson from Seattle, Charlie Carson from New York, Rick Windes from San Francisco, and Tom Reudy from West Hollywood emerged to ensure that regular swim meets would be held between Gay Games. Soon I was representing DSST to the emerging International Gay and Lesbian Association, helping to write the bylaws and, with Tom Wilson of WH2O, became a codelegate to the Federation of Gay Games (FGG), an international body that had formed to ensure the continuity and integrity of the event. Tom and I met at FGG functions in Vancouver, Atlanta, Amsterdam, and New York (in a conference room at the top of the World Trade Center). I regularly shuttled with Mark to meet Jon Bauer and another WH2O swimmer, Rafael Montijo, to develop the IGLA rules of governance.

In high school I had wanted to be a diplomat, and I finally had the opportunity, representing San Diego to the Federation and DSST to IGLA. Mark and I functioned in a quasi-ambassadorial capacity for our team. When Rafael died from complications of HIV/AIDS, we represented DSST at the celebration of his life. Later I would consult closely with Tom Wilson, an internationally traveled flight attendant, about how to bridge the U.S.-European gap when Amsterdam was selected for Gay Games IV and several U.S. delegates to the Federation kept inadvertently antagonizing a solid European/Australian block.

I completely immersed myself in the world of GLBTQ swimming, making friends on my own team and among other cities' teams, finding a sense of belonging that had been denied me by my own high school swim team. Long after graduation, I learned that my teammates had held many parties without inviting me, but then I had been a pariah, among the five least popular in my high school. Despite having had a girlfriend from grades ten to twelve, I faced daily taunts of *fag*, *pussy*, and *wussy* as well as hazing, pushing, and fear of a daily dose of humiliation. I was the

worst thing a boy could be in an athletics-worshipping small town
in central California: insufficiently male identified. Teased even
by other future gays (again, a later revelation), I once was mocked
by one of my swim team members, a junior, in my senior year,
who left a caricature of me on the bulletin board with the caption,
GAY LIBERATION FRONT. Since I had read a daily newspaper since
the age of twelve, I wasn't totally mystified by the reference. But
while I knew in 1973 that people could have a same-sex encounter, I didn't understand that gay people existed or that same-
sex couples might live together, let alone identify as gay. Being
from a naval family and traveling in uncosmopolitan circles, I
simply had never seen it. Through IGLA, I finally got to have the
kind of team and competitor experience I had missed earlier, and
a sense of belonging and support lacking in my youth. More than
happy to claim a position on the front lines, I also understood that
the Gay Games movement was a liberal and somewhat normalizing approach to gay liberation, not a radical queering of society.

But not completely normalizing. Although critics such as Brian
Pronger claim gay athletics does little more than reproduce patriarchal modes of competition, domination, and subjugation, queer
sport doesn't always work that way. Queer sports provide frequent
reminders of how to approach sports differently, perhaps particularly noticeable in swimming and diving because they are both individual and team sports. For example, in 1987 at my first Southern California master's meet, I arrived early only to overhear an
AAU coach repeatedly chiding one of the swimmers for missing
her turn. I can still hear him taunting the young woman in front
of her teammates in a minute-long harangue: "You NEVER
breathe on each side before a turn! Each SIDE before a TURN.
One breath and THEN another before the turn!" I almost quit
master's swimming before I started.

When Frank, our abovementioned coach, tried a similar tactic
on one of my fellow swimmers, Walt retorted from the water: "I
had that in high school. That's not why I'm here." Others on the

team chimed in, leading to a poolside and then a locker room discussion about why we were there at all, doing timed repetitions in an overly warmed pool. Walt's sass certainly queered the coach/athlete hierarchy, but so did the circulation of several of us in and out of the coach role, training one evening and coaching the next.

Other cultural boundaries can break down as queer bodies circulate the globe. GLBTQ athletes become friends, counselors, truth tellers, and even romantic interests within and across teams. (*Caveat emptor*: I have no sordid locker room trysts to report in relation to WH2O.) I'm tempted to say that this regular trading of teammates and the circulation of gays and lesbians throughout major metropolitan areas helps to temper how we view our competition. Perhaps we don't see nonteammates as an eternal "enemy" but as occasional rivals, potential future neighbors, and even prospective squeezes. But is there any marked difference between this lesbian and gay mobility and today's professional sports world, where yesterday's trash-talking opponent suddenly becomes your go-to guy as the team vies for the playoffs? Perhaps in the romance. I know many swimmers—Andy and Scott, Marc and Mike, and even Jeff /Geoff and Mark/Mark—who met, paired off, and fell in love at competitions, causing one of the two to move and join a new team. But apart from romance, affection for individuals on other teams is almost always more than grudging; it is deeply real. Let me talk of one Peter and two WH2O Toms who illustrate the point.

First, there was Peter McCafferty, a tall, striking breaststroke specialist, strawberry blond, freckle faced, with porcelain, sculpted skin and a Crest commercial smile, who coached my underwater turn at the National Master's Swimming Competition at USC in 1990. At regional and national meets in the master's swimming circuit, it was typical for GLBTQ team members to swim for their city's umbrella team, often erasing the official presence of the queercentric teams. Still, we would gather and huddle to critique the sad fashions of our hetero teammates ("Oy! Another Hawaiian shirt?"). Unsolicited, Peter watched my 200-meter breaststroke race, observing my start and each of my seven turns. After my warm-down, Peter told me how much time he thought I had lost, then followed with a coaching session to improve my underwater work. A dreamboat, a sweetheart, and did I say tall? Peter, Mr. WH2O.

Tom number one, Wilson that is, was one of the WH2O determined to keep camp alive. He wrote a column for IGLA's official newsletter, *WetNotes*, called "Moist Towelettes," using the nom de plume Towelette Moiste. Unfortunately the column died quickly, but Tom W. kept it up in person, always a joke, always a smile, with an eagle eye on his role as athlete-diplomat. Being airline personnel had its advantages, so Tom Wilson showed up in any number of venues, my partner in representing IGLA to the Federation of Gay Games. Tom also knew his sport. In my very last swim meet before an injury forced my retirement, he asked me, "What happened, Terry? You were two seconds off your time?" If only two seconds today . . .

The second Tom, Mr. Reudy. My last glimpse of him in the water could have been his ankles—not the anatomy of a fellow breaststroker one wishes to glimpse during a race—in Vancouver in 1990, at Gay Games III. Earlier in the meet, Tom R. had announced that he was going for a world master's record in the 100-meter breast. Chutzpah, you ask? Actually in master's swimming, it is required that you announce your record-breaking intention so that three timers rather than the usual two will be stationed at your lane. Unfortunately, Tom false-started, and in master's swimming, like gay dating, one false start and you're out. But there was an equally memorable moment. As team captain of WH2O at Gay Games III, Tom arranged to have less-adept swimmers mix with highly accomplished ones on relay teams to give slower swimmers a rare chance at medaling. As team captain of DSST, I overly strategized, offering strange mixes and failing

to deliver any relay medals, but Tom's strategy had secured a series of bronze medals. Thank you, Tom. Lesson learned.

I'd like to end my reverie of West Hollywood in, where else,
Laguna Beach. For several years running in the eighties and
nineties, DSST would meet WH2O halfway and have a blowout
beach party in Laguna Beach. Booze, beach, booze, bars, and did I
say beer and beach party games? Although WH2O was supposed
to be the archenemy of DSST, somehow queer sports managed to
massage this sports rivalry into a sixties beach extravaganza.
Think Frankie and Annette with better haircuts. After hours of
bronzing, lounging, wave play, and—one year—a stunning visit
by dolphins, we'd eventually catnap before our rendezvous at the
Boom Boom Room where the chess game of romance, the queen
captured and then the king, played out among the grass shack vi-
cissitudes of a beachside bar.

There were dark moments too: the IGLA meet in Seattle
when they superchlorinated the pool, apparently fearful of AIDS;
the time they ejected us from the Long Beach plunge for our un-
family values after Morrie and some lesbian pals from WH20 appeared shirtless in a Pink Flamingo skit; the time teenagers in Laguna yelled *faggot* at us right after a man had been fag-bashed on a
beach below; and, of course, the steady collapse of fallen camerados—Rafael, Jim, Rick, Hal, Bart, and others—some stunningly
memorialized at the Unity '94 Pink Flamingo performance
through Montreal's red-ribbon water ballet and New York
Aquatic Homosexuals' parade of angels.

At the end, we need no careful weighing of the bad and the
beautiful. West Hollywood, you were good sports and good
friends. WH2O, you know how to move in the water. West
Hollywood, go glow like Esther Williams! WH2O, I love you!

the plush pony

pat alderete

EVEN STRAIGHT PEOPLE KNEW about The Plush Pony. It was a hardcore butch bar located in the El Sereno neighborhood of Los Angeles, just up the street from where my old gang worker, John, lived.

"Damn," John said in a low voice, as though someone might overhear him. "The other night some broad with a Mohawk pulled up in her Harley and started gunning it. Some decent-looking chick ran out of the bar and jumped on the back."

"Yeah?" I prodded, taking a drag on the joint and handing it back to him.

"Well, next thing, another dyke runs out of the bar, pulls the chick that looks like a girl off the bike and busts a beer bottle over the Mohawked broad." John shook his head. "There's always shit going down at that place!"

I stared at John, thinking about what he'd said. I was a Chicana

butch. He'd met me when I was sixteen and he was doing gang intervention as a social worker. John had been a good friend to me
and had helped liberate me from the confines of the varrio
lifestyle. I was now in my thirties, and I was feeling invisible by his
misunderstanding of me as a queer butch.

I was from East Los Angeles proper, so I couldn't hang around
the El Sereno varrio, but I'd heard and wondered about The
Plush Pony over the years. When I was coming out, I wanted to
meet other young butch Chicanas like myself, but our potential
camaraderie as butch women was still overpowered by our varrio
affiliations. Instead of having my ass kicked because I was checking out somebody's girlfriend, my ass would have been kicked because I was from the wrong neighborhood. So I stayed away from
The Plush Pony.

Butch women want the same thing: femmes. There's never
enough femmes to go around, so we're careful with the inventory,
wary of other butches circling like sharks. Then we end up lonely
for someone like ourselves to talk with.

My lack of lesbian homegirls made me entirely too vulnerable,
both at home and in El Sereno. I didn't fit in at home because I
was a lesbian, and I didn't fit in with the El Sereno lesbians because I wasn't home.

•

I'D HAD A CRUSH on Chita for years when her latest girlfriend,
Ana, told me about a women's semipro football team coming together in El Sereno. It was only semipro instead of all the way pro
because they didn't pay and there was just one big game for the
whole season. I'd always loved football but had only played flag,
so I got my ass to the park to try out. Besides, Ana said that many
of the players were Plush Pony regulars and this was my chance to
check them out.

I walked to the crowd of women standing around. There was a

group who must have been the Plush Pony regulars Ana had mentioned. They had short hair like me and were wearing Levi's and T-shirts. There was no mistaking they were not only butch dykes but also veteranas like myself. They stood around like the cholas they'd once been. The other group was straight women; they looked more nervous and unsure of themselves. Some of the younger girls were accompanied by their mothers. Many of the women were about ten years younger than me.

Everyone was clustered around a couple of bulldog-looking men, who were explaining the rules.

"Aw right, my name's Joe Rubalcaba," he barked. "My assistant, Danny Gonzalez, and I are going to kick your sorry asses into football players. How many of you have played contact football before?"

We shuffled our feet, no hands raising.

"Aw right," Joe tried again, "how many of you have played flag football?"

Everyone raised her hand.

"Aw right," Joe kind of smiled, "get into four lines, we're gonna run sprints."

I'd been smoking at least a couple of packs of cigarettes a day for more than fifteen years by now, in addition to taking assorted drugs and booze, and I felt the effects as I sprinted. My thigh was twitching like a rubber band that was getting stretched too thin but I ignored it, knowing I'd have some beers after practice to dull the pain.

Joe had us run, throw the ball, catch, and kick before yelling, "Aw right, not so bad for a bunch of girls!"

From our group a football zoomed out like a laser and smacked Joe.

"Ey, I think I found our quarterback!" Joe laughed for the first time that night and so did we.

"Aw right," he continued, "tomorrow night, same time."

●

THE NEXT EVENING I showed up eager to find my position. I'd quarterbacked and had also been a cornerback on flag teams, but I knew this would be different. I saw a mean-looking dyke eating peanuts and talking to the mother of a sweet-looking girl I'd flirted with the night before. I walked over to the dyke and nodded. She ignored me, tossed empty peanut shells near my feet, and kept talking with the mother. I felt my face get a little warm, but I knew to bide my time and not react. I didn't want to get into a hassle with her unless I had to, and if I had to I wanted to be in a strong position.

"Aw right!" Joe walked up yelling, "get into lines. Tonight you're going to run wearing some equipment."

A ripple of excitement cut through us. Helmets! Shoulder pads!

Joe and his assistant, Danny, started pawing through duffel bags, handing out equipment they thought would fit us.

Joe yelled, "If anyone is wearing earrings, take them off *before* you put the helmet on. Believe me, you're gonna hate yourself if you don't."

I pulled the helmet on excitedly and was amazed to find it was heavy and uncomfortable. It made my head feel wobbly, not safe and protected the way I'd expected. The shoulder pads were better, and pretty soon we were all running around, banging into each other like a bunch of goats.

Joe was right about the earrings. Even though many of us were butch, we were also Latina, meaning that most of us had our ears pierced at birth. I know I wasn't even out of the hospital when my mother had a nurse run a needle through my ears. I didn't notice the studs I'd worn ever since. But I sure did when it was time to take off the helmet, since the damn thing folded my ears up and the earring posts scratched the hell out of the side of my face. After practice that night, a bunch of the butch women walked off together and I wondered if I should catch up with them. I heard the peanut-eating dyke say, "Hey, let's go to the Plush." She turned and saw me and made it clear I was not included. I acted like I didn't care, but I felt like I'd been kicked in the stomach.

•

WE KEPT COMING BACK every night for a couple of weeks. We learned fundamentals of the game, like proper blocking, where we used our shoulders and never our heads. This paid off at work when my boss challenged me to prove I could block and not only did I lift him off his feet but I also knocked his breath out.

We started coming together as a team, learning each other's names and talking more freely with each other. I was made full-back and I loved it. I learned that the big, peanut-eating dyke's name was Connie, and even though she still didn't talk to me, she started nodding.

We still sprinted every night and my thigh kept hurting. Joe would yell, "Make it hurt, girls!" so I thought it was OK. When I would drive home, I'd have to lift my leg with my hands to put my foot on the clutch but I didn't mind. I was loving the game.

"Ey Joe," I asked our coach one night, "what's the name of our team?"

Joe looked up from one of the duffel bags, eyes bright. "The Dandy Lions."

"No fucking way!" a chorus of voices yelled in unison.

"Awright, awright," Joe said, palms up, "it's just a name girls, nothing to get excited about."

"Nothing to get excited about?!" I said. "The fucking 'Dandy Lions!'"

Joe rubbed his chin. "Yeah well, I don't make the names. The league does and that's the team's name."

"Well shit," Connie said, "who we playing against?"

Joe smiled. "The Pussy Willows."

•

WE WERE GETTING BETTER. Carla was this short, quick dyke. Joe put her three steps in front of everybody one night and yelled, "Awright, catch her!" We'd torn out after her, growling and snapping at her heels, but to everyone's amazement, she outraced us all to the end zone. We were impressed and she became our punt returner.

The slow, heavyset girls were put on the line, both defense and offense since we didn't have enough bodies to have different sets. We were especially proud of Kika, who was rumored to be part Hawaiian. She was big, not just fat, and our best hope for stopping the Pussy Willow attack that Joe and Danny said was sure to come.

Connie was on the line too. Before I learned anything about the game, I thought the line was where you put the people who couldn't play, but that wasn't true. They didn't get singled out but they were the ones who made it possible for the backfield to shine. I had a new respect for them.

Our quarterback's name was Josie. At first I thought she had a lot of boyfriends because every night a different guy would come to walk her home, but then someone told me she had seven brothers and no sisters. She acted like it too, like there was no possible competition in the world, but she had a good arm and she played hard.

At practice a week before the game, I was lined up to Josie's right when she passed me the ball and I took off running. I saw Connie coming at me and I turned hard to my left when I felt something snap in my thigh and I fell to the ground. I rolled over and sat up, in pain but afraid of saying anything. I didn't want anyone to think I was a wimp.

Connie was looking down at me, disappointed. "Shit, I didn't even hit you!"

"Yeah, next time, awright?"

Connie laughed and extended her hand, helping me up. We were understanding each other. I limped back to the lineup, then excused myself to use the restroom. I didn't want anyone to know I was hurting because then I'd become an easy target.

By the time I got back from the restroom, practice was over and I went home. I could barely sleep that night. The next morning I was no better. Luckily, one of the clients at my job was an orthopedic specialist for whom I'd done some clerical favors. When I called his office, his nurse recognized me and told me to come right over.

I lay on the examining table, uncomfortable as Dr. Steeple poked and prodded. He said, "Your quadriceps is ruptured."

"My what?" I asked.

"Your thigh muscle is torn," he said, tracing his finger across the top of my leg.

Miserably I asked, "Does that mean I can't play?"

Dr. Steeple nodded. "Yes, your football days are over. Muscles take a long time to heal, I'm afraid. There's nothing we can do except make you comfortable with crutches and let time do its magic."

I got dressed and went to my car. I sat there alone, tears running down my face. I banged my fist against the steering wheel and felt one of my knuckles swell up. Shit! It was bad enough that I'd miss the game, but I'd started to make friends with some of the butches and now I was going to lose everything.

•

THE DAY OF THE GAME I went with crutches in hand and my camera around my neck. To my surprise, I was treated like any other member of the team and given a jersey with the number 15—a back's number.

I watched the team suit up. I'd always thought football players had nice butts, but I found out it was the padding. Man, the pants were a bitch to get on. Tight, tight: pulling them on inch by inch, sliding the pads into sheaths on the tailbone, hips, and thighs.

The red-and-yellow jerseys were put on top of the shoulder pads and then the whole thing was put on. Some of the knee pads went on knees but most were put on the players' breasts and held in place with duct tape. By now everyone had learned to take her earrings off before pulling on the helmets.

"Ey," Connie walked by me, slapping me on the back, "be sure to take my picture, *esa!*"

I turned to look at her and she burst out laughing. I joined her and soon I was surrounded by the butch members of the team, and even some of the straight girls. I was being patted on the back, had arms around my shoulders, and was inundated with yells of "take my picture!" I felt as happy as I could, like I was a part of the team.

•

THE PUSSY WILLOWS were anything but. They were big, hulking women who moved like panthers, hungry and ready to leap.

The game was held on the playing field at Lincoln High School in Lincoln Heights, traditional rivals of El Sereno. The bleachers were mostly empty since it was just girls playing. Mostly it was the butches' femmes and the straight girls' families; there weren't many but they were enthusiastic and I could hear yells of "*Andale mija!*"—"Go, daughter!"

Connie represented our team for the coin toss and elected to receive. The teams took their positions under the clear autumn sky and braced themselves. The kicker from the Pussy Willows punted the football high, right to where Carla waited, tensed and ready. She was our secret weapon and we were ready to show those Pussy Willows who they were up against.

Carla caught the ball and took off. She ran about ten inches, I think, before she was flattened by several Pussy Willows. It was going to be a hard game.

Carla's return turned out to be the best showing the Dandy Lions made during the game. The Pussy Willows ended up kicking our amateur asses up and down the field. In a way it made it easier for me to take pictures, because when our team had the ball we didn't move much.

•

A WEEK AFTER the game I got a phone call from Connie.

"Ey, a bunch of us are meeting at the Plush, wanna join us?"

Trying to be cool, I answered, "Yeah sure, awright."

That evening I showered extra long, trying to calm myself down. I was excited—I was finally going to The Plush Pony and I was invited by one of the *mera chingonas* there. Everyone seemed to know Connie, and I knew she was well respected. It was good to know her and be on her good side.

I was still on crutches but I had lots of pictures to share, I reminded myself as I drove up.

The building was tiny, with rearing stallions painted on either side of the entrance. I thought it weird to have stallions painted on a women's bar but I liked the flames pouring out of their nostrils. It felt awkward pushing the door open with my crutches but that was nothing compared with how it felt once I hobbled in.

The jukebox was blaring Linda Ronstadt, singing "When Will I Be Loved." The cigarette smoke hung thick from the low ceiling, rickety stools were shoved against the bar, with Chicana lesbians slouched on, against, or near them. Everyone turned to stare at me. Balanced on my crutches, I was careful not to look away from anyone and yet not to challenge either. I could feel everyone's eyes on me.

"Ey!" Connie came up to me. "You made it, *cabrona*, come on in."

Everybody relaxed. I smiled and pointed to the pictures in my pocket.

"Awright!" Connie said, pointing to a space at the bar where somebody was sitting, but she moved when she saw Connie point. "Get off that leg."

Everyone perked up when they saw the photos in my hands. I passed some out and sat next to Connie.

"Fucked up about your leg," Connie said, shoving a bottle of Corona beer to me. "We coulda used you out there."

"Yeah," Carla spoke up, "her and a fucking army!"

I was happy. I was drinking more than I needed to, as I always did, when this femme came up to me.

"I saw you practice before you hurt your leg. I thought you were pretty good," she said. She was pretty but her face was as hard as a helmet.

"Thanks," I smiled.

"Your leg hurt?"

"Yeah."

She reached over and put her hand on my thigh. "You want me to get you something?"

I was starting to feel very much at home when I saw Connie's whole mood change. I realized the femme was Connie's girl-friend.

Shaking my head no I said, "Look at this picture of Connie."

I held up a photo of Connie tackling a Pussy Willow. It was probably the best photo I'd taken during the whole game.

Connie turned toward the picture and I could see she was pleased. Her girlfriend, Susie, put her hands on Connie's shoulders.

"Here," I said, handing the photo to Susie, "keep it."

I spread out the rest of the photos, my new friends crowding around me, picking up the ones of themselves.

I drank all night but didn't pay for a single beer.

vito russo does l.a.

john morgan wilson

BORN AND RAISED in New York City, Vito Russo was a New Yorker through and through. But a big piece of his heart was in Hollywood, and his connection to Los Angeles ran deep. He was truly bicoastal, inseparable from either city, a dichotomy that helped define and explain one of the most unique and vital figures in gay history.

I first met Vito in the mid-seventies in the lobby of the funky Fox Venice Theater, not far from the beach. He'd just finished giving a talk, illustrated with slides and film clips, about the shameful portrayal of gays in cinema to a wildly appreciative SRO audience. Now the exuberant crowd filled the lobby and spilled out to the sidewalk, still buzzing about Vito's presentation. Movie lovers all, we would never see film quite the same way again, especially as it had depicted homosexuality through the decades.

Vito had developed the idea for his illustrated lecture after showing camp films during fund-raisers for the Gay Activists Alliance in New York, following the Stonewall Riots in 1969. He began touring with it in 1972, working from a shoestring budget as he took his ever-expanding compilation of stills and clips across the U.S. and later to Europe and Australia. What the presentations lacked in polish they made up for with hilarity, pungent commentary, and trenchant social insight, and he gained increasing recognition within the gay movement. But that night at the Fox Venice, no one could have foreseen the indelible mark he would eventually leave on cultural history.

Vito called his modest presentation "The Celluloid Closet." He said he planned to turn it into a book, if he could just find the time.

•

WHAT I REMEMBER MOST about my first meeting with Vito was his dazzling grin and infectious energy and enthusiasm.

He was on the short side, slightly built, not quite thirty but already starting to lose his dark hair, and a bit impish-looking behind his spectacles and thick mustache. As we were introduced in the Fox Venice lobby, I put out my hand to shake his. He ignored it and wrapped me in a warm embrace. He was formidably intelligent but utterly without pretension, and I felt comfortable with him right from the start.

At the time, I was renting a dilapidated, one-bedroom bungalow for $115 a month in nearby Ocean Park, two blocks from the beach. A mutual friend had told me about Vito's appearance at the Fox Venice, and asked if we could have a little gathering for him afterward at my place. I was always ready for a party in those days, especially if gay men were involved. By the time we got back to my little house, word had spread through the crowd, and more than a hundred people showed up, straining the already buckling floorboards. Gay lib was at full steam and there was a communal spirit in the air, abetted by wine, weed, and music, and enhanced by the special aura Vito carried with him, inspiring and drawing people together. That party remains one of the more memorable of my life.

That night, I glimpsed something in Vito that set him apart from so many activists in those heady days, whose rage and narcissism often left me intimidated and wary. Vito was deeply passionate about gay rights and human rights in general, capable of great eloquence and anger, yet he was just as joyful and effusive about people and life.

I was particularly struck by his unabashed love of Hollywood glamour and old movies. (His favorite was the 1950 camp classic *Caged*, a women's prison flick that starred Eleanor Parker.) At first, I found his infatuation with Hollywood at odds with his keen insight into how its pictures had stereotyped, ridiculed, and demeaned queers in such damaging ways. But as I got to know him better, I realized that this seeming contradiction was what made Vito so unique, such a great activist and communicator, and the perfect choice to write a book about the celluloid closet.

If he could just get the damn thing written.

•

I SAW VITO infrequently over the next few years, yet every time we got together, he was as warm and openhearted as ever.

I always asked him how his book was progressing and he invariably dropped his eyes guiltily and told me how little he'd accomplished. Although he'd earned a master's in cinema at New York University, and his Hollywood connections were many, he wasn't cut out for a conventional job and didn't pursue a career in the film business. Instead, he wrote articles and reviews for magazines and waited tables at night so he could continue his writing and research by day. But he was also devoting much of his time to the gay movement, and his inability to get his manuscript finished became a running joke among his friends. As the years dragged on, I began to suspect the book was a pipe dream, and that he'd never get it written.

One spring afternoon in the late seventies, he called to tell me he was in town, staying at Lily Tomlin's house, and we made plans for dinner. That evening, I drove from the beach to the address he'd given me in the hilly Los Feliz district and parked on the street. Tomlin's huge two-story home, reportedly once owned by W. C. Fields, resembled an old castle and sat on the other side of a ravine, reached by a footbridge. (Vito had no car, leaving him even more isolated.) He met me at the door, looking weary and frazzled. Tomlin had just bought the place, he explained, and had yet to move in. He gave me a tour, showing me cavernous rooms without a stick of furniture in them. Worse, the heating had not been turned on and the big house was frigid. Vito had been writing in the kitchen, standing up with his old typewriter on a counter, while he used the burners on the stove to keep warm. He seemed exhausted and miserable, and admitted that he wasn't getting much done.

In a few weeks, I was leaving on magazine assignments that would take me backpacking and kayaking in Wyoming and Alaska for half the summer. I offered Vito my ramshackle cottage while I was gone. It didn't have the Hollywood pedigree that came with Tomlin's manse, I told him, but it was easier to heat, had a big bed, and a friendly gay bar, the Pink Elephant, just down the street. He jumped at the opportunity.

When I returned to L.A. in early August, Vito had just left. The place reeked of his cigarette smoke but my cat was fat and happy, which meant she'd gotten plenty of food and attention. Just as important, Vito had left me a note on the kitchen table that was encouraging: DEAR JOHN, THANKS FOR THE USE OF YOUR PLACE. I MADE REAL PROGRESS ON THE BOOK! LOVE, VITO.

His legion of friends, including a number of Hollywood luminaries, continued to support him on his mission, offering their houses and apartments for shelter, helping him gain access to archival film clips, and tipping him when they discovered more examples from old movies that might fit somewhere in his manuscript.

There would be more detours, distractions, and procrastination. But little by little, Vito's book was coming together.

•

THE CELLULOID CLOSET: *Homosexuality in the Movies* was finally published by Harper & Row in 1981. It was an instant sensation, hailed as a groundbreaking work by both the gay and mainstream press. Just as there was no one else quite like its author, there had never been another book quite like it.

"In a hundred years of movies," Vito wrote, "homosexuality has only rarely been depicted on the screen. When it did appear, it was there as something to laugh at—or something to pity—or even something to fear. These were fleeting images, but they were unforgettable, and they left a lasting legacy. Hollywood, that great maker of myths, taught straight people what to think about gay people . . . and gay people what to think about themselves."

Although *The Celluloid Closet* never made Vito rich, it greatly raised his profile and influence as a writer and activist. In 1983, for WNYC-TV, he wrote, produced, and cohosted a series focusing on the gay community called "Our Time," which featured the nation's first GLBT hard news and documentary video segment. From coast to coast, he gave countless interviews, spoke at rallies and protests, and wrote political pieces that provoked thought and inspired action.

But Vito didn't have long to bask in the glory of his acclaimed book. The bright promise of gay liberation soon took a dark turn, as AIDS began decimating an entire generation of queer men. How we were depicted in movies now seemed less important than how we stayed alive, or cared for the dying. As the government, media, and medical establishments turned a blind eye to the growing epidemic, along with segments of the gay community itself, Vito's voice became angrier and more desperate. In 1985, he cofounded the Gay and Lesbian Alliance Against Defamation (GLAAD) in response to inaccurate, demeaning, and sensationalized coverage of AIDS by the *New York Post*. In 1986, he lost his lover, Jeffrey Sevcik, to the disease. The next year, not long after my own lover, Jon-Noel, had died from pneumocystis, Vito cofounded ACT UP, which injected new militancy into AIDS activism and took it loudly to the streets.

I'd lost touch with him during those horrific years, but ran into him later in 1987 at Greenblatt's deli on Sunset Boulevard, across from the Directors Guild of America headquarters. Vito had once attended movie screenings there, but now the DGA building was the setting for a panel discussion of AIDS and the media. He was a panelist and I was attending as a journalist. When we bumped into each other at Greenblatt's, he hugged me, as always, but without much strength. I noticed that his face was drawn and unusually pale, and the famous sparkle in his dark eyes was all but gone.

We got our sandwiches and drinks and found a small table in a corner. He asked me how things were going and I told him about Jon-Noel's death. When I asked Vito how he was, he offered a tight little smile and rolled up a sleeve to show me the purple KS lesions on his wrist.

Vito was nothing if not a fighter, and hung on longer than many others. In 1989, he was among those featured in the Oscar-winning documentary, *Common Threads: Stories from the Quilt*. In it, he spoke about his lover's death. "Jeffrey and I dealt with our disease differently," he said. "I got angry. Jeffrey withdrew."

Vito's anger was different now—bitter, corrosive, unalloyed by the infectious *joi de vivre* for which he'd once been known. In the summer of 1990, as I cowrote a piece for the *Los Angeles*

Times on the controversy surrounding the outing of Hollywood celebrities, I called Vito for his input. There was no sense of camaraderie in our conversation, no warmth in his voice. His manner was hard and terse. He was personally opposed to exposing closeted gay celebrities against their wishes, he told me, but he was also furious that more of them were not standing up and being counted, and raising their voices in the fight for more AIDS treatment and prevention.

"I'm tired of defending all the closet queens," he said. "People are dying. We need some help here."

My editor thought the quote was too strong, and wanted it taken out. I fought for it, and it stayed in.

Several months later, on November 7, 1990, Vito died at the age of forty-four. He'd survived long enough to see the burgeoning of independent queer filmmaking, the establishment of successful GLBT film events like the Los Angeles Gay & Lesbian Film Festival (now Outfest), and even the inclusion of sympathetic gay characters in mainstream movies, although he disdained most of the them as well meaning but condescending.

At a memorial gathering for Vito, several dozen of his West Coast friends joined to reminisce at the Hollywood Hills home of producer Craig Zadan. I remember one man in particular, who spoke about the impact Vito had on his own consciousness and sense of integrity as a writer. "Every time I sit down to write," he told us, "I feel Vito looking over my shoulder."

Five years after Vito's death, a documentary version of *The Celluloid Closet*—written by Armistead Maupin, produced and directed by his friends Rob Epstein and Jeffrey Friedman and narrated by Lily Tomlin—was released theatrically. Lighter and less pointedly political than the book, it nonetheless brought Vito's seminal work to the silver screen that had so entranced him, in an entertaining fashion that I suspect would have pleased him.

As for the book itself, it's still in print, used in film and cultural history classes and read around the world.

I never bought a copy myself. Before I could, Vito mailed one to the little house in Ocean Park where I'd first gotten to know him after his jubilant evening at the Fox Venice Theater. The inscription, dated June 24, 1981, reads: DEAR JOHN—THANKS FOR THE MEMORIES. LOVE XXX, VITO.

a remembrance
of rand schrader

ed pierce

ANY RESPONSIBLE HISTORY of the gay and lesbian civil rights movement in Los Angeles would necessarily include the contributions of Rand Schrader, a pioneering activist and ardent advocate who banded together in the early 1970s with a cadre of other gay men and lesbians to champion the cause of equality in Southern California. Through his transcendently open life, Rand significantly heightened the general community's awareness of homosexuality. With his forceful advocacy and inspirational leadership within the movement, he exhorted other gay men and lesbians to follow his example by standing up, being acknowledged, and demanding equal rights.

For a heartening number of young lesbian, gay, bisexual, and transgender people today, the notion of leading open lives is a given. However, as late as the 1970s, the openly gay professional was a rare phenomenon, even in as progressive a city as Los Angeles. Rand was one of the precious few and, as such, established himself as a seminal role model for the rest of us. Rand first became politically active while in law school and continued to pursue the course of justice as a cofounder of what is now the L.A. Gay and Lesbian Center, and also as the first openly gay staff attorney in the L.A. City Attorney's office and one of the first openly gay judges in the State of California.

My partner, Rob Saltzman, and I are grateful beneficiaries of Rand's mentoring. We are also fortunate enough to have been two of his closest friends.

Rob and I met while law school classmates at Harvard in the late 1970s and settled together in L.A. shortly after graduation. Rob met Rand in the early 1980s, when they were introduced by then L.A. county supervisor Ed Edelman. Rob quickly took to Rand for many reasons, including his piercing intellect, political acumen, and extraordinarily kind heart. Rand liked Rob, too, and they became friends, shortly after which Rob arranged for me to meet Rand.

To me, Rand was a revelation. Utterly comfortable in his own skin, he exuded a commanding self-confidence that I had never before encountered in an openly gay man. By contrast, I was, at that stage of my life, an "uncomfortably" gay corporate attorney in a well-regarded L.A. law firm. Rand bowled me over. He quickly, and astutely, concluded that I was in urgent need of mentoring, and discovered that we happened to share a dilettante's interest in the culinary arts. Long conversations about recipes helped us become friends in our own right.

Meanwhile, health-care issues became paramount with the advent of AIDS. During that early, desperate time, Rand devoted himself to the comfort of friends who fell ill and succumbed to the epidemic; he also continued to fight ever more fervently for greater awareness of HIV and better treatment of those affected by it.

In 1991, Rand was diagnosed with AIDS. He confronted the news with the same honesty and frankness that he had displayed in all other facets of his life. On many public occasions, Rand described the self-examination that the onset of AIDS in others and then in himself had forced him to conduct. His candor was sometimes startling. Rand, whose public reflections form the basis of this fond remembrance, died in June of 1993. (Quotations in this essay made without attribution are Rand's own words.)

STARTING OUT

BORN IN LOS ANGELES IN 1945, Rand Schrader came of age when most gay men lived in the closet, or as he would later call it, a "prison of McCarthyite repression." Upon graduating from Venice High School in 1963, Rand attended the University of California at Berkeley and became part of that campus's Free Speech Movement. He returned to Los Angeles to enroll in law school at UCLA, where he formed the university's first gay student union and became part of the vibrant new gay and lesbian community.

Those were heady days for Rand. He "exulted" in his newfound freedom and in his friendships with fellow activists. True to the time, Rand heeded his bohemian instincts and moved into an L.A. commune. He also joined the Gay Liberation Front. Photographs of Rand and his friends from those days show a motley crew, and Rand stands out among them, with a head full of curly hair he once aptly likened to Elsa Lanchester's giant electrified wig in *The Bride of Frankenstein*.

Rand's first gay liberation meeting "set [him] on fire" and led him to work with other pioneers in forming the Gay Community Services Center in 1971. The Center first occupied an "old, dirty and disheveled" space on Wilshire Boulevard with a small, hand-painted sign that, to Rand, "was like a neon billboard on Times Square." The first Center was "a place for us, where we were normal and the rest of the world was different." The Center subsequently moved to a much larger space on Highland Avenue, which seemed at the time "like a palace, a Taj Mahal for our community." The Center, on whose board of directors Rand served for fifteen years, now occupies a still larger building in Hollywood and is one of the nation's largest social services agencies serving the LGBT community.

Critical to Rand's development as a gay activist was his friendship with Sheldon Andelson, a prominent lawyer, banker, real estate entrepreneur, and California Regent—and also a gay man. Sheldon and Rand forged a remarkably strong friendship, despite their fourteen-year age difference, divergent postures within the gay community, and strikingly different circumstances. On the one hand, Rand was a trailblazing, openly gay public servant with student loans to repay. By contrast, Sheldon, through his own efforts, had become independently wealthy and was someone who, "[d]riving up in his Jaguar, with his pair of whippets on leashes, dressed casually in cashmere and hand-sewn shoes, was not [your] typical gay liberationist." Moreover, Sheldon had perfected "the gay skill . . . of being straight with straight people and gay with us" and would "whisper" confidences to other gay men and lesbians in mixed settings.

Rand never tried to master that particular gay skill. Instead, the message that Sheldon whispered, and that organizations such as ACT UP would later shout, Rand communicated simply by stating the truth, forthrightly and naturally, without shame or excess: This is who I am. As Rand put it, "Wherever I've gone, I've been open about being gay. And when I leave, people may not like me but they're not afraid of me." On the circuitous road to gay awareness, Rand, with his quiet dignity and unforced eloquence, was, in the words of friend Torie Osborn, a "militant moderate," whose sincerity rang through his every word, and who simply did not know how to be glib. With Rand, words became action.

While Sheldon provided Rand with access to influential politicians and decision makers, not to mention Sheldon's commitment of significant financial resources on behalf of the gay liberation movement, Rand taught Sheldon that living an open life bore its own additional rewards. Before they became friends, the threads of Sheldon's professional and private lives had run along parallel, functionally independent tracks, while Rand's, in an evolutionary leap, were already intertwined. Sheldon was clearly Rand's mentor, but Rand reversed their roles in demonstrating to Sheldon the value of proclaiming one's own gayness. With that lesson learned, Sheldon ascended to a unique position as an openly gay force among the powers that be, throughout California and nationally.

FORGING AN OPEN CAREER

FROM THE OUTSET, Rand excelled in his chosen profession of attorney. L.A. City Attorney Burt Pines recognized Rand's potential early on when he hired Rand as the first openly homosexual attorney in an office comprising hundreds of other staff lawyers. According to Pines, Rand "was a real pioneer. There was a lot of pressure on him being first." Although something of a curiosity, Rand was, again according to Pines, a "star performer" who worked his way up to leadership of the office's criminal appellate section.

Rand's ascendancy through Southern California's legal ranks continued when, in 1980, Governor Jerry Brown appointed him to the L.A. Municipal Court. David Bohnett, in recounting his ten-year loving partnership with Rand, recalled Rand telling him stories about police officers in the courtroom staring in disbelief at a homosexual judge. Yet, despite his diminutive stature and quiet demeanor, Rand commanded the bench. He exuberantly embraced his new station as jurist and quickly mastered the laws that he had sworn to administer. For him, this was the role of a lifetime.

Rand later described his reaction to becoming part of the L.A. legal establishment, whereupon, suddenly a "career that had begun as an outsider, in protest, moved inside. Inside was as great a challenge. One had the opportunity to enter rooms and speak to people who were convinced that no one like them was gay or lesbian. Together, you and I began to change others' views of us, as we had changed our own views of ourselves."

While Rand's prominence as a judge heightened the general public's awareness of homosexuality, it also proved a lightning rod for young and aspiring gay and lesbian lawyers, who saw in Rand a new breed of role model. Through the years, Rand and David opened their home to frequent fund-raisers for charitable causes. For Rand, the most important of these were the receptions they held for gay and lesbian law students and young lawyers. Many prominent LGBT attorneys and judges in Los Angeles and elsewhere would today almost certainly credit Rand and his purposeful hospitality with facilitating their own open careers.

A Fine Romance

In 1983, Rand exercised a pleasurable judicial prerogative when he swore in a new attorney to the California Bar. The young lawyer invited several friends to observe the ceremony, including David Bohnett, a product of the undergraduate business program at the University of Southern California who had detoured through Ann Arbor to obtain an MBA at Michigan before returning to Los Angeles to begin his career. During the reception that followed the formalities, Rand and David hit it off, and a romance ensued.

Rand soon described to Rob and me a recent "moonlit and magical" evening that he had spent with David strolling hand in hand through downtown Los Angeles, where David resided in a high-rise apartment building on Bunker Hill.

Almost overnight, what began as a courthouse flirtation had grown into a serious love affair that trumped convenience, and David moved into Rand's house on Green Oak Drive near Griffith Park. They lived there together until Rand's death a decade later. Before the sadness surrounding Rand's imminent demise consumed them, those years were extraordinarily happy times for Rand and David.

As Rand and David worked together in refurbishing their ranch house and transforming it into a showcase of 1950s furniture and style, they also had a much broader salutary influence on each other. Among other things, David taught Rand how to relax and appreciate the wonder of any given moment, while Rand nurtured David's activist instincts.

Ominously, Rand and David's happy domestic moments became increasingly interrupted by calls from friends who had fallen ill in ways that baffled not only them but the entire medical establishment.

The Gathering Storm

In time, science historians may conclude that the identification of HIV and the development of medications to treat it were something of a medical miracle, a milestone in the annals of scientific detective work. To those who endured the onslaught of the disease, however, that finding would be hard to accept. At the time, the search for even the cause of the fatal syndrome seemed to take a hellish eternity. Friends were becoming sick and dying at alarming rates, and no one knew why. The horror of the time reminded those old enough to remember of the experience of having seen young men sent off to fight in America's foreign wars. In the age of AIDS, gay men in their thirties and forties became incongruously adept at giving eulogies, and there appeared to be no end in sight to the carnage. It was an excruciating time.

Among those to fall prey to the disease early on was one of Rand's dearest friends, Roger Horwitz, a sweet, unassuming man whose modesty masked an imposing mind that had allowed him to collect both a law degree and doctorate in comparative literature at Harvard before moving to L.A. to practice law. Roger was also the partner of author and poet Paul Monette, perhaps the greatest chronicler of the early years of AIDS.

Roger's diagnosis threw Rand into a tailspin. With David at his side, Rand sustained Roger and Paul through much of their ordeal. In an especially harsh blow, as Roger, blinded by his illness, lay dying, Rand's mentor and Roger's half-brother, Sheldon Andelson, also developed AIDS. Roger died in 1986, only to be followed in death by Sheldon in 1988. Paul Monette himself died of the effects of AIDS in 1995. In a span of nine years, Roger, Sheldon, Paul, and Rand, along with dozens of friends and acquaintances, succumbed to the epidemic.

In a 1990 speech, Rand traced his history as a gay liberator and acknowledged the clash between the freedom earned through the gay civil rights movement and the unconscionable toll exacted by AIDS:

"For me, twenty years ago began the sweet, early years of liberation: marches, meetings, messages of internal pride that convinced us that winning was only a matter of time and that, in time, we would be the first gay people to be open, free, and equal. And it felt that there was no price for this gain, no pain, or, at least, not a price that we could not pay without ease. If there was a sacrifice by coming out or speaking up, the sacrifice seemed almost a reward in itself . . .

"I had no idea what lay ahead, or that the payment was being deferred and would accrue until it was as great as the value of our achievements. I did not know that the cost for developing that internal pride . . . would bring the risk of feeling all the pain of the demise of . . . so many friends . . ."

On another such occasion, he acknowledged that, "comfort and satisfaction are not to be ours in this generation. Instead, the time has come to pay the price . . . After those years of liberation and what we thought was our heroism, we see now that that was the easy part . . . that was the preparation. Today, we must ask: If being gay is good, how could so much that is bad happen? Our courage is in our willingness to live with the contradiction between our conviction that the way we love is right, even as we lose those whom we love."

Within a year, that contradiction would land on Rand and David's doorstep.

Confronting AIDS

In 1991, Rand and David arrived unannounced at my law firm's offices in Century City to tell me that they had just come from their doctor's office, where Rand had been informed that he was HIV-positive, while David learned that he was negative. The doctor had also told Rand that his T-cell count was discouragingly low and that immediate steps needed to be taken to enrich his immune system.

Rand's health declined quickly, and he soon received an AIDS diagnosis. At the time, the promise of the drugs that today stall the progress of HIV was no more than a promise; as a result, a diagnosis in those early years seemed to offer little hope of survival. Thanks to the eventual arrival of somewhat effective medications, however, thousands of persons with AIDS have withstood daunting tests of time and today live active, productive lives, decades after having contracted the virus.

In November of 1991, Rand announced in the *Los Angeles Times* and other local newspapers that he had AIDS. He said that he was making his announcement to show the public that the disease could strike anyone and that he hoped to strip away the stigma then associated with the illness. With his announcement, Rand again became a role model, this time for those living with HIV/AIDS.

When his illness kept him from working, Rand took solemn stock of his professional life. His introspection taught him "how to come to peace with the end of ambition. Lawyers seem to be inherently ambitious; and, to the degree that I have sought more . . . I have been a lawyer. I do not mean to suggest that my efforts have been inordinately selfish—I hope I've worked for our common good—but there has been an awful lot of 'me,' 'me-ness' in that work—my way . . . It's stunning when one faces the end of 'me.'"

Rand insisted that talking publicly about his sadness "should be allowed: a truthful reflection of the inner life of a dying person," the thoughts of someone who has been forced to give up the idea of "someday." He reminded the rest of us that those fighting AIDS are thrown "into the frightening and deeply veiled portions of our minds that begin to come to consciousness when one feels death's breath."

Rand revealed in a late address that he had experienced an unexpected sense of liberation when he met at last his one true self:

"It hurts to give up the competitive activity that I have used to fortify an insecure ego. It hurts . . . to shed the mantle of powerfulness that I have used to obscure my limitations from myself. But now I am getting ready to be sad, and I am sad, and it is setting me free, at last. Not a winner, not dominant, not influential; but free to be alive to enjoy what is, instead of what I wanted there to be, and free to be alive to enjoy who I am, instead of who I needed myself to be."

Feeling Death's Breath

Rand continued to speak publicly about his private journey even after his voice had weakened and the pace of his step had slowed. In December, 1992, at the dedication of the McDonald/Wright Building of the L.A. Gay and Lesbian Center, Rand observed, in what was effectively his valedictory address, that, despite the gay and lesbian community's long-held expectation that "our own building [would help validate our belief that] the way the lesbian and gay community was acting had substance," the reality of AIDS had taught us all that "it's not the building that was the miracle. It was the spirit, the intangible rightness of our belief in our gay and lesbian selves . . . The building has a substance that is important—but substance is what we are getting ready to leave behind. That substance will be yours to manage."

In April of 1993, with six weeks to live, Rand journeyed to Washington, D.C., to participate, as he had done in years past, in a march for gay and lesbian rights attended by thousands of fellow demonstrators. On this last trip, Rand "marched" in a wheelchair pushed by David. By now, Rand's cheeks were hollow, his posture sagged, a sunhat shielded his sallow skin, and he tired easily, but he had insisted on making the trip to take part in a protest that would someday lead to inevitable victory:

"In time, we will win. Unfortunately, it . . . won't be in my time. But I have accepted that our 'time' is not always ours to manage. You will carry on the fight. You will continue to come out and encourage others to do the same."

Rand's strength ebbed further still, and he knew that his immediate prognosis was grim. He addressed his predicament with halting self-acceptance:

"Now I am struggling daily, both physically and emotionally, to reconcile myself to giving up, to giving in to the reality of what is happening to me—facing the end of the cycle of years that I thought would be endless . . . [when] I could hope for all gifts and be ambitious for all achievements. This giving up and giving in to the end of . . . the belief that there is time, in the future, to become who I hoped I would be, requires the sad acceptance that this is all I am, and this is all I have done."

In June, with death at hand, Rand told David that he wanted to leave their home to return to Century City Hospital. Confronted with a dizzying array of medical equipment and medications, Rand was feeling anxious about remaining at home, even though David had long since mastered the ministrations that comprised Rand's regimen. Rand ultimately decided that a hospital setting would provide a calmer environment from which to leave this world than the makeshift clinic that their house had become, and David honored Rand's decision.

As I hurried to their home to drive them to the hospital, David wheeled Rand slowly around the house for a final tour of their private domain. Together, they surveyed the assorted photographs of family and friends, the resilient koi that had survived occasional nocturnal raccoon attacks, the shimmering pool that Rand and David had commissioned when they were feeling flush, the gourmet kitchen that had brought Rand such pleasure, their "California" king-sized bed, and Rand's forever untidy desk.

Upon my arrival, David and I lifted Rand from his wheelchair and carried him down the stairs. Lacking the strength even to sit up without arm supports, Rand lay across the backseat of his noisy diesel sedan. By that time, he was also experiencing considerable physical discomfort.

I cannot recall what, if anything, the three of us talked about during our half-hour drive to the hospital. When he telephoned me shortly beforehand, David had shared with me the purpose of this particular trip, and so I understood its mortal significance. I was at a loss for words. Soon, though, Rand was lying in bed in his not-unpleasant hospital room, where he seemed considerably less agitated, and much more comfortable overall.

Within a matter of days, David addressed a crowd gathered in a UCLA auditorium as Rand received in absentia the university's Distinguished Alumnus Award. In accepting the award on Rand's behalf, David thanked the university and those who had championed Rand's candidacy. He also informed the assembled guests that Rand was on the verge of death. After his speech, David returned to the hospital to recount the evening's events to Rand, and to say good-bye.

As David had predicted, Rand died in the darkness of the coming morning. It was June 14, 1993, and Rand was forty-eight years old.

An Abiding Legacy

As Rand's body was being laid to rest in a plain pine coffin at Mount Sinai Cemetery, official Los Angeles honored his memory. Civic and political leaders spoke appreciatively of Rand's irreproachable integrity and many accomplishments. The several blocks of Hudson Avenue that include the Center's main building were renamed Schrader Boulevard after swift action by the L.A. City Council in an effort led by Mike Woo. The County named the AIDS clinic at County–USC Medical Center, a medical facility that Rand had been instrumental in opening, the Rand Schrader Clinic.

Meanwhile, a generous bequest from Rand to David, combined with David's own visionary genius and the benefit of a nine-month sabbatical that allowed him to consider the future in the face of his wrenching loss, sparked in David an idea for an Internet company that would ultimately give voice to millions of members within a host of cyber communities.

Soon thereafter, David founded GeoCities, which quickly became a thriving nexus of online communities dedicated to the art of self-expression. Within a matter of only several years, GeoCities went public to inordinate success, only to be purchased within a year thereafter by Yahoo! for a price that reflected the euphoric Internet valuations of the era.

Suddenly a man with a great fortune, David took a big chunk of the sale's proceeds and established the David Bohnett Foundation, a private charitable organization dedicated to advancing the goals of the LGBT community, as well as other issues that are close to David's heart. To date, the Foundation has donated eighteen million dollars to worthy causes that continue to advance its several important missions.

Today, David is one of L.A.'s foremost civic leaders, not only within the LGBT community, but citywide and beyond. He has spearheaded and funded, personally and through the David Bohnett Foundation, important social and political initiatives and organizations that have advanced the cause of LGBT rights on many fronts. In addition to running his own private equity firm, David also now holds positions of importance within several nationally prominent artistic and philanthropic institutions.

These achievements constitute, in part, Rand's spiritual legacy to David. Just as David had been hobbled by Rand's loss, he felt invigorated by Rand's lifelong example of service to the LGBT community. Rand was, in David's words, his "inspiration" and "beacon of truth." Although David gallantly took up Rand's mantle of activism, he did so in his own way and on his own terms, and has since crafted a life and amassed a list of achievements of which Rand would be immeasurably proud. It is, of course, a cruel irony that Rand was deprived of witnessing David's stunning financial success, together with the long reach of his philanthropy and advocacy.

to live outside the law you must be honest

robin podolsky

FERD AND I were having dinner, pasta under stagy orange light. He talked about wanting to stay outlaw, about his suspicions of any utopian project that would threaten to make queers into earnest sorts—either rebels or reformers. He'd prefer us to be amoral. I said I'd be happy with any utopian project that accomplished any qualitative improvement along the lines of peace, plenty, and liberty, so long as it really included everybody, not just queers.

Ferd talked abut the amorality of the greenwood, the outlaw's domain. About returning, in the forest, to nature's impersonal, pitiless laws "red in tooth and claw . . ." Reminding him that I was named for the greenwood's chief outlaw, I opined that Robin and his band were *intensely* moral. They robbed the rich to aid the poor. And they may have been pagan religious traditionalists. Thirteen men and a maid: a proper coven. Robin and Marion served as king and queen of the May, of Beltane, with its Maypole and bonfire, the inauguration of spring. A stern moralism, to persist in one's ecstatic rites when people were murdered for less.

Ferd talked about gay men and opera. About his weakness for Richard Strauss. About taking a *perverse* delight in the will-to-power's immolation in its own flame.

What about the fascist misreading of Nietzsche's attack on morality, I asked? Isn't that where amoralism leads? To pink triangles and nights of long knives?

I know, said Ferd, and that's just it. I hate the actuality of fascism and its criminalization of queerness, but I come from a generation of men for whom sexuality is sited in guilt and outlawry.

I come from a generation of outlaws who disdain guilt, I said.

Disdain is a reaction, he reminded me.

I talked about the impossibility of true amorality. We can defy what the dominant culture calls moral; we can see something new, but every replacement or rejection is still a response, shaped by what provoked it. Amorality is like prehistoricity; you can't get there from here.

I'm talking about what gets me off, he said.

Ferd talked about Doctor Faustus and Thomas Mann. It's the moral person who gets tempted into monstrous acts, he said. It's moral people who presume to remake the world and forget that what we know of power is what we've been taught by the people we try to replace.

•

FERD TALKED ABOUT gay men of a certain generation, asking if I'd read *The Boys in the Band*.

I saw the movie, I told him. Hated it.

It's one of my favorites, he said.

I said that my reaction to *The Boys in the Band* reminds me of my dad's stories about his grandmother who came from the *shtetl*. Everything she wore was black, including a shawl that covered her traditionally shaved head. She walked to the market with a huge shopping bag, which she kept filled with candy. When she met my dad, then a child, with a friend on the street, she'd ask the other kid, "You Jewish?" They always said yes and she always gave them candy. Until she died, she never learned much more English than that.

The homosexual lead character in *The Boys in the Band* says, "Show me a happy homosexual and I'll show you a gay corpse."

An ungrateful queer, I respond: "Ma, what's with the accent? You've been in this country twenty years already."

The homosexual wears a fussy little beard and a buttoned-up cardigan. (Ma, why don't you let Tiffany take you shopping?)

The homosexual hands his paycheck to an unreconstructed Freudian who shunts his life story through some object-relations schematic. (Ma, you don't have to be scared over here. When are you are going to learn how to drive?)

Why can't those guys get over it, I asked.

Why can't Holocaust survivors get over it, Ferd said.

Ferd talked about the virtues of compassion, of loving people for their own victories, not the ones we'd wish on them. I shut up for a while. My dad had been scalded with embarrassment at his grandmother's behavior. Safe in Los Angeles, with a living grand-mother who had been a speakeasy flapper, I thought my great-grandma sounded adorable. Younger queers than I are now call-ing *The Boys in the Band* a classic. Crazy kids. What do they know from being an outlaw whether you want to be or not?

•

FERD CAME FROM the Protestant middle-class heartland. I come from Jewish blue-collar L.A. He was drawn to the Romantic side of revolution; I to the moral. He was Prairie Fire, I went proletarian; he to Gay Liberation, I to Lesbian Feminism. Until AIDS brought lots of us back together, united at first by the bottomless indifference of the straight world to the gathering doom, but later by the depth and richness of what would be called the LGBT communities, along with an acknowledgment of Marxism's anti-democratic failures.

Ferd Eggan was only seven years older than I am. I didn't have to help found Gay Liberation—I attended my first Gay Day in Griffith Park before I left high school.

Ferd was just old enough to get in on the tail end of the civil rights movement's voter registration drives in the South. Both of us decided when we were quite young that, however we made a living and no matter what talents we cultivated, our life work would be about leaving the world cleaner, happier, and more just than we had found it. In our respective circles, this was quite normal and normative.

And this is where huge swaths of gay, trans and queer L.A. would come from—out of the Left. We understood, and were proud to know, that we were riding a tsunami of change that reached back to the African-American civil rights movement and encompassed Women's Liberation and opposition to war and poverty. Furthermore, we had learned, in the Left, how to do stuff. How to chair a meeting; to always pass a sign-up sheet in a meeting; to, mostly, keep our tempers when everybody's issues surfaced at a meeting. To define a program—what do we want? To define strategies and tactics—what are steps to what we want? What actions will get us there? To coordinate 'sectors'—streets and suits, for example—without limiting our own perspectives to comport with theirs. To remember that some of us are people of color, women, or poor and that an attack on one is an attack on all. Understand—this was the perspective that guided a huge cohort of those who, in turn, guided Gay, then Queer, Liberation out of its infancy.

There was a particular virtue associated with Ferd's approach to Revolution—he was rarely dour, and he never eschewed 're-formist' victories that would improve people's lives. Ferd was a published poet and an accomplished videographer; he also took a turn as AIDS services coordinator for the City of Los Angeles and helped to bring clean needles to L.A.'s streets. If he flirted with a dangerous infatuation for those streets, he also saved lives which others might have thrown away.

•

THE GREENWOOD NEVER LASTS, but when you get there, even for a little while, it's marvelous. In October of 1991, for weeks at a time, a lot of us got there together.

Governor Pete Wilson (1991–1999) was a forerunner of Rudy Guliani. He styled himself as a 'tough' politician who stayed in power during a recession by aiming public anger at outsiders: undocumented immigrants and people in trouble with the law. He signed the first Three Strikes law in California, recommenced executions and, while gutting social services as his answer to hard times, helped to lay the foundations for the prison industry of today.

Wilson also vetoed AB 101, a bill that would have forbidden discrimination in employment on the basis of sexual orientation. This was a huge disappointment to Wilson's Log Cabin friends. Like Guliani after him, Wilson had tended to make nice with Republican gays, while sporting his own hypermasculine style. AB 101 had been tailored to be a moderate measure by those committed to "working with the governor" to get sexual orientation into a civil rights bill. Such people would insist, later, that Wilson had signaled his willingness to sign such a bill.

In late September, when most of California's veteran queer activists were massing in Washington, D.C. to fight for AIDS advances, Wilson quietly issued his veto on the grounds that AB 101 would be too restrictive on business, his key constituency. Rumor had it that pressure for the veto had come, not only from various business and social conservative groups, but also from the White House.

Everyone expected San Francisco to explode, and it did, spectacularly, for about forty-eight hours. What no one expected, even those of us who live here, was the torrent of people who took to the streets of Los Angeles almost every night for two weeks and continued to demonstrate, off and on, for a solid month, forcing the northern Californians to join us in a culminating march on the state capitol two weeks later.

Upwards of twenty thousand people, most of whom had never participated in any demonstration, marched for miles without permits and without hurting anybody. The turning point was a September 30 rally—on a Monday night! The local leadership had rented a sound truck and worked things out with the City of West Hollywood. The moderate leaders had planned for folks to show up, burn a state flag, vent their anger, and leave while under control. A few Queer Nationals were kind of hoping for a riot. Neither extreme was gratified.

However, Queer Nation did spark what followed by simply turning the crowd around. The late Corey Roberts-Auli, activist and visual artist, simply took the mike and asked the Queer Nationals to meet him in the back. The entire assembly, composed mostly of grassroots lesbian, gay, bisexual, and transgender people whom the activists had never met, turned and noticed that we were surrounded by riot police in full gear. Word passed that Pete Wilson was meeting the president of Mexico at the Los Angeles County Museum of Art (LACMA), not too far away.

What happened next was a moment of extraordinary power and grace. Like ghosts, a group of former strangers moved safely through lines of armed police and into the streets. We arrived at LACMA in time to join with the Mexican nationals who were protesting their president's policies and to be confronted with police on horseback. Without violence and without backing off, this huge crowd *sat down* until we were ready to go.

Not that anyone was docile. My favorite chant that night turned out to be, "Pete Wilson, you fucking weasel, come on down and face the people." The governor ignored the invitation.

Things got uglier when the crowd moved on to the place known by every L.A. organizer for any cause as the vortex of bad mojo—the Century Plaza Hotel. A favorite spot for Republican fund-raisers and a place where demonstrators have been beaten by police since the antiwar protests of the 1960s, demonstrators tried to enter the hotel, and the cops did their thing. Litigation would, of course, follow. And we were off.

The next two weeks proved to be a smaller, localized version of the "people power" demonstrations that swept the globe around that time, toppling dictators of the right and the putative left. West Hollywood, a city that gay people, along with Jewish seniors, helped to found, was the epicenter. But it wouldn't remain so. Soon enough, people who were concerned that the march did not look enough like L.A. put out a flier and pulled the crowd into Silver Lake, a wonderful neighborhood mixture of the Latino working class, various waves of immigration, multiculti Bohemia, and (snap!) Las Queers fabulosa.

Over three thousand people filled the streets of Hollywood to protest a visit by the Reverend Jerry Falwell and to sit in at the Bowl, right as the Sting concert was ending. Night after night, it became a serious game to see where we could turn up next—in the San Fernando Valley; in the unfriendly territory of Orange County; at Los Angeles International Airport, where we wended our way through terminals and down the main traffic artery in and out. (You'd think that would have been a major national story. You'd think so, wouldn't you?)

Yes, people were inconvenienced and, perhaps, lives were changed. People were frightened of us, and they had a right to be. When a group succumbs to that Romantic fantasy of Authenticity and assigns authority to its impulses, dreadful things can happen. We took a serious risk. Fortunately, we never stopped processing, that is, debating in the streets and on the fly, what would be acceptable to do next—we never fissioned off into flying squads or became a mob. We didn't allow our chanting to drown out our capacity for conversation—and most of our impulses turned out to be pretty decent. In the face of extreme provocation, that included one marcher being bloodied by a flashlight, we remained nonviolent. The only documented destruction of property in Los Angeles, on the day of September 30, involved a smashed plate glass door in the Ronald Reagan State Office Building.

The demonstrators were mostly young. While what happened was truly spontaneous, it's worth remembering that these young people had grown up with a set of expectations about their future and assumptions about their worth that are as different from those that shaped me as my own inheritance is different from that which shaped Ferd. Thanks to the activists and social currents that preceded them, these young people had, for the most part, assumed that they were, already, of equal status to their compatriots. To discover otherwise did not shame them in the least; it just made them angry. At the same time, they had, with that anger, nothing to prove and little to vent. They didn't need to be violent; they needed to assert their right to the streets for which they pay taxes like everybody else.

Those moments when we bring the greenwood to life in the city seem miraculous. They are moments of alchemical shift. However, they come as a result of the sometimes tedious, frustrating organizing that only the committed and deliberate can achieve.

•

ON OCTOBER 11, National Coming Out Day, a rally in response to the veto was held in Sacramento on the capitol building steps. Northern Californians had found themselves called to action by people from the region they had dismissed as their fund-raising cash cow. National leaders, such as Urvashi Vaid, had flown in to speak.

We were sharing a cab, Michael, Roland, John, and me, heading to the capitol building from the airport with the radio tuned to news of another spectacle—one that we had almost forgotten but with which most of the country was preoccupied. Michael Weinstein and Roland Palencia were the president and vice-president of the AIDS Healthcare Foundation.

Michael and Roland. One wiseass, ex-Trotskyite Jew from New York and one corporate executive son of Central American pro-labor activists; two men who began as "streets," and, as "suits," were building an international service agency. John Callahan, an Irish-Portuguese working-class intellectual from Boston who had, along with David Hughes, Andrea Carney, and Thea Other, founded Age Of Consent in 1981, L.A.'s first queer rap group. And your faithful scribe.

The four of us were trading protest stories and anticipating the action to come. Just as we took a simultaneous pause, the radio delivered words that none of us, even the most cynical, had ever imagined would come from the Senate floor: "Can you remember the title of the film, Professor Hill?" "I believe it was . . . *Long Dong Silver.*"

What did we just hear? It wasn't the spectre of sexuality that left us worldly radicals bug-eyed. It was the bottomless venality of what was taking place. On the Republican side, a known mediocrity was being nominated to take Thurgood Marshall's place on the highest court; it was the most devastating revelation possible of the then president's opinion of the level of excellence that African Americans might attain. A black woman who had blown the whistle on sexual harassment was being interrogated about moral rectitude by Strom Thurmond. The Democrats were represented through Ted Kennedy's green-faced reluctance to confront that particular sort of scandal just then. Two people of color were being set on one another by a bunch of white guys who would declare the winner—and we already knew that the smart money would be on the black person with a penis.

And all we needed to do about the bankruptcy was turn away. It was time to turn our bodies and our hearts toward the work we had to do. We weren't at the margins; we were at the center of another place, of the greenwood we had made flower in the city when we, in our implacable moralism, declared our passion for each other and our lives to be above unjust laws. For a little while, the capitol building we'd paid for would really be ours.

•

QUEER NATION, the heroes of that hour, rescued us from the imperatives that produced the Clarence Thomas hearings and from fixing our own identities into unchangeable straitjackets. With his very unreliability, Bill Clinton rescued us from the unproductive illusions of assimilation. And with its current assaults on our existence, the right wing rescued us from historical amnesia.

However, we never could make the media give the post-veto marches the coverage we thought they deserved. Twenty thousand people. In the streets of Los Angeles. No permit. Weeks. We took over the frikkin' *airport*, for crap's sake. Later, when L.A.'s streets erupted after the Rodney King verdict and the whole world paid attention, more than one queer activist wondered bitterly if nonviolence had become an inadequate media strategy.

And now? Has it made a difference? Did the post-veto marches become queer DNA?

In California, sexual orientation and gender presentation have both been added to those categories listed in the famous Unruh civil rights act that protects against discrimination in both employment and housing. The State Legislature boasts an LGBT Caucus (although we've yet to elect either an open B or T).

Clarence Thomas has been joined on the Supreme Court by a cohort of conservative judges, thanks to Bush *père* and *fils*. He has had some success with an autobiography.

This year, Larry Craig, a Republican senator from Idaho, was busted in a sting operation and accused of soliciting sex from a male police officer in a bathroom at the Minneapolis airport. Craig continues to insist that he is not gay. That Craig was arrested in the sort of entrapment scheme that would no longer be tolerated in L.A. speaks to our progress as compared to the rest of the country; that someone who appears to be familiar with tearoom semaphore could not only reject the idea that he is gay himself, but vehemently oppose gay marriage and national anti-discrimination laws, speaks to what hasn't changed; that Craig has not been forced from office and that the country is debating same-gender marriage speaks to what has changed indeed.

•

FERD AND I SPOKE for the last time a week or so before he died. He held court graciously—really. No irony here; he knew what was coming and he was meeting it with grace and doing what he could to share, with his parades of visitors, this new peace. He told me that, after all, what mattered were his relationships with the people he loved and who loved him. He said that he had discovered both an interest in Buddhism and, after all again, a renewed appreciation for Christianity. He was giving away his possessions and invited me to leave with a bag of books and a shirt (which I'm wearing now) that he had picked out for me. Red and black, my signature colors; Ferd remembered things like that.

As veterans do, we reminisced and talked about those kids today. (What do they know from oppression?) Ferd, whose video persona was called the Cranky PWA, worried about assimilation. He said, that two gay men who adopt a baby and both keep their jobs and hire a nanny are not good role models for gay parenting. I said, It depends on the men, the jobs, and the nanny.

And there, for the last time, we were again. Ever the romantic, Ferd was worried about losing our essence, about assimilation. Now the committed Jew, all I care about is that we give and receive justice and are kind. What does assimilation mean these days, anyway? When sitcoms include gay couples and their gayness isn't the joke? Haven't we changed the culture as much as it changes us?

Bob Zimmerman once observed that, "to live outside the law, you must be honest." But honesty depends on truth claims, which matter most when justice, that is, laws, are at stake. We demand rights; we accept responsibilities. Our group heritage will never be that of people who aren't us. But each of us belongs to many groups. (Thanks, Ma. If it wasn't for your incorrigible survival, I wouldn't be here.)

•

THOSE MOMENTS AT the barricades never last. The grand illusion of absolute authenticity, of a wild place entirely outside dominant society, can't be permanent, and we only cause ourselves pain when we try to make it so. Such times are always a foretaste, a gift of stimulus, a reason not to mourn the inevitable return to everyday strictures. Because, if we keep imagining new moralities, we'll find our way to the greenwood over and over.

last call

eric gutierrez

AUGUST 1984

"ARE YOU HAPPY?"

"No, not really. Maybe there are moments when I can't think of anything wrong, when everything seems to be going my way. But I figure there's only so much of a good thing, right? So there must be some poor guy out there really getting dumped on.

"I don't know. Sure. I'm happy. Why shouldn't I be? I see friends, I go out, I flirt. Sometimes someone will flirt back. I like people. They like me. I mean, what do you want me to say? Am I happy? Sure. Insanely, profoundly, truly happy. Really, what can I say?"

"Are you happy?"

"Shit, what's with this guy and his happy? Look, are you trying to depress me or something?"

He took out ten dollars, left it on the counter, and excused himself inaudibly.

I often go to bars and pose disturbing questions. I don't know why, but I feel very strong and certain in these narrow, shadowed clichés open 'til two. I never leave with anyone. It would surprise me terribly if I did and I would feel angry and ashamed with myself afterward. I am always angry and ashamed afterward. I take that to mean it is not love.

I really don't know why I come to these places. I know real people to go out with if I want company; I have real friends to talk to if I want conversation. These people don't interest me, not really, and they never come to places like this to talk, their heads revolving in a continual demi-tour of the room like radar each time they begin a new sentence.

I don't really know why I come to these places. I should go home to Anne, let her feed me and lead me to bed.

I have total access to her body. We make love since that is what she prefers to call it. Our sex takes imagination; I call her Anne of the thousand ways.

It's last call, and I don't want to go to Anne's bed smelling of smoke and sweat and bottled beer. The lights flare up to a full two thousand watts, exposing bad skin, gray hairs, and other telltale signs. Like trolls and cheap whores, the remaining patrons retrieve discarded shirts and leather jackets and scurry from the light.

In the parking lot outside there is a scene in progress. I love a good scene and create them often. The last of the good-timers either gather around the fighting men or strike anxiously to their cars. I'm in no real hurry, so I join the onlookers. A man dressed in zippers is chasing another man, who is short enough to be a jockey, around a Datsun 280Z. The jockey is trying to maintain a good attitude while dodging wild swings of a pool cue.

"Michael, stop it."

Michael is just warming up.

"Michael! What in the hell are you doing?"

Michael swings again, misses. "I'm trying to kill you."

I turn toward my Volvo and climb in, inspired. Fastening the seat belt, I sober up at the thought of Anne. I don't want to go back to her sunny apartment and her future plans. This morning, before tying my tie and going to work, I could have had her any way I wanted. But I didn't want.

It is now eleven days since we've worked the mattress, become dumb with pleasure, and lay in the dark with chapped, thirsting tongues. This morning the romance and the erection did not spontaneously generate. There is a chance this might become an issue.

Sometimes in bed, in traffic, standing in line at the movies, I drew away from her kisses. Maybe our lips did touch. But they would immediately part. My hands probably did rest on her hips, but I didn't pull her to me. Instead, my hands were steady and noncommittal. Now I stay out late and stare at fat girls in the street. I browbeat my colleagues. I jostle the blind.

I lie. Occasionally I do accompany drunken strangers home. I did it last Tuesday. I think I may have contracted herpes. Or syphilis. Or worse. Maybe not. But maybe yes. I never worried about it before but now, with Anne, maybe I worry a little. But casually, in passing.

The Book of Revelations somehow seems like an appropriate reference: from decadence to disease to doomsday. The Lord sees fit to keep a balance sheet on my life. It reads: "Give him six figures per annum but temper it with genital sores. Allow him that promotion but at the expense of peaceful sleep. Numerous unhappy sexual encounters. Plague and pestilence."

Once a year, on a Sunday no less, the people in places like this celebrate with a parade. Abomination Fest. I read about it. Like a pileup with fatalities, that's something you can't help wanting to see.

Inside my Volvo I'm well protected. I have a better chance of surviving here than anywhere else in my life. Damn glad to be here. What more could I want than to make it through traffic, smile wryly, and swallow my own sour spit before falling into clench-toothed sleep?

This steering column collapses on impact. The headrest protects against whiplash. I talk a good relationship. Anne has yet to find me out. I see through her, though. She thinks I'm witty when I'm merely sarcastic and insists I have a sense of humor.

I wonder if Michael has killed his friend yet.

I'm smarter than Anne and can get what I want without bullying. She thinks I'm troubled. Actually, I'm cunning. She pampers me and tries to make up for the gruesome childhood I told her about but never had.

The blonde in the next lane catches my smile and thinks it's for her. I nod, accelerate, and cut her off. I'm well protected in my Volvo and fear no collision. I flip off cabbies and run waitresses ragged.

Sometimes I make Anne cry. She still believes I'm sensitive as she trembles barefoot quite late in a puddle of light, as she cries with enough feeling for both of us, as she burns all two hundred watts on the porch for me. Swollen with tears and rage, she sometimes becomes a woman I can admire, lancing accusations that I respect. I don't argue. I don't agree, either. I don't compel her to prove her point, so Anne talks to wood.

This car still smells new and not a speck of dust is lodged anywhere in the dashboard. The waxed hood throws clean reflections.

Anne is not very pretty, but men can't seem to leave her alone. Right now, though, she's home, waiting for me.

I smell like the bar I was in. I'll shower before crawling beside her. I'll go to her in the dark the only way I can, a way I know well. It goes like this: stripped naked, I press my skin, not to her, but to the one I saw tonight. Rubbing cheeks, I feel only stubble, breathing deeply I taste smoke, and the voice I hear is deep and choked in my own throat. Finding my place inside her, I talk to him, see my muscle as his muscle, grip her hands as his hands. We lock and separate until we shine, until she's gone, until he and I can't ever separate and our mouths crush together and I push his shoulders hard into the wet sheets.

It's late. I somehow hurt her last Sunday and have been meaning to apologize since Tuesday when I probably got herpes. It's funny how intentions can fill a whole week.

There's a twenty-four hour convenience store on her block. I'll buy her a giant Heath bar, I'll crinkle the wrapping under her nose, and I'll make love to her while she chews.

JUNE 1987

WE DID NOT PLAN IT. I did not plan anything then. But he was my first boyfriend anyway. I had been in love before, at nineteen—I can admit it now—but that first love was a secret and, like most any living thing, could not survive the dark. This time it was different. There was air. There was light.

We got tested together at the Center on Highland. Neither of us could believe we were negative. We spent the whole afternoon and the next day in each other's arms. When we finally got up and left the house, it was Sunday.

If he knew it was Gay Pride Day, he never let on. I thought we were just walking to the boulevard to find a place for breakfast, but the floats and groups milling on the side streets for the parade sent us in search of our friends from ACT UP. He and I had attended the initial meetings in Plummer Park, and the L.A. group would be marching for the first time in the parade. We joined them. I remember I was in black shorts, Doc Martens, and an open chambray shirt. I remember starting out tentatively, handing out flyers to spectators along the parade route, afraid of being seen. Someone took my picture. Still, the applause, the whistles, the chanting, "Fight Back! Stop AIDS! Act Up!" seemed to give me shape and form. I felt grounded in my boots, and before we had gone two blocks I had stopped looking for my boyfriend in the crowd for reassurance.

By the time we reached the fire-and-brimstone brigade at the intersection of Santa Monica Boulevard and La Cienega, I noticed how they looked right through me, through all of us, and perhaps more than anything, that convinced me I would never be invisible again.

SEPTEMBER 1992

WHAT'S THE POINT? When it's all over we just claim insanity anyway. Pretend or actually believe that it wasn't really what we thought it was. "That wasn't what I meant by love at all," we'll claim. "This is what I mean. I was mistaken before. It was all a mistake."

But it wasn't. How could it be when everything now has changed? Perhaps what I called love then isn't what I would call love now but it was love, nonetheless. I still remember it. I still dream it.

In this dream there's a Spanish-style bungalow and a mossy concrete pond with a few mottled carp drifting beneath two lily pads. Flowering desert grasses and beds of rosemary surround us while we sit and think and stare in the sunshine. We are shirtless and graze each other's skin in passing. He reaches out to finger my bicep; I come from behind to stroke his belly, in this dream.

I trust him and leave my journals and unfinished manuscripts on the table by the window where I work. He doesn't bother with the headphones when he plays the keyboard anymore; I even get to hear the false starts and mistakes. Our house is home to words and music.

In this dream we are naked. His skin is smooth and looks even whiter against my black hair and rusty skin. It's not a racial thing. I found him that way. In this dream.

There's no point in wanting to "be sure." Who's ever sure? "I'm sure it was this way." "I'm certain you told me seven o'clock." "I'm positive I put my keys right here." "I am 100 percent in love with you."

I am 100 percent in love with you. What kind of person would say that or believe it for long? As if love were an unchangeable mathematical certainty. As if love were something you knew instead of believed. As if there were not more to the dream.

In this dream he isn't so passive and I'm not so juiced up. I don't ask the kinds of questions I used to. I let him feel safe. I drive a convertible now and he lets me feel giddy. We don't dilute a drop of this discovery and we don't make any of it up, either.

Maybe in the beginning we were lonely and horny and that has to be a part of this dream, but it isn't the part worth telling and it isn't the part that still lasts. Maybe it all starts from lonely and horny. Or ready and willing. Or even indifferent and lucky. Who cares how it starts. Does it matter? Does it matter that the dream starts at last call in a smoky bar, or in the sunshine among the waves? Does it matter if it starts on the warm asphalt of the boulevard under the gaze of riot police or in a kitchen with friends looking on? Will it change the wetness of the kiss, the things that were said, the look in his eyes, in this dream?

In this dream we are past the most difficult parts. The part of earning his trust, of him earning mine. We are past how hard it is keeping my hands off and my mouth shut. We are past the moment we needed to identify love or the moment we gave up trying. In this dream we kiss a lot and our cocks are always hard. We aren't much interested in "love."

We make each other laugh and think of unexpected things, and, since the dream is complete, we fight. It's important to me that we fight, that we do it well. I don't care even if it gets loud or comes unexpectedly. This is where the proof is, whether we are fighting each other or fighting to get back to each other, and in this dream we fight like Queer Nationals in order to hold each other again. It is this part of the dream that makes me believe the most.

We are healthy in this dream. We have family and friends. We have each other. Our sleep is peaceful and deep. But in this dream we are awake, so wide awake. In this dream.

NOVEMBER 1998

I DRIVE OUT OF my way now to avoid West Hollywood. There's not much there anymore that heats or cools my blood. And besides, the traffic is devastating. I hike in Griffith Park. I live in Silver Lake.

They say that if you live long enough and sip your café or kir royale on the terrace, everyone you know will eventually pass by the Café Flore in Paris. In West Hollywood, it's an unspoken assumption that if you work out hard enough and have managed to stay alive, everyone you've slept with will pass by The Abbey. It isn't true, of course. Only the young go to The Abbey or Rage or Here Lounge just as once only the young went to the Rawhide, Revolver, and Studio One, places that no longer exist, places where former patrons are forever twinks and newbies. Places where others like me hid in the dark corners until we learned some truths, let down our guard, and marched in the open sunlight to be seen, in the process becoming kinder and becoming men.

That corridor of bars and restaurants, party boys and porn aesthetics, rapidly came to define the city, and so the city became an epithet not just for fundamentalists and late night comedians but also for those of us who had had our politics, our spirits, and our blood tested. We marched and volunteered. We dedicated plaques. We overspent on tributes to our own gay identities. But did we love? Did we learn to love?

On the side streets where people had sex after last call, neighbors in red-tile-roofed cottages complained until signs were erected: No CRUISING. The dictionary definition of cruising, the one before "to search (as in public places) for a sexual partner," is "to travel without destination or purpose." A time finally comes when we all need to find someplace else to go.

Everything is packed away, now, even the dreams and the truths. I am moving to New York, but I have amends and apologies to make before I go. Some mistakes cannot be corrected, and reconciling with loss and love is not easy. We cause pain and we hurt. We learn too slowly. We fail our dreams. But we forgive one another anyway.

In finding sex and self-respect, destination and purpose, and—yes—finally love, a new generation is now passing through West Hollywood. It was a safe place for me and for that I will always be thankful, but in leaving I will not miss it. I no longer need a safe place or a gay city. Others might. In fact, I am certain they still do, and I am glad it is there for them. But I am moving. And I am happy.

gay is good

an essay too personal and otherwise

winston wilde

For Don Allen

EVEN THOUGH I'M a native homo Angeleno, I'm not really being gay in our City of Angels these days or nights. This is not about West Hollywood or Silver Lake or the other gay scenes of Los Angeles today. En Nuestra Pueblo de la Senora de la Reina de Los Angeles, I have lived many lives: my years in Malibu with John, in the Hollywood Hills with Paul. Instead, what follows is a fragmented account of growing up a gay boy in Santa Monica, from about 1960 to 1974. The sexual stuff might be a bit racy for some of you. There's your warning.

•

MANY OF MY childhood amigos had lesbian moms, or I should say moms who became lesbian. I ran into my favorite one recently and asked her how she was doing. Tita answered: "Well, I'm now seventy years old, and I'm having an identity crisis." I just love my Californian moms. They've played a positive and influential role in who I am.

My childhood was in fact idyllic, but not without the shadows of fate. Like the Kennedys (only without the big bootleg bucks) and like Tennessee Williams (only without the Southern sensibility), I grew up with a disabled sister. This changed everything. We were never a normal family, thanks be to God. I have always been disability-aware, as was my last husband Paul Monette, who had a disabled brother. It bonded us in our love of each other.

I was painfully aware at times that we were living privileged on pill hill in Santa Monica. We were expected to eat everything on our plates, waste nothing, because children in Biafra were starving. We boycotted grapes and marched against the war. My nose pressed to the giant den window, I dreamed and watched the sailboat races go up and down the coast from Marina del Rey to Point Dume. What a view from my favorite room in the house, with its polished cork floors and Moroccan carpet, a wet bar with West Coast lighting, and floor-to-ceiling bookshelves: psychology, anthropology, theology, a travel section, encyclopedia, Dr. Spock, *On The Road*, Ginsberg's *Howl*, Baldwin's *The Fire Next Time*, Gloria Steinem's *Open Marriage*.

My first conscious recognition that I was different than the others, and homosexual, was at a picnic at Rancho Park in West Los Angeles when I was three-and-a-half (1960). On the grass, on a single blanket next to my family was a gay couple with good vibes. They were muscular and handsome and of archetypes my curiosity was attracted to: the smooth blond in white trunks with a single gold chain around his strong neck, the hairy darker dude in black. I looked at them. I watched them. I moved my towel closer to them. They smiled at me and were nice to me. There was a mutually acknowledged kindred spirit that I would later learn to call "gaydar," our God-given umbilical cord for the survival of queer spirit.

There were many childhood obstacles to overcome, but mine could never be as significant as my sister's. At five I had to stop liking the color pink. After several months of gnarly pleading, my groovy mom finally compromised and bought me a Ken instead of a Barbie at the toy store in the Brentwood Country Mart. I later scored big time when I saved up enough allowance for a G.I. Joe. But I was then reduced to tears when my mother came home from a sociology class at UCLA, during the Vietnam War, having been convinced by a professor that we should throw away all of our "war toys," even my dearly beloved comrade, G.I. Joe. The premature death of Joe was but a prelude to what was in store for me.

•

MY BROTHER GREG and I would go to the Berkeley/Wilshire Barber Shop for our "boys' regular" or a "butch." From the age of five, I got my hair cut by this hot guy with hairy, tattooed arms. Ed had been in the Marines. He was tough. No fidgeting. Pay attention. I remember once in that bastion of testosterone picking up a *Playboy* and getting all hot and bothered by the naked chicks with tits. This was a lot better than the *National Geographic*. The barbers were all looking at me and smiling, approvingly, as no one's mother was around. That's about as close as I ever got to being one of the guys—getting a boys' regular.

One day after school I was helping Greg with his paper route. I was telling him some fag jokes I'd recently learned on the playground of Franklin Elementary. I was nine, Greg was thirteen. If there was ever a defining moment in my life, this was it. Greg got really mad at me and told me that it was not OK to make jokes about gay people. He reminded me that our mom's hairdresser

Jimmy was gay, and didn't I like Jimmy? And that important people in history like Leonardo da Vinci were gay, and would I make fun of them? Mom and Dad taught us to not make fun of Negroes, or Chicanos, or Orientals. Why should the gays be any different?

•

MY FIRST CRUSH was on my best friend's dad. He was a tough, handsome, short, fat, confident, hairy Jew who walked around the house naked eating fistfuls of raw salami, shoved into a mustard jar before each gluttonous bite. He barely ever noticed me. The few times he said anything nice to me were like golden showers of warm radiant affection. But alas, he was unavailable. And I mean completely unavailable.

If you asked any kid in Santa Monica, or most of So Cali what their idea of a totally bitchin place in heaven was, they would have answered, "POP." Pronounced PEE-OH-PEE, it stands for Pacific Ocean Park. Now long gone, POP was an amusement park that was mostly on the broad, sandy beach, but some parts, like the roller coaster, jutted out on piers in the water. Sometimes the powerful waves would go rolling under the park, thundering as they passed under your feet. *Hijole*. There was the funhouse distorted-mirrors attraction of Davy Jones's Locker and hundreds of skill games to play. By far, my most libidinous childhood memory of POP was King Neptune, a big muscle-daddy god of great power. And boy did he have a body! Waiting in line for the King Neptune ride I had to hide my little boners. In a giant fountain of splashes and bubbles, the bare-chested and pectorally endowed King Neptune emerged like the glans from a foreskin: trident clenched in one manly hand, the other commanding the reins of a half-dozen energetic dolphins cavorting. From the gay couple at Rancho Park, to my barber Ed, to my best friend's dad, to King Neptune, I knew by age ten that I was a daddy hunter. I wouldn't learn until years later how common intergenerational love is with queer folk. I had thought it was just another perversion upon my homo perversion.

At fifteen, I hitchhiked a few times from Santa Monica to the unincorporated badlands of L.A. County, which would later become West Hollywood. Just past Barney's Beanery and their sign that said FAGOTS STAY OUT, a porn theater on Santa Monica Boulevard was my destination. With my fake ID and a little chutzpah—at fifteen I looked about twelve—I ventured into the early 1970s porn scene. Hitchhiking back to Santa Monica that Friday night, I was picked up by a dude in a Karmann Ghia with a bumper sticker that read WAR IS NOT HEALTHY FOR CHILDREN AND OTHER LIVING THINGS. I was pleasantly surprised to find that it was my former teacher: so handsome, so cool, and I had such a huge crush on him. I asked to go to his apartment for some herbal tea. I totally seduced him. He resisted, showing me pictures of his fiancée. I kissed him anyway. I pulled his pants down and had my first suckfest. He reciprocated hesitantly. I know that many people will look at this with terrible judgment as they did at Mary Kay Letourneau and Vili Fualaau. But I can tell you that I left there in the morning, and I sang all day long: "Let It Be," "All You Need Is Love," "Blowin' in The Wind." I shared libidinous caprices with this gentle man many times over the following twelve years. We had a delicious, loving, and mutually satisfying affair which I still hold dear to my heart. Only problem, the object of my seduction was an unavailable, mostly straight guy on the DL.

At fifteen-and-a-half I came out to my parents at the Mayfair Theater. My father—who was a Boy Scout, a World War II Air Force lieutenant, successful real estate developer, accomplished hiker, equestrian, camper—responded to my coming out with, "Well, I don't know much about homosexual tendencies, but you're my son, and I'll love you no matter what." Ain't that something? That's the kind of "good enough parenting" I've been so blessed with in my life. Thanks Dad. Thanks Mom.

A few months later my parents informed me that they were separating, and my life as I had known it was shattered. Everything changed that year. On October 31, 1972, I was the first applicant in line with my dad at the Culver City DMV. I had my driver's license in hand by 9:30 a.m. Waiting for me at home in dogtown was my mom's radical 1965 Mustang convertible, gray with a black-and-chrome interior. I thought I was so cool, so boss, with my long blond hair in a black suede headband, cruising up PCH, with Led Zeppelin's "Whole Lotta Love" blaring from the AM radio.

Santa Monica High School (aka Samohi) was a hellish place for me: thirty-two hundred students and I couldn't find one other hippie homo. The sadistic gym coaches were really uptight and would bark at a few of the nelly guys who couldn't pass: "You're doing those push-ups like a girl. What's wrong with you, ya faggot? Are you a sissy? A homo?" I knew I had to escape from that mental institution pronto. I started to ditch PE and go to my dogtown beach, a few blocks away.

By this time POP was closed down and locked up but not patrolled by guards. For a while there were no fences on the beach under the piers, and it was a happy hunting ground of homosex. I was warned about the unspeakable activities that occurred in the dark shadows of the underworld. The scent of tar and wet sand was punctuated by the dank stench of piss and the punch of fresh man jizz. Dig it. These seaweed smells salted by the air whipped through those playchambers of Lord Poseidon. And dude, don't forget the ever-present sweet aroma of pot, MaryJane, the dime bag. I must admit that I was too cowardly at the time to loiter under POP, to exercise my gaydar, and instead walked through the haunted maze of sticky fat tree trunks at a quick, uninterrupted clip. Only once did I pause to see if I could spy anything, but immediately picked up my pace for fear of being forever sucked into the vortex of homosexual orgiastic reefer madness.

Not wanting to choose among living with my dad, who moved

to Malibu, or my mom, who moved to Westwood, or living alone in the now empty house I grew up in, at sixteen I told my parents I wanted to get my own apartment, and they approved. A funky Victorian studio in Venice on Ozone and Pacific at $120 a month gave me privacy and sanctuary. A block away was the boardwalk, a few blocks more and I was at the gay beach, and just down from there was the pit at Muscle Beach. I quickly learned the fine arts of tricking and was dragging older muscle guys to my crib for, as we used to say, French and Greek.

The Venice gay beach was between the first and second lifeguard towers just north of the Pavilion. Most of us regulars during the week had night jobs and night lives, and we knew each other. Lesbians, like Martha, brought guitars and went topless. Gay guys began stripping their suits once in the water, or, more boldly, at their towels and then running into the sea. People shared food, joints, and music as we mellowed out together. Groovy times of the hippies were alive and flourishing that year at Venice Beach. We called it Free Venice, and we volunteered at the Free Venice Food Collective and the Free Venice Free Theater. There were house parties every night, and we frequented local bars like the Roosterfish in Venice, the Pink Elephant in Ocean Park (which was my home away from home), and the S.S. Friendship in the Canyon. The Friendship's decor was in the groove: an authentic local history of long boards, fish nets with found beach ephemera, and pics of gay surfers from days long gone. This was all lost when the Friendship was sold in the mid-1980s to an immigrant homosexual and underwent a disco redecoration to beige linoleum.

Our little summer nudism at the gay beach in Free Venice turned into a politicized fandango. The LAPD at that time had no all-terrain vehicles. They hadn't started wearing shorts or even short-sleeve shirts yet. Poor guys, stuck in the heat of summer in full-length wool. So when the cops began coming onto the beach and hassling us naturalists, we got all uptight, and a war broke out. To walk from the boardwalk to the edges of the gay beach by the shoreline, one had to traverse a Sahara of sorts. It was easy to spot the cops approaching, and so we set up sentinels, taking shifts to warn our comrades that the pigs were coming. We then felt righteously empowered by our cooperative vigilance, and so almost everyone felt more comfortable and safe to be completely naked, all the time, and even to move around towel-hopping in the buff. The lifeguards weren't selling out, they were cool, and totally on our side. It was a free nude-in, on the beach, every day. At the first battle cry of "PIGS!" we scurried to retrieve our bathing suits or a towel to wrap in, or we ran into the ocean.

At some point a topless dyke was arrested and charged with "Lewd and Lascivious Conduct." She chose to fight the charges. She argued in court that being naked was an affirmation of her being, not an invitation to sexual behavior. The judge agreed with the defendant, and the next day the *L.A. Times* read: NUDE IS NOT LEWD, JUDGE SAYS. For the rest of that summer, the Free Venice gay beach was a legally nude beach. After the media got ahold of it, our utopia was destroyed, smashed by the imperialists and culture vultures. Thousands of tourists, Angeleno and otherwise, began slumming at our beach, with cameras and telephoto lenses. It was horrible. I think it was hardest on the lesbians because the straight male tourists were the most pernicious. The camera crews from the networks were there almost every day fishing for sexy clips to boost their capitalist pig ratings. Many gay men fled north to Chautauqua, what's now called Will Rogers Beach (or Ginger Rogers Beach). This beach at Chautauqua has been a gay beach since the nineteenth century, but in my time Free Venice had surpassed Chautauqua as the happening place. To this day there is an historic poster up at the Roosterfish. It is a collage of photos from the Free Venice Nude Beach days. I'm proud to say that I am in it, at age sixteen, wearing a brown suede loincloth I'd made, with feather-and-bead tassels, the twelve zodiac signs, and I-ching coins sewn on. I was a gay hippie. I am still a gay hippie.

•

BY TENTH GRADE, I was either totally into the class or not at all. Either the teacher was a Democrat, against the war in Vietnam, for a free dress code, and pro-gay, or, a Republican, for the war in Vietnam, against the free dress code, and a homophobe. Looks like some things haven't changed much. I knew I needed to get out of there.

I interviewed at Crossroads and a few other alternative private schools, which we called "free schools." Only they cost a lot of money. I randomly chose a free school called Pacific Hills on the corner of Fifth and Broadway in downtown Santa Monica. It used to be a beauty parlor, and over the entrance was a sign that read, NOT A SCHOOL. Our administrators indulged the irony and left the sign in its place, and so we generally referred to our school as Not-a-School. When I signed up there I had no idea that so many of the students were lesbian and gay, as were at least a third of the teachers (whom we called "facilitators"). I was in heaven. No one cared if I liked pink, or played with dolls, or had weird ideas, or acted dramatic. For the first time in my life I could let my little gay light shine. I know it's cliché, but my life went from black-and-white to Technicolor.

One coastal June-gloom day at Not-a-School, a few lesbians and I were having a heated discussion about God and being gay, so we decided to go on a field trip. This was to be a theological-anthropological research adventure. We hopped in my Mustang and headed east on Santa Monica Boulevard through a purple rain of jacaranda in search of the Reverend Troy Perry, who had recently been on the news as a happy gay minister with his own gay church. We never found Troy, but we did have juice and cookies with his lesbian mom. I can't remember her name, but I'll never forget her friendliness and her hospitality. She told us that God loves gay people, and that God made us gay, and that God wants us to be gay because He needs gay people. She said that gay people are good people, and God makes good people gay. There are a lot of hateful people in the world, she said, and it was our duty as loving gay people to spread love and to try and help the haters turn into lovers. Troy's mom instructed us: this was the work God wants us to do. What a bitchin profound moment in my queer spiritual development: a reconciliation of theology and sexuality. She gave us some stuff as we were leaving, handing me a bumper sticker that said: GAY IS GOOD. Outside in the parking lot my lesbians and I said a few quick pagan prayers as I stuck it on my Mustang bumper.

From there we went to the newly opened Pleasure Chest, an adult toy store in a Craftsman bungalow on Fairfax. I bought a pair of handcuffs. I still have them, and I still use them (but not as often as I'd like). In the sixth grade I had had sexual fantasies of tying up my gym coach spread-eagle on the floor of the girls' bathroom and cutting his clothes off with a switchblade. Buying the handcuffs was the beginning of a third coming out: a perversion on top of a perversion on top of a perversion. I was an under-aged homosexual daddy-fucker into bondage and domination.

Living in Venice I cultivated my beds of desire. As a young queer boy I was in the groove, learning about fuck buddies and the value of being around a bunch of different older gay men, learning from their stories and their tricks. Plus, I've always been curious about the sexualities of others. One of my fuck buddies taught me about fisting; another about bondage; another was into wrestling. I was heterosexually active as well. At sixteen and seventeen I had a robust, energetic, and diversified sex portfolio.

My most beloved fuck buddy was Don Allen, a twenty-nine-year-old photographer who drove to Mexico several times a year to shoot. He documented and embraced indigenous ritual from

Jalisco to Campeche and Yucatán. He made his living photographing eye surgeries for Saint John's Hospital and lived in this far-out bungalow in Venice. His yard was lush and verdant, abuzz with dragonflies and faeries. His balcony was a screaming greenhouse of orchids he'd snuck back from Aztlán. He wanted to do whatever turned me on, and I usually wanted to slip him the sausage. Don had dark hair and a beard, and he was a really great kisser. He was the first person I learned how to dig sleeping and snuggling with. Don took me to many places of queer interest, introduced me to Harry Hay and the radical faeries, encouraged my drumming. This bohemian homo turned me on to buttons and native ritual. He showed me glimpses of a leather world. Don taught me about making love. Many years later I fathered and cared for him in what little ways I could as he scratched out a last couple of years before dying of AIDS. So many of my handsome G.I. Joes fought valiantly for this country and for their freedom and for the dear love of comrades.

When I got the drip I went to a doctor in Century City who I'm sure was a former Nazi now in some kind of witness protection program. He jabbed an instrument halfway into my penis to collect a sample, which was totally unnecessary, as he could have just swabbed the ooze. I was in so much pain that I swore I would never have sex again. That lasted about three weeks. A couple of months later I got nonspecific urethritis again. Don said that he'd heard of a new place downtown on Wilshire and Union called the Gay Community Services Center. He dialed up, and the folks there told him that the Gay Men's V.D. Clinic was on Tuesday and Thursday nights. Don made me an appointment for that night, and we headed downtown eastbound on the Tropic of Venice Boulevard.

It was another Technicolor moment. Although the place was shabby at best, and in another time zone from the Westside brass-and-marble health care I was accustomed to, what hit me right away was that the secretaries were gay, the nurses were gay, the doctors were gay, the patients were gay. Everyone was acting campy and silly and making this painful medical necessity a joy. I knew I'd found a home and couldn't wait to get involved. A nurse, and I mean a bearded guy in jeans with a little white nurse's hat on his head, told me that they were going to start their first Volunteer Training Program, and would I be interested? Next week I was sitting on the floor with twenty other gay men, all older than me, learning about syphilis and antibiotics and condoms and how to be culturally sensitive. I was sixteen, and I was helping to build my community. The holidays and rituals of my family had fallen apart, and I was learning how to reinvent my gay self.

The Gay Men's V.D. Clinic played a big part in my life for the next two years. The guys at the clinic empowered me. They had me making charts and doing initial intakes. I learned how to take cultures and run VDRLs. And because of my genetic enthusiasm, they soon had me giving all the patients the nightly Welcome Rap. I had learned enough gay humor to make a clinic full of homos laugh out loud. Which was really important to me, because I was so insecure and constantly ashamed of my ever-present acne, and I was the skinniest twink on the block. I just wanted to be able to grow facial hair, to have some muscle on my arms. I just wanted to be older.

When the Gay Center moved to Highland Avenue, I went with it. After we closed the clinic each night, the staff and a few specially-invited infected ones would go to eat at Arthur J's on the corner of Highland and Santa Monica. There were always drag queens there, day and night. What really got my blood pumping at Arthur J's was when the bikers came in. The leathermen usually arrived late at night on choppers, making a much more dramatic entrance than any single drag queen could possibly pull off unaccompanied by an elephant. These leather daddies had handlebar moustaches and lamb-chop sideburns. Handcuffs on the right, black hanky on the left. I soon learned about Griff's on Melrose, the Old Guard ways, codes and ethics, and to me this all made gay life look kind of normal, like vanilla.

My brothers at the Center also turned me on to the baths, or as Don always called them, the tubs. One night after we closed the clinic, the director, Jack, a skinny white guy with a big dick and a Southern accent, suggested that we go to the Wilmington Baths. Another night they took me to the Hollywood Spa, then the Roman Holiday, and eventually to 8709. My life as a bathhouse connoisseur was born.

There were a lot of places to go at night in 1974. But usually I stayed west of longitude Sepulveda and went to the Pink Elephant. Most of us beachfolk needed to summon a lot of energy if we wanted to go clubbing in town. There was the Sugar Shack in Van Nuys, an underage disco that always disappointed me because everyone was my age: a total boner killer. Across from the Paradise Ballroom on Highland was the underage disco The Other Side. The Other Side was right on. At the Paradise they had a juke box with old hippie rock standards. But upstairs across the street we had live DJs, and they were playing all the happening hits.

When Studio One opened on Robertson, I had a gay identity crisis. It was my first glimpse of what would later be called "the cloning of gay culture." It was a shift from the hippie individualism to a more congruent uniformity. People were wearing the same things, like Izod shirts, and acting the same way and saying the same lame stuff. I found myself unable to conform to the dominant gay culture and its lack of people of color, who were often not admitted to these mostly white clubs in town. Not so at the Pink Elephant. My beach friends were Chicanos and blacks and whites and everything all mixed up. White fags were shocked that I was going to The Catch One (a black homo club) and to a *puro latino* bathhouse in *pinche* East El-lay. Soon after I found this L.A. gay community, I felt alienated from it. But I was also unwilling to accept completely the Old Guard ways of the leather community. I was up to my ears in identity formation.

The turning point for me was the summer of 1974. Friends

had moved to San Francisco, mostly to go to school, and I visited them often, falling in love with the Emerald City. But I was still living in L.A. and creating a fabulous rich gay life.

That year I had marshaled the courage to attend the L.A. Gay Pride Parade which was on Hollywood Boulevard. It started, if my memory serves me, at Cherokee and headed west, turning down Highland and ending at some famous hall on the west side of Highland where there was to be a little celebration.

I was standing on the sidewalk watching the parade go by, clapping and cheering and seeing friends from the Gay Community Services Center and friends from Free Venice and my friends' lesbian moms. And as the parade went by, people were stepping in at the end, noncostumed "normal folk," gay men and women, like me, who had been watching from the sidewalk. Only problem was the LAPD. They started swinging their batons and cracking heads and beating the shit out of my brothers and sisters for stepping into the street. A small riot ensued. I was fortunate enough to escape without injury, but I clearly remember seeing bloodied lesbians crying and angry fairies being beaten to the ground by the fuzz.

The next week I went to a newspaper vending box to get my copy of the gay newspaper called *The Advocate*. In this issue was a centerpiece of photojournalism, comparing the parade in Los Angeles to the parade in San Francisco. The pictures of the parade in L.A. were of the LAPD brutalizing their peaceful citizens. The pictures in San Francisco showed two male cops in uniform holding hands, dykes on bikes, and a much more colorful and creative parade than its southern counterpart.

I knew what I had to do. There was no choice. Soon after moving up to the City I met a cop who became a fuck buddy comrade, and I was taken under the wing of a female pervert named Cynthia Slater who radically changed my life. But that's another story.

queer by nature

greta gaard

AS AN ADULT I've given a lot of thought to place and identity, yet it's surprising that my view of my coming out years is so entangled with the built environment. I know my coming of age in 1970s Los Angeles was deeply connected to the natural and cultural topography, the flora of Los Angeles.

From ages eight to twenty, I hiked the hills of the San Fernando Valley, Malibu Canyon, and the Santa Monica Mountains for solace, for a breather from social interactions where I felt the outsider, though I couldn't pinpoint the reason. Growing up south of Ventura Boulevard in the San Fernando Valley, I climbed the hills behind our house all the way up to Mulholland Drive, where I could get a wide panorama of the city stretching to the ocean on the south, and the mountains to the north. On a clear day the Valley looked like a lush garden of trees ringed by tawny purple mountains, sprinkled with yellow Scotch broom and mustard flowers. The trees whose names I knew—eucalyptus, jacaranda, bottlebrush, lemon, orange, avocado, blue spruce—grew thickly amid oleander bushes, ivy, rose bushes, gardenias, azaleas, geraniums, birds of paradise. I knew about sweet williams and how they attracted bees. I knew not to eat the long shiny leaves, the pink, red, or white flowers of the oleanders. We knew the names of cultivated nature, but not the names for wild plants which are still a blur to me, forty years later—the low scrubby bushes on the hills where I climbed, the blue sage, the yellow flowers, the types of rocks, the soil. We didn't know the name for my sexuality either.

In eighth grade social studies, I was shocked to learn that Los Angeles was actually considered high desert, and its soil was clay. This explained the marginal success and failure of my backyard garden. The carrots I pulled out were stunted, unable to penetrate the thick clay, while the green beans, red-leafed lettuce, scallions, and radishes flourished. These plants worked with the surface of things, while the carrots tried to go deeper. They weren't well suited to Los Angeles culture, a city based on appearance, trends, and movement. I empathized with the carrots.

My love of the natural world began in Los Angeles, in a very managed environment with Japanese and Mexican gardeners shaping the lawns and landscapes according to their white residents' desires. My sexual nature was also managed by the social environment, a complex interplay of Hollywood actors, metaphysical spiritualities, WASP values. When my parents drove Ventura Boulevard, they pointed out familiar landmarks for me: the Hot Dog Show, the Orange Julius, Von's grocery store, the deli, the gas station, and then a blur of independent retailers until the Sav-On drug store parking lot at Laurel Canyon. Without my parents, I learned the names of other places on Ventura: the Queen Mary, the Dummy Up, the Apache bar.

The endlessness of Los Angeles, the way that one community blended into another and you could drive for hours in most direc-

tions without ever leaving the city—no wonder people felt everything you could want was here for the asking. People in Los
Angeles had a strange sense of U.S. geography: there was California, New York, and a few places to ski in Colorado or Montana.
The rest was "flyover country." Marginal. Unimportant.

Social spaces like gay bars weren't on the usual maps, either.
We didn't call them "queer" bars in the 1970s, and the lesbian
bars weren't dyke bars or girl bars either. The Gay Yellow Pages
listed the bars as gay, lesbian, or "mixed"—and then specified
whether it was gay and lesbian mixed, or gay and straight mixed.
There were sex shops and bookstores, but the main places to meet
people were the bars.

Yes, I drank too much, if you consider nine drinks a night as a
problem. But the night began around 8:00 or 9:00 and lasted until
2:00 or 4:00, so there was plenty of time to dance, pee, cruise, and
be cruised before last call. You had to drink to be there, and the
drinks were small anyway, and maybe they were watered down
too, and to manage the chaotic pulses of fear, elation, arousal, and
disco there was no other means but alcohol. Some people tried
pot, but I hated it. A marijuana high reminded me of spinning too
much on a playground. Poppers were fun for a one-minute bump
to higher grounds if you were dancing, but they didn't offer a
steady high, and too much of them made me sick. Alcohol was
simple, reliable, sociable. I stuck to the same type of drink too: a
tequila sunrise, with a cherry and stem I learned to tie in a knot
with my tongue against my teeth, proof that I would be a good
lover. Sometimes I had vodka tonics or lite beer after a long
evening of dancing, but these were the only variations. I made and
followed my own rules: no mixed drinks, no whiskey, no liqueurs
or wine. Violating the rules always ended badly, and those times
are not worth retelling.

In retrospect, the strangest thing about coming out in Los
Angeles was the mythical one-night stand which would serve as
your entrance ticket to gay life. Somehow I believed that I was not

a "real" gay person until I had sex with another woman, a stranger
I would meet in a bar, and leave with for an hour or an evening,
our sex becoming my induction ceremony into lesbian identity.
Never mind that I had fallen in love with my best girlfriend at age
fourteen, attempting suicide when our friendship ended after a
year. Never mind that I had searched for and read Radclyffe Hall's
Well of Loneliness in my Catholic all-girls high school library (what
was it doing there?). Never mind that after expulsion from private
to public high school, I chose the captain of the girls' basketball
team, the girls' softball team, and the girls' athletic association as
my best friend, walking her home from school each day with my
arm locked through hers. I thought my identity was something
someone else would give me, like a title or an honorary degree.

It was legal to be gay. It was simply illegal to be young and gay.
So I used a lot of fake IDs at the bars, borrowing my roommate's
ID from Puerto Rico, using other friends' second driver's licenses,
getting a driver's license from a friend who gave it to me and
didn't want to answer any questions. We were carded outside the
bars after nine o'clock, so I went to the bars at 8:00 or 8:30 and
tried to be inconspicuous. Sometimes when I made it past the
bouncer I was still carded by the bartender and had to count on
the dim lighting, the crowd, the loud music to blur the license
dates, the photo, and my face.

The Dummy Up was the lesbian bar closest to my parents'
house, just off Ventura near Laurel Canyon in Studio City. It was
in an alley that functioned like a driveway into the Sav-On parking lot. The sign was inconspicuous and the door always seemed
locked, but at night after the drugstore shoppers had gone home,
and the parking lot had cleared out, the D.U. woke up. Cars began appearing, and women walked singly or in pairs, disappearing
inside the door in a wall. How did I ever get the courage to take
my parents' car when they had gone out, drive illegally, park in
the lot, walk down that alley, and pull open that heavy door into
darkness? Only desperation could have given me the power. I

know I went there early, I went there often, and I watched, wondering if I would find myself there. How could I be sure?

The obvious answer was to ask someone who knew. Somehow I got my hands on the Gay Yellow Pages, found the Los Angeles Gay and Lesbian Community Center listing, telephoned them, and asked for directions. There were weekly meetings for lesbians. All I had to do was get there.

My transportation showed up unexpectedly one night when I went to my boyfriend's apartment to play guitars. Rick's apartment was in Studio City, in a sixties two-story, white-and-gold glitter stucco building with exterior stairs to the upper apartments. Rick took me out to view his balcony and all his potted plants, then disappeared into the apartment. After a reasonable time of waiting for his return, I went looking for him and found him in the bedroom. He had completely undressed and was lying naked on the bed, waiting for me. I had two immediate reactions. At eighteen, Rick was an Italian god, with curling black hair, dark brown eyes, dark skin, and a perfectly muscled body over six feet tall. He was Michelangelo's David, come to life in bronze flesh before me. What a piece of art! That was my first reaction. My second reaction was to ask to borrow his car so I could drive to the Gay and Lesbian Community Center meeting for lesbians. Rick rolled off the bed, dressed, and handed me the keys to his VW.

The Community Center was in an area of Los Angeles that I never frequented. At sixteen, I had given no careful thought to race and class segregation; all I knew was that the area seemed seedy, but the urgency of sitting in a room with other lesbians was more compelling than crumbling architecture, vacant landscaping, and litter. Walking into the Center, I was directed to a room where the meeting was already in progress. Thick clouds of cigarette smoke greeted me when I opened the door to enter a circle of women seated in chairs or on the floor. Uncomfortable at once, I sat down and wished for invisibility. Now reviewing the mental tapes of that meeting, I see a smoky room crowded with black and

Latina women, women in blue jeans and T-shirts, baseball caps and short hair. In my white ribboned sundress, with my hair in a ponytail, my white middle-class upbringing clanged loudly against the circle. These specific differences were not clear to me; all I could grasp was that I would need to wear different clothes and cut off my hair if I were to be a true lesbian. The facilitator welcomed me to the group and invited me to introduce myself. With the shamelessness of youth, I asked everyone how they knew they were gay. A low chuckle ran around the room. One woman joked that she would take me home and show me. Another woman suggested that I should just live my life and the answers would appear. No one had any clear guidance, and at the end of the meeting I left, disappointed. I had hoped that the rumored predatory sexuality of lesbians would indeed inspire one of them to take me home, and I lingered in the entryway of the Center, but no one offered.

What the meeting did confirm was what lesbians looked like— flannel shirts or T-shirts, jeans, short hair, chunky or athletic build. This wasn't how I looked, nor how I wanted to look to feel attractive. These lesbians were like a third gender to me, somewhere between women and men, in a place I couldn't go. How could I present myself as lesbian, and available? I didn't want to be a woman if it meant wearing lots of makeup and sleeping with men. I didn't want to be a man. I wanted to touch a woman who dressed like a man, whose energy overtook me, a woman with short hair and strong hands. I didn't know what type of lesbian that made me, or how I should dress to attract such a woman. If I had come out in the 1950s—if I had been born twenty years earlier—I would have fit right in to the butch-femme culture, would have known who I was and who I wanted. But 1970s lesbians were not my scene, and 1970s lesbian feminism was not a safe place to be a teenage femme.

Once I got to college I did have lovers, mostly women who were suitably "androgynous" for the time. The middle-class girls didn't know enough to treat our relationship as a relationship, and they continued to date men as cover or became involved with several girls at the same time and then wondered why everyone seemed jealous. The upper-class girls knew enough to realize that our relationship couldn't be brought home. ("You'd use the wrong spoon," Anne would explain to me patiently. "You'd probably break your dinner roll in pieces and butter them all at the same time.") The working-class girls weren't girls: they were butches or jocks, and they went to community colleges or they joined the military. Our class differences made it difficult for us to hook up.

After coming out, my choice of bars expanded. At first I frequented The Queen Mary on Ventura, a quiet little bar for drag shows, not two miles from my parents' house. When I was finally able to go there, armed with a fake ID and my first real lover, I was still unprepared for the electric power of drag. The show's audience was mostly heterosexual couples, which surprised me and made me uncomfortable. I had gone to great lengths to arrive in gay territory, away from heterosexuals, and here they were, effortlessly entering our space. There must have been other gays in the audience, though I don't remember them. What I remember were the queens—their long hair, fishnet or silk stockings, high heels, lusty glances. They lip-synced the songs of the day: Evelyn "Champagne" King's "Shame," Aretha's "R-E-S-P-E-C-T," Donna Summer's "Love to Love You, Baby," or Sylvester's "(You Make Me Feel) Mighty Real." Sometimes the queens pole-danced or came out into the audience and lap-danced with married heterosexual men, who laughed with their friends, flirted with the queens, and tipped them well. I became a regular, hoping for nights that were less well-attended, nights when the queens would dance for me. The flirtation and electric attraction I felt for one dark-haired queen exploded all my maps of gay identity. I didn't think I wanted to have sex with a gay man (did I?). I wasn't attracted to femmes; I *was* one, for goodness sake. When I left the bar one night with friends, I tried to be offhand in commending the queens for the sexual chemistry they could evoke through their performances. "Yeah," one of my friends, a butch, replied. "It's why people come." There were no words for this kind of attraction.

When I heard about a real working-class gay bar in Wilmington, I began driving the freeway, an hour each way, to dance at the Diamond Horseshoe. Friends said it was dangerous. There were fights in the parking lot. The police raided the bar. The area was industrial and abandoned. All of this was true. What friends didn't mention was that there were real butches at "the Shoe" and I could watch them, even if we never spoke. One blurry evening of dancing stands out as typical. I brought Lynn, a married heterosexual woman, with me, someone with Farrah Fawcett hair who waitressed with me at the deli in Santa Monica and said she just wanted to go somewhere to dance without being hit on by men. So we went to the Shoe, where the butch I had lusted after for months finally approached me on the dance floor—but she cut in between us, dancing with my friend, and finally kissing her full on the mouth while I stood by. Ordering an extra drink from our table, I put my friend's hat over the drink when last call was announced. Some time between 2:00 and 3:00, the bar was raided. Foggy with poppers and too much alcohol, I saw three men in police uniforms walk onto the dance floor. The music continued, but the dancing stopped. I grabbed my friend's hand and started moving for the door. That seemed to be the point of the raid, or maybe there was more to it. We didn't find out.

Other bars I attended only once, but the evening was so spectacular that the bar left its mark on me forever.

I was introduced to West Hollywood's hottest men's dance bar of the day, Studio One, as an underage, unwitting messenger to a drug deal. My college friend, Cat, had lived in Hawaii and had a regular connection there for Kona Gold, a high-quality strain of marijuana, which was regularly delivered to her via air transport to the L.A. airport. Cat drove us to LAX in her BMW and waited as I ran in to the package office and claimed the box in brown paper wrapping, bound with plain string, and no return address. Relieved to get back to the car, I sat in air-conditioned coolness as Cat sped us down the I-10 to West Hollywood, wove down streets I had never driven, and parked at the front of a block-long, two-story, white building. Bouncers greeted Cat at the arched doorway and waved us through the tunneled entrance without IDs or cover charges, and we entered an enormous high-ceilinged dance hall. What I remember most clearly in that flashing disco-lit darkness was not the beautiful men dancing shirtless and crowded on the large floor, but the beautiful men dancing on the balconies, in Greek and Roman loincloths and laurel wreaths, dancing amid palm trees and tiny white lights. Cat and I were whisked up to the owner's level where I could watch the balcony dancers enticing the floor dancers, and the evening spun in my head with the strobe lights, poppers, and pot. I don't know how we got out, or how I got back to campus for my eight o'clock course in Greek philosophy.

With Trisha, my first lover, I was introduced to The Palms, L.A.'s oldest lesbian bar. The Palms was a hole-in-the-wall bar like many mirrored discos I had seen, with an intimate dance floor, a long history, and a good mix of women. One night, Trish picked me up and drove me to her West Hollywood apartment, a lovely walk-up with red clay tiles and lush palm trees filling the tiny patio. After a few drinks, Trisha and I drove to the Pleasure Chest, a sex shop on Santa Monica. I marveled at black leather masks and whips, hammocks and tunics, soft synthetic vaginas, and an entire glass case of electric penises. You could press the buttons on the case and the corresponding phallus would plunge, rotate, or vibrate. There were cases and cases of clips and wrist restraints, studded collars and bracelets, strap-on harnesses and two-way dildos. It was impossible to look at all this paraphernalia without getting aroused. "What should we do?" I murmured meaningfully to Trisha. "Let's get some vibrators, and we'll go park," Trisha suggested. Impressed by her knowledge, I waited silently as Trish spoke to the clerk, examined a few different models, and then chose two hand-held vibrators. She even asked for batteries. I could hardly wait to see what happened next.

Trish drove us to a neighborhood near a classic bar, The Palms, which she assured me I would have to see. We parked on a quiet street, away from the streetlamps, and Trish shut off the engine but left the battery going to play some John Klemmer for ambiance. We unpacked our vibrators, plugged in the batteries, and unzipped. After about fifteen minutes of heavy breathing, I finally said, "It's not working for me." "Me either," Trisha snapped, obviously irritated. "I think the batteries were old." Frustrated with our purchases, Trish said, "Let's just go to the bar." And then she warned me that the bar was strictly a butch-femme bar, and we wouldn't get in unless we passed. "What!?" Still the unsuspecting novice, I watched, baffled and impressed, as Trisha reached into the backseat of her car and pulled out a tie, rolled her sleeves up to the shoulder, tucked a cigarette behind one ear, and greased down her hair. This was not Trisha's public gender presentation, and I definitely liked it. "What should I do?" I asked innocently. "You're fine," Trisha muttered from the backseat, where she stashed our jackets and locked up the car. We passed inspection from the bouncer and danced away our frustration amid mirrors and glittering lights.

By the time I was twenty-one, it was all over—I had moved out of state, started graduate school, slept with a man. The landmined and barb-wired territory between gay and straight meant I would struggle another ten years to name my identity as bisexual, and in ten more years I wouldn't even care about definitions, my life becoming its own explanation. My identity came naturally to me—but I had to work at it for a long time.

Visiting Los Angeles years after I'd moved away, I gathered with some close friends for a reunion walk on the Santa Monica beach. We were older, established in our careers, confident in our sexualities. As we chatted, the *whoosh* and *aahhhs* of the waves, the crunch of the sand under our feet, the damp salty air, and sunlit mountains behind Pacific Coast Highway almost made me question my reasons for leaving this beautiful coast. A flock of birds darted above us then, not gulls or sand plovers. I squinted but couldn't recognize their markings. "What are these?" I turned to my friends, who stopped chatting and turned faces upward to look at where I was pointing. Finally somebody said it. "Oh, it's just *birds*." And the faces turned back to eye level where the culture was, and the conversation closed behind my interruption as if I had thrown a pebble in the waves.

As someone who needs to know the names of things, I was probably right to leave Los Angeles. When I come back to visit now, it's the land that greets me first—the waves off the Pacific, the brown and purple Santa Monica mountains, and the flowering jacaranda trees along the street where I grew up. Then, it's my ex-lovers.

color bonita

seeking collective tangible intimacies

christopher angel ramírez

His gaze is feverish, almost animal-like, as if his very heart were beating in it. You realize that he feels just as you do. His pain has disappeared and has been replaced by a sensation of happy fatigue, of being accepted. And you ask yourself if you could accept his friendship, his love, and at the same time give yourself to him.
—Luis Zapata, "My Deep Dark Pain is Love"

AS A FIFTH-GENERATION MEXICAN AMERICAN, I grew up in Perris, a small rural environment nestled between Los Angeles and Palm Springs, California. I come from a very strong Catholic home where homosexuality is perverse and an act that condemns you to hell. Latino male homosexuality has to be "hidden." I remember becoming more familiar with my own sexual desires—"hidden" sexual desires for the attractive Chicano boy, for example—the one who always sits across from me in church on Sunday, the same one who sits across from me in class at St. James elementary school. I begin to ask myself, does his feverish gaze, his "almost animal-like" gaze want to devour me? I ask myself, am I projecting these feelings and thoughts—is this "real"? What am I doing? Remember, hombres Latinos can't desire other hombres Latinos—I will go to HELL for it! So what do you do? You suppress those desires and they slowly poison every part of your being because there is no outlet. But, what if "you realize that he feels just as you do." What if the poison and pain disappears and is "replaced by a sensation of happy fatigue, of [finally] being accepted." What then—"you ask yourself if you could accept his friendship, his love, and at the same time give yourself to him." What then? Does the church condemn you to hell? Does your family disown you? Does Latino culture turn its back on you with disgust? Can you ever overcome those hateful words that are thrown out at you—faggot, joto—when you wait innocently at the bus stop? And now at thirty-two, you think, aren't we over this homophobic shit yet?

I remember how much I anticipated the day that I would get out of Perris; how I grew alienated and disenchanted by high school. Normally I would show up to campus dressed all in black and walk around with my shoulders slouched. I suppose this way of acting makes one a prime target of high school bullying and homophobic slurs. I had absolutely no confidence in myself or in the world that existed around me. Confidence came with drug and alcohol abuse, particularly the days I spent in the underground club scene. By age fifteen, my freedom came in the form of a white capsule, Ecstasy. Total liberation from the affliction and chaos I bottled up inside my mind and heart. For two years I went back every weekend to release my angst on the dance floor with other confused, lost children of darkness. Pain and suffering have an interesting way of revealing awareness, and for a spilt second there were endless possibilities floating amidst the holograms and radiant beaming lasers and throbbing techno beats.

The best way I can explain this liberation is in comparison to a film, Julian Schnabel's *Before Night Falls*, an episodic look at the life of Cuban-born poet Reinaldo Arenas. This sensation of being totally liberated from both self-inflicted and cultural oppression occurred when Reinaldo entered America for the first time—he sits with his head tilted back on the edge of a convertible with snowflakes crashing against his beautiful exile skin. I was free.

My own arrival to New York City in the fall of 1998 had similar overtones. Growing up in Perris did not afford much opportunity for snow, given its desert-dry climate. I remember walking alone outside a club one early morning and feeling refreshed by the glistering snowflakes against the soft fluorescent city lights. I took my beanie off and let the snow slide off my shaved head. The first snowfall's gentleness encouraged me to walk instead of taking the subway. A lone civilian on the streets of Manhattan imagining how he might experience this someday with another soul. The snow provided comfort from the radiant, warm, empty spaces of the club I left tucked in the background several blocks away. The city in all its multiplicity provided a sanctuary.

•

FOR ME AS A LATINO GAY MAN, moments of liberation have always come by way of art, mostly in the form of visual imagery. When I think deeply on this realization, I notice that it comes largely from the pain of knowing how rare and precious those ephemeral moments are. Where does the Latino history of men who love other men reside? Instances that evoke the intangible intimacy I crave and desire to have with another Latino man. Instances that have only existed in intangible, intimate spaces of cruising zones such as Elysian Park in Los Angeles and now the virtual space of

Craigslist and AIM chat rooms. Polymorphous slippage: an intimate life that exists in multiple, but rarely tangible, forms.

I walk up to the park by foot, only a couple of miles away from the Promenade Towers on Figueroa and Second in downtown L.A. where I live. I sit up against a rock and observe all the Latino men driving by, noticing how they glance over slightly at me. Just across from me is a parked truck. I debate nervously whether I should approach him. How long before he decides to get impatient with me and drive off. I ask myself, *why doesn't he get off his truck and approach me?* I anticipate my next move and finally decide to take the risk of being rejected.

"What's up?"

"Nada," he says.

I notice a rosary hanging off the rearview mirror as well as a gold necklace pendant with the name Santos written on it. I stare deeply into his eyes and with my penetrating gaze tell him, "*Sígame!*" He follows a few feet behind me, through rugged terrain, until we settle for an area where we both feel we won't be caught. His eyes so close and near to mine, his body hungering for physical abrasion. He gazes over—between the branches that we pass through, the sun glares partially through, the way light sometimes flares through the lens of a camera. He signals a plea to vanish. However, anticipation returns him to the moment and fills his entire body with joy, freedom so endless it burns—burns so intense it leaves him living outside his body. Until . . . his hand reaches over to the branch and pushes it slowly to make his full entrance, an arena of love and intimacy occurring simultaneously. His leg freezes (almost in midair) in a sort of freeze-frame. He stands there still—and looks over toward me so deeply that the foreground of his face becomes blurred, the background in focus. I then enjoy the warm, sunlit glow that surrounds his smile, lean over, and begin to kiss him. This deep embrace makes my whole body tremble. Kisses to the mouth and nipples, pants and briefs pulled down, our half naked bodies coiled up against each other.

Multiple frames, movement, our hands moving sequentially. My desire to hold on to this intimacy fades away when I open my eyes and find myself alone in this space: a sacred intangible realm.

So I often ask myself how I can arrive at a space of social understanding and healing that transcends the intangible intimacy and love I have with other Latino men. I am invested in opening up possibilities that may transgress the temporal quality of cruising zones. I realize this trajectory does not illuminate the histories of all Latino gay men. Rather, it sheds light on the reality that we are still living in a homophobic, racist society where intimate acts between men remain invisible. Because so much of our vibrant and complex history goes unexplored or arrives in limited forms, I feel it is our responsibility to contribute to our history equally (in whatever shape or form that may manifest). This possibility can lend itself to richer individual histories and collective action.

•

IN 1997 I SAW the film *Star Maps*, another rare treat of a visual medium to transform my life. It was a glimpse into a rich individual history that did not exist for me until I sat practically alone in that dark theater with my popcorn in one hand and ice-cold Coke in another. I recognized in myself a big, more-than-life-sized character on the screen who provided me with some hope that I would overcome my own adversities in this world. The film gave me inspiration and the tools to think more critically of the world around me and to dare to imagine that I could contribute in some positive way to the history of Latino gay men. Intentionally or not, the director Miguel Arteta provided a testimony for me to witness the voice of a Latino gay character on the screen. A tangible history existed somewhere; I went searching. A tangible history that provided some perspective on many issues that affect our lives, including the societal violence brought on by the family, religion, and culture. The representation of the protagonist Carlos reminded me of my own invisibility—sexually and racially, but also my working class background and my personal spiritual practice, *catholicism* (with a small c).

I realized I wanted to witness a more evolved Carlos, a resilient Carlos, one who participates in a cultural landscape that offers him openness and freedom to interact with the world without defamation and discrimination. A Carlos that I also see in myself, who seeks the courage and confidence to push for more real change. There is no real space for Latino gay men to discuss freely and openly their emotions. So I took it upon myself as an artist, teacher, brother, and friend to use witnessing as a mechanism for trans-formation: Color Bonita was born—an interactive new-media dialogue performance, illuminating the lives of Latino gay men. Equally important, it is a venue for multiple histories, including the larger gay community and public testimony from heterosexual audiences. There's a great need to bring Latino families and the Catholic Church into this dialogue.

I interviewed twenty-nine Latino men in Whittier, California. Hearing these stories brought me even closer to understanding my own history as a Latino gay man. The intimacy that came through those dialogues echoed a lot of pain and suffering for many, but also healing. I remember meeting one of the participants, "Genero," at a New Year's Party in Los Angeles in 2005. The following testimony reflects the normalizing gender dynamics that occur in the Latino household:

And I think in my family, especially in our Puerto Rican household, kissing between men was just not a cool thing, in public at least. I remember exactly when I knew that I was very different from the other little boys my age. When I say different I mean knowing that what I was feeling for other little boys was not a good thing. I must have been probably four. I know I wasn't at school yet—I was in school when I was five years old.

We were in the boys' room. My older brothers and I
shared a room with bunk beds. We were watching TV, we
were watching an Elvis Presley movie, and I don't know
why or what possessed me, but I got up and went to the TV
screen and kissed Elvis Presley on the TV screen. And all of
a sudden I hear screaming, "What are you doing?" "Oh my
gosh, you're a *pato*!" A *pato* is a very bad derogatory statement to tell a Puerto Rican person . . . it's like saying *faggot*.
I knew at that point that I did something very bad. I cannot
be kissing men, especially in front of other men. And they
went and they told my mom and my mom questioned me.
And she said, "Did you kiss the TV screen and kiss a man
on the TV? Why did you do that, do you like men?" And I
knew I had to say no because that was a bad thing. And I remember that very distinctly.

For Genaro, kissing between men is not a good thing, "in public at least," meaning in front of other people in the house. Hostility toward same-sex desire in the home is explicitly rejected. It's
also in direct conflict with the family unit. Genaro knew he was
different from other boys as a result of this incident. He is very
explicit in the way he defines his difference here—"what I was
feeling for other little boys was not a good thing."

The home is a place where your heterosexual public persona is
performed and where sex outside of marriage is not condoned.
Because many men who engage in sex with men in public have a
deep desire to keep that part hidden from their public persona,
the act of having sex in public space becomes a private affair—
especially in the context of how the home becomes a public performance space of normalizing gender roles for Latino gay men.
The home also acts as a form of oppression toward Latino men—
having to "act straight," or in our inability to express our queer
desires, and these have long-lasting effects on our lives. Genaro
felt that derogatory words toward gay men have the power to

send him into a "downward spiral." In fact, the consequences of these words and home experience for many Latino gay men can seriously compromise their agency and authority over their own lives. Genaro continues:

I have to say . . . so that statement makes sense . . . that I am in recovery of alcohol and drug addiction. I have been sober for the past ten years actually. So I think that consequently because I grew up in a fear-based home, that if you are gay you are going to burn in hell.

So growing up with that feeling plus the feeling that society doesn't accept you at all, and you are despicable and then growing up in Chicago in the ghetto, where that is absolutely a no-no, being gay, it kind of fucks with your mind. You grow up thinking—I'm a mess!

And I knew I was a mess in my head. How I came to a healing . . . it started in my first day of sobriety where I came to terms with so many issues in my life. And I knew that I couldn't go on unless I worked those things out.

Resilience can occur on multiple levels as another participant, Hector, reveals:

When you live your life in truth and you see the world through the lens of truth then nothing can destroy you, nothing. One's happiness is dependent on one's self solely, and no one and no object can destroy that. And that happiness and truth has given me strength to stand here today and be proud of whom I am.

The strength and vigor that I heard come out of his mouth provided me with yet another opportunity to share and put forth these stories into the world. When one views the world "through the lens of truth," it's possible then to see new worlds. My earlier ideas that those rare glimpses from the media can be transformative was unfolding before eyes and ears. Narrative has transformative potential—it can awaken the collective memory of minority subjects. Equally, what I call "participatory narrative," a collective narrative we can all take part in through mobile digital technologies, can ignite interconnectedness and a sense of belonging beyond the confines of a heterosexually normative narrative.

In the case of Tony, dreaming of other transformative possibilities began for him as a child in the fields as a migrant worker. He says:

> I allowed myself to create stories in my head and daydream about living in Los Angeles, going to school, being an actor, a lawyer, a doctor. I would put myself in situations. I would run with it.

Tony's vision to create other worlds in his head allowed him to experience multiple ways of achieving new ones. His ability to think through his everyday reality critically would later be vital in-dealing with the dominant heterosexual world he encountered through his own parents' homophobia:

> My family being Latino, being of Mexican descent, they do not appreciate me or accept homosexuality. It's very difficult, so my family they don't know, they just assume I am in-between girlfriends, and I led them to believe it.

Perhaps, his motivation to "lead them to believe it" is the thought of a future possibility not yet here. I remember listening to his testimony and being astounded by his intuition and insight. If he hadn't arrived yet, he was about to:

That's the most important thing: Who you really are in this world. Because if you don't really know yourself you're nothing in this world, you are zero and you can't move on—you can't be successful.

These words provide me with a sense of agency and willingness to believe that I can overcome a world filled with hate and delusion. They produce in me a willingness to understand and interrogate the gay community and my own Latino roots. They ignite a need to memorialize the death of my best friend Jorge, an immigrant from El Salvador who died of AIDS in 1998, as well as the urgency to continue transforming every aspect of intimate space so that our brothers don't continue dying in silence.

I am crossing to the other shore, where the Latino man standing across from me at the bus stop feels as I do. And where an incredible sensation of happy fatigue drowns our senses, and we realize that we can accept each other. I can accept his friendship, his love, and give myself to him. We can make worlds where our difference thrives, not just around the curves and terrain of a Latino gay historical landmark, Elysian Park. This is my declaration to the world: a life mission, Color Bonita.

around 1980 in silver lake

eloise klein healy

AROUND 1980, a neighborhood street festival in Silver Lake took the name Sunset Junction, but when I moved to that neighborhood in the seventies, it was long before any moniker of that sort had attached itself to what was a fairly marginal neighborhood. I lived on Sanborn Avenue north of Sunset, and in five minutes I could walk to A Different Light Bookstore. But it had taken me years to find that I belonged in that spot.

I didn't come out officially until 1980. I had been married, been carried from the feminist movement into the lesbian feminist movement and landed not too far from a bookstore that seemed to be the beacon for all the searching souls who populated the area—indeed, the whole world of gay L.A. My life was changing as rapidly as the traffic signals at the intersection near my house. I was becoming not only somebody new, I was entering into a movement with sister and brother writers, all of us trying to make a public space as writers and artists who were unabashedly gay or lesbian.

In that time, I was teaching at Cal State Northridge and holding private workshops at my house. Many of those writers I worked with went on to read their work at the Lesbian Writers Series that Ann Bradley initiated at A Different Light Bookstore. One time, I counted up the number of my workshop participants who were on the ticket and it numbered around forty. Terry Wolverton, Aleida Rodriguez, Bia Lowe, Jacqueline de Angelis, and Sharon Sumpter, among others, claimed the public arena and made some waves.

But when you're in the middle of an energy field, it often doesn't seem to be anything *but* normal, the "daily life" of a movement. In retrospect, it was a spectacular display of alternative energy to be writing and reading and creating a new consciousness that turned like pages do, the content filling the mind, changing the very substance of the body. It was an otherworldly experience, but it was just what we were doing then. Trying to make something totally new that recognized us and that, in turn, we recognized in one another. It was pretty new to be so gay, so "out," so completely interested in shaping a new way of being.

My time was also increasingly being spent at the Woman's Building in downtown Los Angeles on Spring Street. A wild mix of women from all over the world had converged to participate in the Feminist Studio Workshop. I taught writing, helped arrange a reading series, swept floors (no hierarchy at The Building!), and hung out with the book designers and typesetters. I also took a class from lesbian-feminist art historian Arlene Raven and, using that lens, started to reread and reconfigure whole periods of literary and art history. Instead of Hemingway's Paris, I found Gertrude Stein's salon on the rue de Fleurus and Natalie Barney's Temple of Friendship.

I came to suspect that the people I met in Silver Lake and West Hollywood were as significant as the characters in the history I read about in Lillian Faderman's *Surpassing the Love of Men*. For example, Gil Cuadros, a poet of great promise, was often found just down the street at 3226, a gay bar with a fantastic patio. His poetry was a clear-eyed delineation of gay male desire, wonderfully articulated and totally new. He lived long enough to create a great book, *The City of God*. But he died too young, one of the victims of the HIV/AIDS pandemic.

Likewise, Judy Grahn and Paula Gunn Allen, writers and activists from the East Bay, lived right in our midst for a year. When their apartment was burglarized, a group of women led by Geraldine Hannon sprinkled salt around their building and told stories of strength to ward off any more intruders.

It was the Temple of Friendship all over again, this time set just south of Sunset.

The poem I'm concluding with, "On Lesbian Writing," is the direct result of seeing slides of Romaine Brooks's paintings of the lesbian circle in Paris. These were the layers of history I'd missed in my "straight-girl" literature studies in college.

On Lesbian Writing

In the interests of examining the connection to the lives
we are living we must ask does the bond run in the blood
or is it as some believe directed by the power of the moon
or as others say by the power a woman effects on your an-
gle of vision but of course some don't bother to say or
didn't say but even in casual photos the distinctive tilt of
the chin speaks volumes and the incredible glance that
lives on in the one standing next to you who has as well included as a personal style just the most impossible shading
of arrogance which indicates and welcomes an understanding that goes beyond cultural boundaries as when the
lights go off and one fingertip after another gauges the di-
mensions of sensation on the surface of the naked skin or
under cloth or leather or beaded and gathered stuff

arranged ever so wonderfully you can't believe in looking at the photographs and the paintings that nobody thought anything of the display and took no opportunity to comment on the distinctive manner of ornamentation and posture which acts almost but not quite as an affront to the received and applied rules of behavior while making a territory alongside of or just out of reach of the norm in which she and whomever she wanted to be with simply blossomed

—*Passing* (Red Hen Press, 2002);
reprinted by permission of the author.

l.a. incog-negro

daryl keith roach

ONE: THREE STRIKES, YOU'RE OUT

"YOUR SON'S A FAG," hissed Miles Davis to my father. It was 1969. I was returning from a Christmas trip to Europe. Europe was wonderful. Europe opened my eyes. I was beautiful, black, and proud. And I was gay!

I grew up in New York City. I learned I had advantages that some black kids did not have at that time. My father was Max Roach, the late, great jazz drummer who pioneered bebop and was one of the founders of modern jazz. It was a world rich in experiences, some that I did not understand, some that prepared me for the rest of my life.

When I returned from Europe, all hell broke loose. I sat in the living room in our fourteenth-floor apartment on the Upper West Side overlooking Central Park and listened as my father raged: "*FAGGOT!*"

My parents, who were divorced by this time, were not primed for this. My mother, the former Mildred Wilkinson, was one of the Danzler Models, a part of the new post-war period of Negro advertising. It was said that my father stopped playing the drums and walked up to my mother in a club and declared, "This is the woman I am going to marry." My parents had primed me for being educated and being fully equipped to function in a white world. The idea was that opportunities open to black men were, up until then, limited to numbers runners, drug dealers, or pimps. They were not having any of that. They were not having any of this, either.

"Do you get fucked or do you do the fucking? Do you wear dresses and hats?" My father raged. I was sitting in this great, carved, wooden armchair that my grandmother, who cleaned Park Avenue apartments as a maid, had left him. Dad was stalking around, yelling obscenities at me. I actually had the thought, *how does he know all this stuff?* Meanwhile, my mother said in her best high Negro tone, "You already have two strikes against you, why would you want a third?" This puzzled me. I asked what the other two besides being a fag were. Mom said, "being black and being a black man." The problem was that my parents never let me entertain the idea that being black would ever be a liability. So I was a BLACK MAN FAGGOT.

Years later in Los Angeles, I was becoming increasingly irritated about the way casting directors, TV writers, and producers were stereotyping black male actors. We were playing pimps or lowest common denominator street thug types. I grew up reading Langston Hughes, whose "Semple" stories had always intrigued me. They were so human and everyman in their way. Although Jesse B. Semple was street, he held such great wisdom and his philosophy was just "be simple" in life. I started to do the short stories as audition monologues because there was a lack of material then for black actors.

Rae Allen, the Tony Award-winning actress for *And Miss*

Readon Drinks a Little, was my acting teacher and coach in the early eighties. She'd worked and studied with the greats of Broadway. She asked me where the monologues were from. I said they were from a collection of short stories by Langston Hughes that my father gave me, and I had adapted them for auditioning. (Dad used to say he gave me the stories because "Goldilocks and the Three Bears were not part of the African-American experience.") Rae wanted me to bring more in to class and work on them in addition to the scene work we were doing. The great thing about L.A. is that, despite being restricted and terrorized racially, I also felt creatively liberated and entrepreneurial. Groups like est, the Erhard Seminar Training, and *The Advocate* Experience shifted this BLACK MAN FAGGOT to a human being who happened to be male, gay, an actor, black, and all the various parts I chose to include in my life.

Thus, *Semple: A One Man Show* was born, directed by Rae Allen with music by Max Roach. One night, as I leaped out into the audience to do "I Will Now Obituize Myself," there in front of me was the great Ruby Dee, beaming. When I was a child, Ozzie Davis and Ruby Dee were my idols. To have Ms. Dee there at the theater in Los Angeles was truly wonderful.

Because of my extraordinary circumstances growing up, certain events and people had a great impact on me. When I was sixteen, a few years before the Miles Davis bomb, Dad had a cocktail party filled with all sorts of colorful people. At one point, the novelist James Baldwin grabbed me and said, "Max, Daryl is beautiful, man." Well, the *way* he grabbed me, pushing his pelvis into mine, made me uncomfortable and I made a stink about it. Dad said at the time, "Homosexuals are some of the most creative people we know." Bingo! I thought, *how cool*.

Maya Angelou, whom my father considered a sister, believed that words have vibrations, psychic vibrations, and certain words would take redefining every time you used them. So, the word *faggot*—which originally named a bundle of sticks that was used in the dark ages to burn suspected homosexuals, whether male or female, as witches—carried so much pain and evil with it that to use it lightly was a mark of unconsciousness. And *consciousness*, black consciousness, was central to how I was nurtured. Even the word *nigger*, which my father said often when angry, was only to be used with a great deal of conscious attention.

So, in their quest for consciousness, my parents went to see a black psychiatrist. Homosexuality was classified as a disease at the time (speaking of the *dark* ages). Furthering their pain, the doctor's advice was that "all homosexuals are suicidal" and to "take him out of New York City." I was sent to San Francisco with my father on one of his gigs.

TWO: STRAIGHT TO SAN FRANCISCO

MY FATHER SAT IN FIRST CLASS while I sat in coach. Coach! There is a term, now widely used, which encompasses a lot: entitlement. I felt entitled. I was number-one son, the heir apparent. We never talked, and we were not talking now. In fact, we had not really talked since I was eight, when he walked in on me dancing over the living room furniture to Tchaikovsky's "1812 Overture" in my mother's crème silk and black chiffon negligée. That incident sent me *straight* to Sugar Ray Robinson's Boxing School.

We checked into the St. Francis Hotel. When he emerged from his end of our shared suite, Dad informed me that two friends were coming by to keep me company. At about 7:30, two very sexy ladies, Mercedes and Beryl, arrived. I couldn't have been more depressed and cut off. Two black hookers to straighten me out was the fix my father had come up with this time? They looked liked pros, full-on Afros, beads, platform shoes, and the sexiest dresses.

Dad left to go to the club. "How are you doing, baby?" Beryl said, after a long, awkward silence. "Not much of a talker, are you?"

"My father found out I am a fag!" I startled myself with this pronouncement.

Beryl and Mercedes burst out laughing, furthering my descent into despondency. Gathering herself, Mercedes said, "It's, OK. Baby, we're lesbians!" I'd always felt lucky, and luck struck again. We ordered champagne and caviar. Pearls of perception flowed from Beryl and Mercedes as the champagne flowed. They clocked my parents in surprisingly astute ways: "High yellow mother, father too full of his press releases. You have to take control of your own life. You need your parents to get through the next bit of time, especially school. You have to start lying to them. You are being far too honest."

Beryl and Mercedes said that my parents had not prepared me in a *real world* kind of way. Sure, I knew our history, our struggle, but did I know how to survive?

When Dad returned from the club at about 3 a.m., we were all in various stages of undress. Beryl and Mercedes had gotten quite amorous with each other with all the talk of "Freedom now! *Right now!*" Dad must have thought his plan had worked. Nothing was said of it, again. Beryl and Mercedes were my teachers, and, for that moment, they taught me to look beyond the terror I was undergoing with my Dad.

Terrorism is pernicious, whether inflicted by parents, communities, or governments. One is highly injured, and the intent is to close one down. I was told by my father at one point to change my name, that I was a disgrace and would be disowned if I didn't change.

My father's second wife, Abbey Lincoln, who referred to herself as our wicked stepmother, said, "Never let anyone tell you who and what you are." She had to say this very quietly under her breath one day in the apartment while all the drama was unfolding about my lifestyle.

Years later, I had the moment to address my lifestyle with my father when we worked together on one of his tours, "Max Roach's

America." We were at the George V in Paris, playing to a sold-out house at the Cité de la Musique. Again, we were sharing a suite, and again I traveled by coach with the chorus and orchestra.

My father's European agent, Victor O'Gilvy, who set up the tour, remarked how good I looked. I had long since adopted my father's declared stance. I remember as a child sitting on the toilet seat watching Dad do his toilette before work. As he finished he'd say, "Daryl, I can't wait for tomorrow." "Why, Daddy?" I'd ask, my legs swinging back and forth from my perch. He'd say, "'Cause I get better looking every day!" I still laugh quietly at how tickled I became when we played that game.

Victor asked me what I did to remain so youthful. He asked my age. I said fifty. Dad said, "Hold up! Don't tell people that because women will know how old I am." Victor said, "I bet you don't do drugs," and I said, "No, my father did enough for us all." "Alcohol?" I said, "I drink *Caucasian-ally*."

Victor went on, "Obviously, you go to the gym, you eat well. What else *don't* you do?"

I looked at my father and Victor. I said self-assuredly, "I don't do women!" With that they fell off their chairs laughing and went on a riff about how chasing "pussy" will age you. Dad said, "If I'd had a taste for dick, I might not have gotten into so much trouble . . . but I couldn't wrap my lips around the idea." Considering where Dad and I began on this journey, it was a great moment.

THREE: ESCAPE FROM NEW YORK

I CAN REMEMBER going into my first gay bar in New York City and the sheer terror of that first visit. It was around the corner from the famous Village Vanguard, where Dad played and where my sister had her sweet sixteen birthday party. The nearby gay club was Julius's Bar. It had a big bay window in the front. I was terrified that the jazz club owners or friends of my parents would walk by and see me in there.

For what should be obvious reasons by now, I had to get out of New York and set up a life for myself. I wanted to pursue my dream of acting. I had encouragement from Sidney Poitier one night at the Russian Tea Room. It was after the premier of *For the Love of Ivy*, in which he starred with my stepmother. Sidney purred, "I welcome you to the game."

Los Angeles is where I ended up. I was to face another kind of terror: the LAPD. Within five days of my arrival, after returning my rental car on Wilcox Avenue in Hollywood, I decided to hitchhike to my apartment. When I stepped out into the street, a police car made a U-turn. Two white officers emerged and said that I was not supposed to be hitchhiking and didn't I know this was a bad area. I said I'd just arrived from New York City. They looked at my driver's license and wrote me a ticket for "having one foot in the road."

Over the next few months, incidents with the LAPD escalated to the point that I referred to my situation as DWB—driving while black. It seemed that every time I "DWB'd" into Beverly Hills at night, I was pulled over. I spent one harrowing evening in the Beverly Hills police station under suspicion of being involved with a homicide in Venice. Being new to L.A., I didn't know of Venice Beach. I remarked about how thorough the police and Interpol were to be working together on a case from Venice, Italy. "Well," a police officer said, "we have a smart nigger here!" This was the first time, other than my father using the "N" word, that I was referred by that epithet. I knew they were serious. It scared me and I would never again DWB in Los Angeles unconscious of my new knowledge.

DWB was not the only form of terrorism I experienced in L.A. When I was not harassed by the police, I discovered that getting a place to live and even getting into a gay bar presented other terrors.

I was dating the magnificent Brahm Elmendorp from Holland. He recently moved to Los Angeles, having enjoyed an illustrious European career as a dancer. One night, Brahm said he wanted to "experience" me in this bathhouse, 8709. I wasn't particularly interested in doing this, and to explain to white men how such things operate takes too long on a date. So, with resistance, I agreed to this visit. We ascended the steps to the bathhouse. Brahm got in without even showing any ID. Did I say that he was magnificent looking? I stepped up to the window and was asked for my driver's license, passport, and another form of government-issued ID with a picture. Brahm moved beyond the front doors and assumed I would follow him. After a while, Brahm emerged to find that I didn't have the "right" credentials to enter. When he realized the entire deal, Brahm was incensed. Europeans knew of our racial history but couldn't really understand, so he was completely thrown by these conditions.

Bars, in L.A., were restricted by color and gender. Women and people of color were routinely required to have three pieces of picture ID. Even if I did get in, I knew that men couldn't touch one another in a bar for fear of getting arrested for lewd behavior. Entrapment was a big issue into the early seventies with the LAPD.

These obstacles were a dare to me and the kind of thinking I was trained to defend against. My life experience had created a kind of vision such that I could see these terror techniques intended to limit groups and keep people from intermingling. We, as a world community, were just beginning to emerge from restricted, racist thought patterns created and generated to keep us "separated." None of these obstacles deterred me. My father use to say, "Where did he come from? He thinks he can do and go anywhere." But Los Angeles, in those years, tried to make me screen myself. Racism and homophobia were the standard fare. Decades of this kind of fear, dread, terror produced the Rodney King riots in the early 1990s.

The residual effects of terror are resentments and hostilities, which in turn destroy creativity, communities, and lives. Being terrorized can cause one to hide, thinking of ways to be left alone. I thought of displaying a contraption in the rear window of my car: a black man's hand mounted on a spring attached to a suction cup. The hand would wave back and forth with a caption: NICE NEGRO ON BOARD.

I had a slow year in 1977. The secretary at my agency really took a liking to this "nice negro." The casting director for *Little House on the Prairie* had called for a white actor whose name was Harold Rose. The secretary at my agency somehow heard "Daryl Roach." She was so excited at me having this opportunity. I grew up watching *Bonanza* and fell in love with Michael Landon as Little Joe. When I arrived at the casting office, the staff looked a little distant. I found out later that the staff at Paramount had called my agent and said I had "crashed" this audition, which is a no-no. I was doing my "nice negro" routine and was called in to a meeting with a Ms. Sukman. After some polite chat, she said, "We don't do any shows with black stories." I took the moment to ask, "What years is *Little House* set in?" She said, "1860s." I said, "They fought a whole war about us then." We laughed, and I suggested that if in the future a script came across her desk in which she could conceivably place a person of color, she could take the chance.

A script did come across her desk about an Irish itinerant boxing family. She told me that in one of the production meetings she suggested that the characters could perhaps be black, instead of Irish. When Ms. Sukman called me in to read for it, she said that she was "hot" that week for coming up with the idea, and she wanted me to get the role because the idea had come from me. The episode was called "The Fighter." Mr. Landon, whom I have so much respect for, called NBC while we were filming and said he needed another half hour for this story. They gave it to him on the spot. That episode went on to win an Emmy.

My early life in Los Angeles was like trying to live L.A. INCOG-NEGRO. Coming out to myself, my family, and friends was a process that I discovered in Los Angeles. Thank the Gods and Dad, it worked. I refused to let terror work. And like Dad, I get better looking every day.

8709 w. third street

sean church

I CAN'T REMEMBER a time when I wasn't obsessed with movies. My mother has told the story many times that she started taking me to movies when I was six weeks old. She started graduate school when I was less than a month old. She would study like mad during the day, while I was with my grandmother, and several nights a week she would come home from school, eat a quick dinner, and take me to her favorite refuge, the movies. Since I was a good baby who didn't cry much, she was able to take me without disturbing people around us in the auditorium.

Cut to: my senior year of college. I decided that I just had to be in the movie or TV business. I knew I had to go to Los Angeles or New York. I decided to move to New York, since I'd been there often during my teenage years to visit family. I loved the city (and still do); however, I'd only been to visit during summer vacations, and after two snowy winters in the Big Apple, I learned I was by

no means a fan of winter. Since I was getting nowhere professionally after a few years either, I decided to go make a new start
where the weather was at least warmer. I'd never been to Los
Angeles before, and of course, having been in New York for a
while, I'd heard nothing but horror stories about its lack of culture, sophistication, good food, and intelligent people. But at that
point the thought of warmth and sunny beaches was enough to
get me to make the cross-country trek.

I arrived in Los Angeles a few days after Christmas, 1978. The
temperature was in the eighties, and I was in heaven. The next day
the Long Beach Earthquake struck. Fortunately, the tremors
weren't too serious, and I felt inexplicably exhilarated rather than
terrified. In town less than twenty-four hours, and I was no longer
an earthquake virgin! I had one good friend in L.A. Phil had moved
here from back home in Texas about the same time I'd moved to
New York. There was an opening in the apartment building he
lived in, so I was able to move into an apartment just across the hall
from him. It almost made me feel like I was home again.

Other than going to Grauman's Chinese Theatre to see the
movie star footprints and taking a drive by the Hollywood sign, I
was not much interested in doing the sightseeing thing. For a place
I'd dreamed about going to my entire life, I was just strangely not
inclined to explore it. Maybe it was those nasty rumors from New
York making me feel that I might find out that they were true, if I
delved into the city too closely.

But Phil decided that there was one distinctly nontourist spot
that we *had* to visit. It was called "The 8709." That was the address on West Third Street. It was a gay bathhouse not techni-
cally in the West Hollywood city limits, but it was only a stone's
throw away, and, as I would quickly come to learn, very much a
part of the gay West Hollywood scene of the late seventies and
early eighties.

My first visit happened in January, 1979, when gay people were
starting to feel more comfortable about coming out and express-

ing their true selves. Many were also very free about expressing their sexuality. While I was in New York I'd dated a couple of guys (including an Irish seminary student and a nice man who later became a recognizable, if not famous, TV actor), and I'd been to most of the gay bathhouses at least once, if not several times, so going to a sex club was not a new experience.

I'd known Phil for almost ten years, from working at the same place before we left home. Otherwise, I might never have met him. Phil was a tall, gorgeous, blue-eyed blond hunk—and I was *not*. I suppose no one would call me bad looking, but usually I just blended into the woodwork. I was not someone who stopped traffic, whereas Phil did. Despite Phil's looks, he was friendly, warm, and intelligent. You may ask, "Why didn't you two get together?" Mainly, because when I met him he had a boyfriend—a tall, gorgeous, brown-eyed hunk. Even after they split up, I knew Phil was only interested in me as a friend. Usually guys as stunning as Phil would never give someone like me the time of day, but he was never one to lord his looks over anyone. Maybe that's one of the reasons I liked him so much. Going to a gay bar with Phil was a two-sided experience. On the one side, it was fascinating to follow a little behind him as we would wander through dark, smoky nightclubs. I would see men notice him, then walk into poles, stop talking in mid-sentence, or drop their drinks, or at least their jaws, as we would walk by. Of course, he must have known he was blessed with extraordinary looks, but he was never rude to anyone who spoke to him, except maybe to creeps who deserved it. On the other side, I would usually feel disheartened walking alongside him because no one ever even noticed me. I was a mere shadow to the Golden Boy.

So when Phil suggested that we go to the 8709 bathhouse I said, "Oh, really?"—especially after he explained how the place worked. It was a bathhouse that never advertised. One knew of it only if one were recommended for membership by a current member. The management only wanted clients who were attractive enough to keep the members "satisfied," and they wanted to keep riffraff out. It sounded somewhat elitist to me, but hell, here was Phil thinking I looked good enough to get in, and the thought of not being attacked by the many less-than-attractive ogres I used to encounter at New York clubs made the chance to join the 8709 quite appealing. I said, "Let's go!"

Back in those days it was easy to find street parking at night, despite its proximity to Cedars-Sinai Medical Center. We parked in the alley behind the building. There was a sleazy-colored light above the door. There was no sign of any sort, no indication of what loomed inside. Phil opened the door, and we entered. There was nothing there but a staircase leading up to a glass window. There were several men lined down the staircase, waiting to pay their entrance fee. I was somewhat expecting to see clones of Phil, but at the same time I didn't want to be the worst-looking person in the room. It was quite dark even at that entrance, so I couldn't see what the guys looked like. On later visits, I don't recall the staircase ever being that dark again. Maybe it had been my imagination working overtime, maybe not.

When we made it to the check-in window, I showed the attendant my brand new California driver's license to prove I was old enough to get in. (I looked about sixteen from the time I was eleven until I was almost thirty.) When the attendant asked me for the cash to pay for my membership and entrance fees, I breathed a sigh of relief, realizing that I had passed the "looks examination." Wow, I was good enough to get into the most popular sex club in town! We heard a loud buzzing sound at the door, and we were able to pass through the security door to enter the sex paradise of West Hollywood.

As we entered I noticed the TV room, where guys could take a break from all the activities going on elsewhere. We walked a short way to a staircase that led us down to the locker rooms and showers. We took off our clothes, stuffed them into a locker, and put on towels so we could start prowling around. I can't tell you

exactly how big the place was—I'm terrible with spatial concep-
tion—but it seemed fairly large to me, especially since it had two
levels. Phil gave me a tour of the place—the steam room, the
Jacuzzi, the showers. We passed a row of small rooms. Some had
open doors, with naked or nearly naked men lying on hard, thin
mattresses waiting for prospective partners to enter and get down
to business. Other rooms had closed doors, behind which I heard
men who were definitely getting down to business.

There was another "TV room," but this one showed gay porn
videos. VHS machines hadn't been on the market all that long,
and I didn't have my own home machine yet, so this was a rare
opportunity for me, and for others, I suppose, to see this much
smut outside a dirty movie theater or bookstore. The fact that
there were bunk mattresses in the room made being a voyeur and
a slut at the same time a definite likelihood.

Back upstairs, there were more halls of small rooms with
doors, and there were a couple of large playrooms. One was a
completely dark room, which scared the hell out of me. I may
have been a playful type, but I drew the line at having sex with
anyone I couldn't see. Holding Phil's hand as we slowly passed
through, I entered that room only that one time. The other large
room, a maze, had a little bit of light, and I do emphasize little bit.
Over time, that became my favorite place in the club to meet
someone (or two, or three). Then I preferred to run off to one of
the free small rooms for a bit of privacy. I admit to being a voyeur,
but I've never been an exhibitionist.

I honestly don't remember what shenanigans I got into on that
first visit. But I can tell you that I wouldn't have missed out on it
for the world. My second visit was only a week or so later. I soon
became quite the regular. Phil had a car (I didn't) so I couldn't go
there, except for the times he asked me to go along with him. One
time he fell asleep with some hottie in one of the small rooms. I
waited for hours, not knowing where he was exactly. I ended up
having to walk the four miles home in the middle of the night, so

I could get at least a few hours' sleep before going to work the next day. Before I woke up in my own bed that morning, Phil came crawling on his hands and knees into my bedroom to beg my forgiveness. What more of an apology could I have asked for?

After I'd been in Los Angeles for about five or six months, Phil started working in Laguna Beach. He was spending more time there than in Los Angeles, and after a few months, he fell in love in Laguna Beach and decided to move there. For a while, I couldn't get to the 8709 very often, unless some other friend who had a car was willing to give me a ride. But my first summer in town I got the chance to move to West Hollywood, and I was at last able to buy a used car. I was free to go wherever I wanted, whenever I wanted. Finally, this meant I could go to the 8709 on my own!

I *did* have a life outside the bathhouse. I had a job. I went to movies and the theater. I would go to restaurants occasionally—especially for Mexican or Japanese food.

I had good friends. In fact, I had a number of straight friends, male and female, who enjoyed hearing about my most recent ex-ploits at the 8709. I could understand why the straight women might be interested in sexploits between gay men, since men are their sexual interest, but I never quite understood why the straight men enjoyed the stories. I'm not stupid enough to think they were all closet cases—maybe they were just liberated enough (this was not long after the hippie movement) to be interested in something so different from their kind.

One thing that the 8709 gave me, which the "real world" rarely could, was sex. I functioned well at my job, and I enjoyed a lot of activities that I participated in, but the one thing that was lacking in my life was a relationship. Even before I'd moved to Los Angeles, I wasn't all that successful in finding and maintain-ing romantic relationships, but after coming here, that got a lot worse. Looking back on that time, I can see that I didn't have much self-confidence. Growing up, I had always been an A student and teacher's pet, but most of my peers didn't want to hang out with me. My few friends were other nerds and geeks. To say I was unpopular would be an understatement. By the time I was in college my skin cleared up and I started to fill out a bit, so people didn't cringe at the sight of me. I actually had a very sexy boyfriend my last year in college, and when I was living in New York, people appreciated my intelligence and sense of humor. But who in West Hollywood gave a damn about those things? (Some of those New York rumors *were* accurate.) All I had to do was look around me on the street, at the gym, in the clubs, at my best friend—and I always felt so inferiorly unattractive. This was the town where movie stars, porn stars, and models are a dime a dozen. I was certainly not the type that other gay men ran after, and on the rare occasions when I would get up the nerve to ask someone out on a date, I always got the same response, practically verbatim: "Oh, Sean, you're one of the nicest people I've ever met, but I could never think of you *that* way." I would either end up being their best friend, or they would never speak to me again.

Most of my friends knew that if I wasn't at home, I was likely either at the movies or at the 8709. Once a frantic friend even called the place trying to find me when an emergency situation came up. And yes, I was there. Since none of the guys I wanted to date in this town were interested in me, I could go to the 8709 and, for a few hours, have a good time with some stranger(s). I can't even imagine doing that kind of thing now, but back then it was my oasis of pleasure. One time I had sex with a famous pro-football player, another time with a TV sitcom star, and once with a *Playgirl* centerfold. But the best time I ever had there was with a guy named Kent. I had never seen him before, and I never saw him again, but for the couple of hours we spent in one of the small rooms at the 8709, I was in sheer heaven. It didn't even occur to me until I was on my way home that I didn't ask him for his phone number as we left the room. Maybe I'd been disappointed

too many times before, and I didn't want to get turned down
again. Then too, he hadn't asked me for mine either, had he? For
the same reason? I'll never know, but I'll never forget him.

The 8709 must have been the same haven for many others. It
was "live and let live" at the time. Yet who could have possibly
known what was lurking around the corner? However, of course,
in the early eighties gay sex life as we knew it was about to change
more drastically than anyone could have foreseen. Although the
club had always been predominantly "white," there had been a
few good-looking men of other races who passed the looks test at
the front window. But I think around 1982 I noticed that the strict
door policy was beginning to relax a little. I started being aware
that the crowd was a little more mixed, and, surprisingly, that
some slightly paunchy, not-so-attractive older men were being allowed in. I suppose that this was to keep business up. Obviously,
the word that there was a newly developing, sexually transmitted
disease that was killing gay men was not good for bathhouse business. I remember reading in several magazine articles at the time
that one was less likely to get the disease if one didn't fool around
as much as before. Of course, it only takes once to get the virus,
but at the time I just cut down on the number of times I went to
the 8709. I don't remember ever hearing anyone talking at the
club about the scary new disease. There was a lot of denial going
on with any of us who continued to go to the baths.

It was nearing the end of an era, one we may never see the likes
of again. The 8709 was an early casualty of the AIDS era. Sheldon
Andelson, a wealthy leader in Los Angeles's gay community,
owned the club and the property it sat on. The local medical community started trying to get him to help fight the epidemic, but he
felt the club was a symbol of hard-earned sexual freedom, so the
place stayed open a while longer. However, when Governor Jerry
Brown appointed Andelson to the University of California Board
of Regents, Andelson's name suddenly disappeared from the bathhouse's ownership papers. By 1984 Andelson, having become an

important figure in Democratic politics, yielded to pressure from party concerns and closed the 8709 forever. Andelson died from complications from AIDS a few years later. His obituary in the *New York Times* on New Year's Day, 1988 mentioned highlights of his distinguished career as a lawyer, banker, member of the UC Board of Regents, and fund-raiser for Teddy Kennedy and Walter Mondale, but of course, it did not mention that he had owned the most notorious gay bathhouse in the whole country.

The 8709 closed before any of the other local bathhouses and sex clubs did, before many gay men "got" how serious the new epidemic was. I had tried other bathhouses like Mac's in Silver Lake and the Hollywood Spa a few times, but Mac's just really couldn't compete with the 8709 crowd, and even after the 8709 closed, Mac's could rarely get a hot crowd, or any kind of crowd, really. And the Hollywood Spa—well, I hear it's just as dull now as it was all those years ago.

Even before the 8709 closed, I had gotten scared of the mysterious new virus. If I had the virus, I didn't want to give it to anyone else. If I didn't have it, I certainly didn't want to catch it. My dear Phil died from AIDS, as did a number of my close friends. I went back into the closet for years, at least sexually. I was still openly gay, but you'd never know it from my physical behavior. And when I did start having sex again, I only had safe sex. At first I really hated having to use condoms and to watch out for risky bodily fluids, but I eventually got used to it. I can honestly say that I haven't had unsafe sex in almost twenty-five years. But for a brief period of a few years, the 8709 was my oasis of unbridled sexual fantasy. My recollections of it are a cherished memory in my heart that I never want to forget.

a

ghalib shiraz dhalla

HE MARKED THE END of even a fleeting affair with a ritual of personal destruction. Some punish plastic, others gorge on food to fill the infinite void left by love, the hope of it, but he needed to raze something, to actually remove something from him, his realm.

Just as an amputated arm continues to inflict phantom pain, so too the fading of something as precious as a feeling for another must be marked by a corporeal act of obliteration, no matter how small.

Sometimes this took the shape of something as inconsequential as the breaking of a cocktail glass, seemingly accidental as he poured into it a shot of warm, unpalatable vodka at the end of a bitter night and before climbing into bed without praise or gratitude for a God that had deprived him yet again.

At other times, he cut himself as he was slicing the onion into

slivers for his breakfast omelet, and his eyes would brim with tears
so that it looked like the rivulet of blood, red enough to paint lips
or the parting of a bride's head, was drowning the whole world in
scarlet.

Then there were cruder nights, nights when he would swallow
life whole, like a man ravenous for something so specific, that its
dearth had driven him into an astounding and insatiable binge for
all else, and in the process, suffocate all agonies in the cacopho-
nies of carousal at the bars and nightclubs of West Hollywood,
where vulnerability guised itself in arrogance and those who were
still foolish enough to hope for a different outcome and linger
through the changing guard of youthful faces, had learned how to
smile and mask any disenchantment with expertise.

At the end of such nights, he found himself kneeling, not re-
pentant in prayer or ready to take another man into his mouth,
but over the cold, porcelain rim of a toilet, regurgitating not only
the poisons of life but also the toxicity of what he had thought of
as love.

A. changed this. On their last night together, A. reminded him
that they had a deal, not so much with words but with that magnificent tilt of his head as he touched his mouth and looked into his
eyes with so much pain in his own. It was an impotent gesture, one
that could rescind nothing but conceal none of the longing he felt.

He wanted A. to stay as much as he wanted to see him go. If an
impending disaster cannot be diverted, then it was better that it
came to pass so that he could go about the business of rebuilding.
The end was near and he grew anxious more than fearful.

So he responded—with the same tacit though awkward jerking
of his head, letting his eyes wander from A. while he was still
where he could be seen, touched, and felt that—yes, we had a deal
and now you must go to that other desert, one filled with palms
and mosques and burning resin instead of ours with the concrete
snake and smog and me. You must go to a wife waiting to bear

you children so that I can be quickly reassigned to a world of bars and new men and freedom.

You will be grounded by your commitments. I will be suffocated by my freedom. You must go. Look—but only ahead—not at me to change your mind.

But if A. stayed, it had to be his decision. Disowned by kin and country, he would never be able to go back. The land of the free would imprison him for good. Love came at a cost. It was not free and it didn't, contrary to baroque, romantic notions, multiply inherently. It had to be reallocated, detoured, compensated for. No such thing as love without casualties.

He cradled A. into his arms and stayed awake through most of the night, watching him sleep, running his hand over his head, ministering gentle kisses not as a lover would another but as a father would his child. For the last month they had stopped making love, having decided it was better for bodies to be prized apart before the heart would have to follow suit.

Sometime in the night he found himself ensconced by A. and he let himself be sheltered and warmed, terrified of the breadth of the bed, already feeling the space A. would leave behind on it. *Let me know more of this*, he thought. *Hold on to the way we are before I know anything else.*

Winter had come early and the sky wept, drenching the parched city with its waters and promising to paralyze the runaway and the winged creature that would take A. away to the ends of the earth. They were rooted in the middle of the terminal, surrounded by so much luggage, by A.'s suspecting friends around whom they could not steal the intimacy that had unfurled between them for a year now. And he thought, *how can they not see? We, our emotions, are like an ancient tree in the midst of all this bustle; our roots thick and gnarled like the legs of a giant wooden spider about to be uprooted. Will the ground not shake? Maybe they will, but like us, they too will hold equilibrium, not speak.*

As he watched the distance between them grow, first as A. walked through the boarding gate as if entering a portal to the afterlife—a life without him—and then, as the plane surmounted nature's wrath and pulled A. into the stony sky, he could think only of life's cruel irony: that somewhere at the end of his lover's journey was someone waiting breathlessly; that a parting must take place at one end so that a welcoming could take place at another. This must be what Beckett meant when he talked about the constant quality of tears, how for each one who begins to weep, somewhere else, another stops.

He entered not just a house that screamed its silence at him, but also a life he thought he had deflected.

Glasses waited to be shattered, knives glinted along serrated edges, memories remained trapped and muffled behind glass frames. But now that the one true love of his life had left, he did nothing because no conceivable act could express the gravity of his grief. Nothing could exorcise it. He could not bleed A. out of him like a humor or cut him out from the marrow of his being.

Every act of love and the cruelty inherent in it would remain like the fingerprints on a mirror, imperceptible to most but always there, reminding him of being touched.

He would observe no ritual this time; do nothing to bring closure. Perhaps the world doesn't end cataclysmically, it dies with a whimper.

He would throw himself into life once again, yes, and soon, the features that he had started to see as his own would fade into a sea of other faces unless he looked into old pictures; the sound of that voice too would become warbled by new voices, thank God, so that their promises would no longer even echo in the air around him; and although he would always remember how comforted he felt enveloped in A.'s arms, surely he would also forget just how warm the skin felt against his own, as if burning from somewhere within.

the love that dared speak its name

teresa decrescenzo

For Betty

THE QUESTIONS ARE ROUTINE and predictable. This is by no means the first, or even the tenth, hospital visit for us since our cancer wars began in the spring of 1986. Mumbled rote responses to each question about age and general health and insurance follow one after another, in a bureaucratic *pas de trois*, with me as the Greek chorus, commenting, correcting, clarifying answers. We have done this too many times over the years.

At the question about marital status, Betty answers, "none of the above. I am in a domestic partnership."

The clerk, a young, dark-haired woman wearing a beige blouse and pants that match her blank expression, responds that she will just check "single."

Big mistake.

"No," Betty says tartly, "you will not check the box marked 'single' because I am NOT single." The clerk's reply is polite, but encourages no discussion. "I understand," she says brusquely, "but we don't have a box that says 'domestic partner,' and you are not legally married, so the easiest thing to do is just to check the box that says, 'single,' so we can go ahead and get you admitted for your procedure today."

Bigger mistake, suggesting that it would be "easier." Easier for the clerk, maybe. I suppress a giggle as I find myself remembering the old Señor Wences comedy routine on the *Ed Sullivan Show*, where Wences and one of his imaginary characters would converse about a problem that would always end with the same line, "is easy . . . is easy for you . . . is difficult for me."

Predictably, Betty reacts sharply. "Easier for whom?" The question was obviously rhetorical.

Now speaking in a low, deadly tone, Betty delivers a brief lecture on the history of gay rights in America, followed by a synopsis of the same-sex marriage efforts of various public-interest law firms both within and outside of the LGBT communities, then gets to the big finish: "If you think for one instant that I will sign a document that describes me as 'single,' you are mistaken, young woman. That is simply not going to happen."

Then, as if just remembering that she is ever the conciliator, known for being reasonable, Betty seizes upon a compromise position. "I suggest that you simply leave that question blank. Leave it with no response, or write in, 'patient declined to state,' so we can just go forward."

The bureaucratic expression fades, the admissions clerk's lip begins to tremble, and moisture gathers in the corners of her eyes. She turns the monitor around so that it faces Betty. "Ma'am, can you see this screen? It is locked. It is programmed so that I cannot go to the next question, or to any other part of this admissions form until this question is answered. The same is true for every question. Each question must be answered before the program allows movement to the next question. That way, it is 'idiot proof,' and an admitting clerk can't accidentally overlook a question. So, please, won't you just let me check the 'single' box? Please? We cannot go any further if you don't."

Which is where we are now, at 9:45 in the morning, in March 2001, together twenty-eight years, we are two ordinary people fighting a life-threatening illness, with our long relationship invisible to this hospital.

The admitting clerk is in semi-tears. I am slumped in my chair, head in hands, taking very shallow breaths. Betty looks as if she were twice as tall as her five-foot height. Crossing her legs and folding her arms, she leans back in the swivel chair in front of the Cedars-Sinai Medical Center admission desk. "Well, I guess you'll just have to send for someone, won't you?"

The clerk is now in tears. She has tried everything she knows how to do to persuade Betty to answer the seemingly simple question every hospital admissions form asks about marital status.

This issue is our donnybrook, on this no longer typical day, as we do the necessary paperwork for Betty to have a procedure, yet another in her by then nearly fifteen-year battle against an aggressive cancer that had threatened to devour her more than once since the initial grim diagnosis that gave her two years to live. The surprise this day is on us, to learn that a hospital in the middle of West Hollywood, a facility once considered ground zero for patient care during the AIDS holocaust, does not have a box marked "Domestic Partnership" available to check among the marital status choices.

"Honey, please," I beseech. "We can work on this issue later. I agree with you a hundred percent. So does the clerk. Can we please just focus on the important thing we need to do today, which is to push back on this cancer again? We can deal with this next week, or next month. Please."

She fixes me with a cold stare. "What bullshit, Terry. Pure bullshit. That's just an excuse for not doing the right thing. I am a gay activist. I have devoted the past thirty-plus years to making things better for our people, and you think I'm just going to overlook this insult? From a hospital in West Hollywood? Just forget it. They will find someone, whoever is the head of this hospital, and they will change this form, or I will not consent to be treated here. And I'll write a column about it, and I'll post it on my PlanetOut site, and on my own Web site, and I'll contact the Joint Hospital Accreditation Committee, and the West Hollywood Mayor . . ."

I sigh. We wait.

•

IT REALLY DID SEEM strange that a hospital in the middle of the gayest city in the world, one that had a dedicated AIDS unit during the plague years, would have committed such a gaffe. Yet, here it was, and here we are, waiting, with Betty sitting with arms crossed and her mouth in a tight line.

Betty was not always the determined activist. In fact, ironically, it was while we were driving to Cedars-Sinai back in the mid-1970s, where she had a procedure to reduce the discomfort of benign but painful fibroid tumors, that she chastised me about my tendency to disclose our relationship on medical forms. "After all," she said, "I just want to get some relief from these fibroids, so please don't get into that gay activism thing you always seem so eager to do." By that time, Betty had become the nationally known psychotherapist who was first to declare herself as a gay mental health professional, when she stood on the stage at UCLA in 1971 during a program called, "The Homosexual in America"; who was beginning to shape the launch of numerous organizations that would lastingly impact and promote the well-being of the lesbian and gay community; who would, in the ensuing years, become the well-known author of *Positively Gay* (1979), the perennial bestseller *Permanent Partners: Building Gay and Lesbian Relationships That Last* (1988), and a Lambda Literary Award-winning memoir, *Surviving Madness* (2003); who would, by the time she reached her late forties, become a fire-breathing, intimidating, indomitable activist.

I decide that it is probably not a good idea for me to use that earlier time as an example of how to handle this situation, so I say nothing, and we sit in silence.

Eventually, a hospital administrator appears, and after some discussion about policy changes, Joint Commission on the Accreditation of Healthcare Organizations (JCAHO) regulations, and moral relativism, another administrator is summoned. Still later, a third hospital official, subsequently identified as a senior vice president, made a commitment to look into changing the policy.

During the various conversations, one of the three discloses to Betty and me that he is gay. This disclosure is one of the most amazingly common experiences both Betty and I have had when doing advocacy work—people with fears ranging from losing credibility, to losing a job, will whisper somewhere during a conversation that they are gay and admire what we are trying to do. I'm always seduced by that revelation. Betty could not be had as easily as I. If anything, in a situation like that, she would be more likely to confront the closeted person.

A compromise is reached, a truce declared. Unyielding in the matter of using the "single" designation, Betty will allow the "married" box to be checked this one time only. The hospital, admitting the error of its ways, will make amends to the LGBT community by changing its policies, though the computer reprogramming will take a while. The deal struck, cancer can now be defeated, and peace will once again reign in the land of WeHo.

We complete the admission process, and Betty undergoes her procedure.

•

A FEW WEEKS LATER, Betty is on the telephone at home, talking with prominent civil rights attorney and advocate, Evan Wolfson. Evan is the founder and executive director of Freedom to Marry, the national nonprofit organization working to gain equality in marriage between same-sex couples and straight couples. During their chatty catching-up-with-each-other conversation, Betty mentions our experience with Cedars-Sinai. Always an engaging raconteur, she savors the details as she recounts to Evan what happened, moment by moment. When she finishes, Evan asks her what proof she had received—he might even have used the word "evidence"—that Cedars kept its word, that they actually did what they promised to do.

Betty is smart, sophisticated, a wise teacher, talented psychotherapist, and writer, but politically savvy she is not. Why? Because it never occurs to her that someone would promise to do something, and then not do it; or that someone would look another person in the eye and deliberately lie.

Though she is stunned by his recommendation that she find out if the hospital administrators intend to do what they said they'd do, Betty follows Evan's advice to follow up with Cedars, and calls the next day.

Turns out, the hospital administrators are indeed working on the policy change, but it will take more than just a signature on an internal policy memo. They promise to be back in touch. On April 10, Betty receives a letter from the vice president of medical affairs, thanking her for "the opportunity to review and respond to your concerns," and further offers that "the information regarding our patient database entry options" had been communicated to the management responsible for the registration and admissions process at the Medical Center.

The same day, Betty writes a polite letter of response, thanking the medical affairs v.p. for his letter. His letter is two paragraphs long. Hers is two pages. After thanking Mr. V.P., she puts it simply, "Good. So what is happening now?" She asks whom she can contact and what specific corrections they are planning, and then delivers the most important message, which reads: "My concern is not just about an unpleasant experience I had at Cedars. It is about what every gay man and lesbian in this country goes through when visiting a doctor or health-care organization for the first time."

Recognizing that if you don't connect the dots for them, most bureaucracies won't figure it out by themselves, and for most large health-care agencies with their studies, analyses, and the dreaded Diagnostic Related Groupings that drive how much third-party payers will spend on a patient who is hospitalized, data are what will impress them, Betty goes on to cite studies that support her point. "We have data," she adds, referring to the just released Witeck-Combs Communications/Harris Interactive survey, "that tell us that gay men and to a larger extent lesbian women, actually *avoid* seeking medical care at all because they don't want to be subjected to exactly the kind of experience I had at Cedars."

After a couple of further paragraphs, she closes with a simple sentence, "I expect to hear from you about what is being done."

On June 6, 2001, Cedars management sends an e-mail informing her that they had "conducted a due diligence review." As a result of this review, they say, the Medical Center "shall revise our Admission Intake process to include a marital status encompassing the category of Domestic Partner."

She cries. I put my head in my hands again, this time with relief and pride.

•

IN ONE OF THE MANY EXCHANGES of letters with Cedars, Betty
cited the famous Robert Kennedy quote from a 1968 speech in
which he observed that "each time a man stands up for an ideal, or
acts to improve the lot of others, or strikes out against injustice,
he sends a tiny ripple of hope, and crossing each other from a million different centers of energy and daring, those ripples build a
current that can sweep down the mightiest walls of oppression
and resistance." A piece by the artist Corita honoring that quote
and Bobby Kennedy still hangs on the wall in the home that Betty
and I shared for twenty-five years.

In August 2003, once again we find ourselves at Cedars-Sinai,
once again embattled by the cancer that has by now spread to her
bones. This time, the admissions clerk, a different one, asks Betty,
"What is your maiden name?"

We are both so startled that we must appear to be like bobble-
heads, looking back and forth at each other. The clerk repeats the
question, adding, "I can't go any further with the process, unless
you disclose what your maiden name is."

Déjà vu. How can this be? Once again, the frozen computer
screen is back.

Well, it seems that on the day of the initial face-off in 2001,
when Betty agreed as part of the compromise to allow the staff to
check "married," a trigger was pulled that sent the computer into
action, and the program was on a seek-and-destroy mission. If
Betty was married, then where was her maiden name? The system
could not rest until that blank was filled in, and her file was forever frozen at that spot on the intake form.

On that summer day in 2003, we didn't know it then, but

Betty had less than two-and-a-half years to live. I point that out here to acknowledge that we were both pretty beaten up and exhausted—still fighting, but very tired. This time I insisted. I got my Italian up, and I said, "Just let her put whatever she wants in the fucking file. Don't argue. Don't push it. We can deal with it later."

And we do.

In September 2003, Betty writes another letter to Cedars. She might have been tired, but she still had plenty of fight left. She warns them that there will be media attention from both the gay press and the straight press if they don't fix this problem now and forever.

The return letter from the admissions manager is one-page long and uses bullets to detail their actions. By now, the matter of "domestic partners" as a marital status option on the admissions form has been codified by state regulators and is now an official part of the California OSHPD (Office of Statewide Health and Planning Department) regulations. What a rush we get from reading that—what gratification.

The letter goes on to explain that the admissions rep, upon seeing the computer prompt to get the maiden name, looked back at the prior admission, saw the box checked as "married," and understandably assumed that information to be correct, so was being reasonable in her request for the maiden name information. The admissions manager indicated that he had *personally* made the change of marital status to "Domestic Partner" on all of Betty's accounts, etcetera, etcetera. I just bet he did, and I bet he checked the forms twice.

Bobby Kennedy also famously said, "There are those who look at things as they are and ask why . . . I dream of things that never were and ask why not?" Betty did that regularly, asked why not. She didn't live long enough to tackle her next project, which was to work with JCAHO to require all its accredited hospitals in the country to offer the "domestic partner" choice among the marital status choices available to patients.

•

AND SO IT CAME TO PASS in the little village of WeHo that LGBT hospital patients will forever be allowed to proclaim the love that dared speak its name, thanks to a little but mighty advocate named Betty Berzon.

an ephemeral life

dan luckenbill

BEFORE ATTENDING a recent board meeting at the ONE National Gay and Lesbian Archives, I passed some time poring over our duplicate books, which are for sale to the public. The illustrated dust jacket of a book I have known my entire adult life but had never read caught my eye.

In an indistinct space, two handsome men sit on a bed. Each is beefy—muscular, but not with the abdominal definition promoted today by men's fitness magazines and Abercrombie & Fitch advertisements. One wears a form-fitting white T-shirt and khaki trousers that fit the shape of his genitals. On one thigh he holds a ukulele pointed downward toward the second young man's blurred crotch. He is shirtless and his right arm is behind the other's back, seemingly at his shoulder. Physique magazines of the 1960s showed body builders posed to display their development and might even show two men together—usually with a discreet distance—or show body contact between men in poses of staged wrestling. I had seen nothing like this suggested affection between men in a sequestered and luminous space where the thrill of sex between men might occur.

This illustration set an image of romance between men for the rest of my life, but how did I discover it and eventually meet the artist?

I probably first saw the book about 1965 when I was a student at UCLA. It would have been wrapped in plastic and for sale in downtown Los Angeles at a sleazy tobacco-and-magazine stand opening off the grimy sidewalk of Main Street between Sixth and Seventh. When I got the nerve to buy such books or the few magazines displaying male nudity (also wrapped in plastic, with dots covering the genitals), cigar-chomping sales clerks paid no attention to my age. They were happy to take my money.

In the 1960s, for someone underage who couldn't enter a gay bar, there were no community centers, no student centers, no places to meet except restrooms or stairwells for furtive sex. I certainly had plenty of that at UCLA. I surprised one of my English professors doing the same cruising on campus—I got an excellent grade in his class. Gay communities or neighborhoods were difficult to discern. From John Rechy's *City of Night*, I learned there was a circuit of bars on Main Street, but Rechy didn't use the real names, and the activities he depicted—although enticing and adventurous—were intimidating, if not scary. The magazine stand was on the edge of this area I didn't venture into. I had happened upon Rechy's gay milieu, but how did one find out about other neighborhoods or hangouts?

Several decades later, I look back to see that I have played a supporting role in creating community space for young people. My work began with the UCLA Lesbian & Gay Faculty/Staff Network—I was cochair for much of the 1990s—which then led to the creation of the LGBT Studies Program and the LGBT Resources Office. Through my job in the UCLA Library I have helped to get the personal papers and manuscripts of authors like Betty Berzon, Paul Monette, Michael Nava, Mark Thompson, and Terry Wolverton. To honor Paul, I organized an exhibit and conference about his life and work. I serve on the board of directors of ONE and the advisory committee of the Monette-Horwitz Trust. This abundance of services and resources can make it difficult to put myself in the place of that young man who didn't know where to go.

Few landscape clues remain the same. The newsstand and all of the downtown bars mentioned by Rechy have closed. Most have been demolished. Gay neighborhoods shift, although in Los Angeles, Silver Lake, Hollywood, and West Hollywood they have remained fairly constant. Bookstores and gay bars close, reopen, or adapt, and façades of buildings are remodeled to create a bewildering urban palimpsest. How do I spark my memory to recreate what I experienced and to relive my feelings when I saw that book?

I work in or for two archives, so I ought to be able to do this.

Few conventional published histories or geographies exist: oral histories and memoirs remain the primary resources for a culture that was hidden and even criminalized. The pioneers of the 1950s generation—what might be called the greatest gay generation— are largely gone. The activists have mostly all been documented, but the texture of daily life and its institutions are often ignored. Gay bars leave little for research except flyers and matches. The logos and graphic art for these are particularly evocative of their times. Other daily life can be recreated with gay guides, ticket stubs, tourist brochures, and menus—throwaway items usually with addresses but seldom dates. Archivists call these "useless" objects ephemera, after the brief life of the fly which also gives us the adjective "ephemeral." Collections of these materials are perhaps my favorite at the Charles E. Young Research Library Department of Special Collections, where I have worked for over thirty-seven years.

West Hollywood businessman Sheldon Andelson (half brother
to Monette's lover Roger Horwitz) noted that West Hollywood
came about because of the railway. Moses Sherman and Eli P.
Clark (Sherman's brother-in-law) owned the Los Angeles–Pacific
Railway, founded in 1898. The area was first called Sherman, and
Santa Monica Boulevard was Sherman. San Vicente was Clark
Street. For years now, this core area of "Old Sherman" has been
known for its gay bars. The usual explanation for this clustering is
that, until 1984, it was an unincorporated area of Los Angeles
County, meaning that it was under the jurisdiction of the sheriff's
department rather than the notoriously homophobic LAPD. This
arrangement also allowed for the speakeasies on Sunset Strip during Prohibition.

One item of ephemera at UCLA led me to believe, or possibly
just fantasize, that other reasons supported this proliferation of
gay bars. I discovered a folded flyer: Sherman Business Directory
. . . July 10, 1925. It promoted "an ideal climate, frostless and
fogless, fanned by cool refreshing breezes from the Ocean," and
it urged those who picked it up to "trade at home and help build
a city."

When I entered the business names into a database and in-
dexed the street addresses, I obtained on paper an idea of what
someone getting off the trolley in the 1920s would see. Realtors,
decorators, barbers, two tobacco stores within two blocks, mar-
kets, banks, coffee shops and lunch rooms, and even a baby store
and a feed-and-seed store, mixed in this working-class neighborhood of small clapboard cottages.

I didn't know there was a hotel close to the corner of Santa
Monica and San Vicente. I've never seen a picture of it. Across the
street were the railroad yards and barns where now the hulks of
the Pacific Design Center loom. Hunky workers would have
played pool (one pool hall listed in the directory), drunk or dined
in taverns (none listed but photographs document them), and lived
in rooming houses or cottages in the area. I see the hotel as run-

down by the 1920s. Sexuality was constructed differently in that period, and gay men could mingle with this trade or rough trade and cruise to obtain a prized trick. Two men could check in to that hotel and be in a room like the one on the cover of the book.

This stolen sex was also romantic, and the book could illustrate such a romance.

Residential life at that time was divided. At the top of the hill above Sunset Boulevard, movie stars and motion picture directors built their homes. In 1932, George Cukor moved not to Beverly Hills, but to 9166 Cordell Drive in that area, so that perhaps he, too, wanted the shelter or the benefit of not being under the LAPD. The Sunset Strip speakeasies had already opened, and with the end of Prohibition, former speakeasy La Bohème's exterior was remodeled slightly to create the Trocadero. Harold Grieve, who in 1927 was the first decorator to move from downtown Los Angeles to West Hollywood, decorated the interiors in a "Gay Paree" style. These chic clubs, often with bisexual or gay or lesbian entertainers, spread just a few blocks below Cukor along Sunset.

John Chase's *Exterior Decoration: Hollywood's Inside-Out Houses* gives the best history of how, after World War II, gay men began to remodel their cottages into maisonettes, primarily following the taste of 1930s Hollywood movies and the Hollywood Regency style. This had been promulgated by gay actor-turned-decorator William Haines, who with his lover and partner Jimmie Shields, had an office on the Strip, in a building designed for Haines. Much later, this building became famous as Le Dôme restaurant. (The name is still on the remodeled building.) In 1935, Haines, architect James E. Dolena, and landscape architect Florence Yoch (who lived with her partner Lucile Council), began to redesign Cukor's house.

Serving this area and adjacent areas was a market named Shermart, which was where the sheriff's department is now. I don't know the date of the market's opening, but it didn't close until the early 1970s. It was like Jerry's Market in *Double Indemnity*, large and dimly lit, but upscale, with a butcher, fresh produce, and other products for the finicky clientele. Shermart served as gay central. I don't remember cruising in the parking lot, but I certainly recall a lot of stopping to talk, gossip, dish. Actor John Carlyle mentions the market in his memoir, *Under the Rainbow*. This neighborhood landmark meant so much to Carlyle that when it closed he framed one of its shopping bags.

But that was later. My first visits to West Hollywood were when I was a student, and it's difficult to recreate exactly how I knew to go there.

One clue resides in the physique magazines of the 1950s and '60s. I had begun buying these digest-format publications, such as *Tomorrow's Man* and *Grecian Guild Pictorial*, in high school in central Illinois, when I would sneak them home tucked inside copies of *Theatre Arts* or *Dog World* checked out from the public library. Through various retro publications, their layout is familiar today, but these did not show any full frontal nudity. The male genitals were discreetly tucked into posing straps—G-strings by any other name. I saw an abundance of corn-fed male nudity in my high school locker room during mandatory physical education classes, but the first time I saw unruly male pubic hair escaping from a posing pouch in a physique magazine I nearly fainted. Soon after, the owners of the magazine store came to their senses and realized they had better stop selling these publications to a minor. I was busted.

The makeup of the physique magazines generally included innocuous articles on Greek sculpture, the ideal Greek physique, and body building. The featured models followed in two- to five-page spreads. The back pages of the magazines had ads from the studios producing these photographs, and they also had ads for what could only be called "gay" clothing. You could buy your own posing strap! Or a see-through tank top. Or a bikini. Items certainly not sold in America's middle-class department stores.

A West Hollywood clothing store named Ah Men was one of these advertisers, and that may be why I first started roaming the area. I've recently seen one of these ads, featuring physique model Bob Gentry. Actor-photographer Roy Dean used him as the model for his first ever "coffee table" book of the male nude, published in Los Angeles by the Rho-Delta Press in 1969. Titled *A Time in Eden*, the text beckoned: "And into nature's naked paradise came [naked!] man." It is possible that Dean took the photographs for this ad, which features Gentry in a "fishnet swimsuit" and posing strap "for that well-dressed 'undressed' look." Ah Men opened in a loft at Melrose and San Vicente "upstairs, down an alley, in an industrial area and finding it was half the fun." It moved to other locations in what is now "downtown" West Hollywood, or Boystown. I probably visited the location at 8933 Santa Monica, where in 1925 L. C. Poor sold "cigars, tobacco, etc." and where the drugstore is now on the north side of Santa Monica between San Vicente and Robertson. It had been remodeled in— what else?—the Regency style, with an awning in alternating stripes of light green, white, and light blue. I pawed through the racks of thongs and G-strings, eyeing the clerks who I hoped were eyeing me.

On one of those occasions I looked in the window next door and saw the canvas that had served as the basis for the dust jacket illustration. The shop was also the studio of the painter (whose name I don't recall). I asked if the painting was for sale, and it was. The friendly artist talked to me and quoted a price I couldn't afford as a student on a scholarship with only a part-time job. I can't recall his other paintings.

And the book the painting illustrated? It was *The Invisible Glass* by Loren Wahl, a pseudonym of Italian-American novelist Lawrence Madalena (1919–1983), first published in 1950 in New York by Greenberg (who published several gay novels beginning in the 1930s) and reprinted in Washington, D.C. in this edition by the Guild Press in 1965. *The Saturday Review of Literature* gave

this gay novel a favorable notice: "another story of man's inhu-
manity to man." It depicts an interracial romance between American officers in American-occupied Italy at the end of World War
II. The African American attended UCLA but is condemned to
serve in the segregated "Negro" Corps. The cover probably
doesn't illustrate any scene in the novel but was done or repro-
duced to sell more copies. The artist is not credited.

The first gay bar in West Hollywood was likely the Four Star,
which in 1961converted from a working-class tavern. The "sensa-
tional" paperback *Hollywood: Gay Capitol of the World* (sic), by L.
Jay Barrow, gives this speculation without naming the bar but lists
its location as a few blocks east of Clark Street (San Vicente). Gay
bars seldom opened directly onto the street, and neither did the
restaurant Por Favor (where the Mother Lode is now), which, as a
friend of mine quipped, served the "sour cream school" of Mexican cuisine. It had no windows on the street and its "speakeasy"
entrance indicated that to be caught dining in a gay neighborhood
was a blemish on one's reputation. But nearby Norma Triangle
resident Carlyle recorded what might be called mixed but fond
memories of the restaurant where he had fights with his longtime
friend Judy Garland.

The existence of a market, a restaurant, and a clothing store
shows that the gay male community had more arenas for socializ-
ing than just the bar scene—even if one went to a bar before or after going to one of these places. To my knowledge, no newsstand
or bookstore was open in the area when I first knew it.

Here we have several ways to begin to reconstruct—if only
sporadically—the quotidian and ephemeral history of West Hollywood: through hardcover books marketed as "soft porn," through
matchbooks, through advertisements, and through paperbacks intended to be read and, no doubt, thrown away.

ONE National Gay and Lesbian Archives and the June L.
Mazer Lesbian Archives preserve these items along with the more
expected records of our lesbian and gay lives: literary and histori-

cal and psychological works, musical recordings, posters, and works of art. The Mazer is proud of its T-shirt collection and softball memorabilia of the 1950s, items as meaningful to the lesbian community as are see-through shirts for gay men of the same generation.

ONE and the Mazer not only preserve this fragile and ephemeral history, but form significant parts of the political and cultural history of Los Angeles and West Hollywood. Formed in 1952, ONE is the longest-lived lesbian and gay organization in the United States. It is one of the oldest such archives in the world, and it is the largest in the world. Lillian Faderman has written that the Los Angles lesbian scene she first encountered in Los Angeles forty years ago (roughly the time I was discovering Ah Men) "seemed . . . to exist only in darkness." But for her an archives such as the Mazer, the largest on the west side of the continent, proclaims "not only our immediate presence but the fact that many went before us, that we did indeed have a history."

The first homophile organization was the Mattachine Society, founded in Los Angeles by Harry Hay and others in 1950. He was ousted from the Communist Party for being gay, and, after only a few years, ousted from the Mattachine because of being a communist. Early gay histories were written in the years when scholars and academics identified more with the left, and ONE was perceived to be more accommodationist—it really wasn't—so that it has only begun to receive the attention it has long deserved. The best praise for ONE may have come from R.E.L. Masters in *The Homosexual Revolution*. Masters and others wrote what might be termed soft-porn anthropology and sociology with case histories of titillating sexual experiences combined with censorious statements about homosexuality. He called ONE "the largest, most powerful, and most militant of the homophile groups in this country."

Masters derided *ONE Magazine* (first published in January 1953), calling its covers "homo-sexy" and accusing them of "imparting . . . fruity aromas." Cover banners of the magazine actually show the variety of serious issues addressed: Homosexual Marriage (the author actually wasn't for it); Homosexuals in the Military; The Feminine Viewpoint; and, What About Religion? In 1958, ONE secured from the Supreme Court the only gay rights victory for the LGBT community of the 1950s when it won the right to distribute published material with the word *homosexual* in it, material previously declared obscene just for mentioning the word. Without this victory there could have been no further gay and lesbian activism. Founders of ONE stated that they were not the forerunners of the LGBT civil rights movement; they began that movement.

A member of ONE envisioned the first "gay church," but that was not realized. ONE did put into place a variety of social and educational services. It granted the first advanced degrees (master's and doctorate) in "gay studies" and organized the first gay tours of Europe. A driving force behind ONE, Dorr Legg (under a pseudonym), in 1958 declared on the cover: "I am glad I am homosexual."

Jim Kepner wrote the first recurring column for such a publication, called "tangents, news & views" for *ONE Magazine*. He began collecting lesbian and gay books as early as 1942 and continued to collect until his death in 1997. He opened his collection to research in the early 1970s and for a time rented a space in Hollywood. When West Hollywood incorporated in 1985 and elected the first majority gay and lesbian city council in the United States, the city provided numerous LGBT benefits. In 1989, Kepner's archives were housed in the city's Werle Building at 626 North Robertson Boulevard. Dorr Legg died in 1994, and in 1996, Kepner's archives merged with ONE; together they form the ONE National Gay and Lesbian Archives. Along with the Mazer Archives, ONE still maintains collections in the Werle Building. (ONE does not open the collection in West Hollywood, but materials can be obtained through its space at 909 West Adams near USC.)

If I had discovered at least one area where I could find gay men, what did I do after that? The next question was not where, but how do you "be" gay? *Hollywood: Gay Capitol* indicated the plethora of styles when it described "fluff" bars and leather bars. Neither of these seemed to be the niche that I wanted. Further clues remained in the old physique magazines, such as photographer Bruce of Los Angeles' *The Male Figure*, where Bob Gentry was identified as an "ex-Marine." As I turned the pages, even more models were identified as "ex" of this branch of the military which was becoming sexier and sexier for me. Even *ONE Magazine* discussed this identity dilemma in a cover article with the banner, THE MARGIN OF MASCULINITY. I solved my problem by letting myself be drafted to become what I then considered masculine, and I became an officer in the U.S. Army. Gay clones solved the problem by creating "gay macho" in the 1970s, and gay style seldom looked back to fishnet swimsuits and bikinis.

The author of *Hollywood: Gay Capitol of the World* noted the stream of traffic flowing between gay bars on weekends. That traffic is almost constant now, and walking the recently widened and tree-shaded sidewalks of downtown West Hollywood gives mixed feelings to someone of my generation. On the one hand, I rejoice in the openness young lesbians and gay men are privileged to have, won for them by pioneers such as Harry Hay, Jim Kepner, Dorr Legg, and the women members of the Daughters of Bilitis. On the other hand, as with any back-to-back generations, there is often little knowledge of or respect paid to those who forged such a positive geography. And while openness is easygoing, it is also a little suburban. The gritty train yard and hotel and bars one sneaked into also meant adventure. This adventure is now perhaps invented through clubs and drugs. Those clubs wouldn't admit me now, but it is the turn of persons of another generation to gather flyers and buttons and other ephemera for memoirs to be recorded when it is time to recreate their lives.

departures and arrivals

malcolm boyd

ONE: OLD HOLLYWOOD, YOUNG MAN

"HOW DO YOU KNOW MARY?" Marion Davies, holding a martini glass, asked me. We sat together in the downstairs sitting room of Pickfair, Hollywood's most glamorous and famous home. It was 1950. Mary Pickford was giving a small party. Soon we'd move into the elegant dining room for dinner.

Director D. W. Griffith, the father of the film industry, was another guest. Mary's butler, Mr. Fenton, had earlier explained to me how sorry he felt for Griffith, a fallen mogul and now some-what shabby man whose shirtsleeves were embarrassingly frayed. Other guests included MGM's Adrian and Janet Gaynor. She had won the first Oscar for Best Actress. Mary won the second.

At the dining room table Mary reigned over the assemblage a bit coquettishly, a bit imperiously. She remained properly re-served in her evening role of Great Lady. However, she sparked

the occasion with alert humor and personal warmth. Her moments of pure cinema magic shone when she surreptitiously read-
ied herself for close-ups, making a familiar *moue* with her lips.
What Webster's describes as a "pout, a grimace expressive of
petulance" was a trademark of Mary's. As was her wont on other
occasions, Mary slipped into two favorite roles: Queen Elizabeth I
and Mary, Queen of Scots. She was perfect in the contrasting
roles of Elizabeth as the strong monarch, and Mary, Queen of
Scots as the vulnerable royal victim of power. Long absent from
the screen, Mary Pickford loved to playact at home.

Table conversation ebbed and flowed. Since we were an ensemble at the dinner rite, no guest starred. No speeches or out-
bursts or ungainly laughter. While the mood stayed convivial, it
was not relaxed. Nor fun. It was a performance on everyone's part
and at every level.

I was in my twenties. Incredibly, I was Mary's partner in the
production firm of PRB, Inc., Pickford–Rogers (Mary's husband
Charles "Buddy" Rogers)–Boyd. I had come to Hollywood after
graduating from college, worked my way up in the film and television business rapidly, met Mary, we'd surprisingly clicked, and
now I was seated atop my own particular world.

Old photos show I was attractive in a Montgomery Clift sort of
way. I knew I was gay, of course, but didn't yet have any real understanding of what meanings might be attached to that. Gay was
one of the most obvious stereotypes in the world then. Everybody
"got" it right away and either snickered at fairies or became en-
raged at faggots. The closet was larger than Madison Square Garden. It preserved professional reputations but not human lives.

Sex was the red-hot neon sign in this tableau. I was prepared to
place my toe in the water, but was not about to immerse myself in
unknown swift currents. Whom could I trust? I was in a goldfish
bowl surrounded by gossip, celebrity, and the harshest competition on earth. I wasn't about to risk the loss of my kingdom for an
errant folly. Besides, the only men I came in contact with were

driven, overworked, highly competitive men like myself. I didn't like myself very much! Nor did I like those who were similar and surrounded me. I had no glimpse of anyone or anything that would be understood today as gay in a liberated sense. I couldn't figure out what to do with such insoluble factors in my life. I worked harder and harder, moved ever deeper into glamour and celebrity, and placed meaning on hold.

The easiest, best sex was with someone warm, open, decent, and honestly caring. This had to be someone who did not work in the industry. So this meant sex with a nice guy lacking access to power, gossip, raw competition, and the bitchy confrontation of an old Bette Davis movie. Sex mixed up with ambition and business, with getting ahead and office politics was, in my view, bad sex.

Always, I felt that there really weren't any secrets in Hollywood. Gossip was legion. It neither kept people in line nor made them paranoid or afraid. Gossip was simply omnipresent. It was an enemy of such things as kindness and romance.

Lavish parties in great homes were the best Hollywood scenes. But two celebrated playgrounds were highly publicized clubs on the Sunset Strip in West Hollywood, Ciro's and the Mocambo. A night at either place was like no other. Each had tables that became symbols of status, the best and the lowest. They had dance floors and stages for entertainment. Ciro's was darker. Tourists could seldom get in. The owner was one of the most powerful men in Hollywood because he instantly established one's status or took it away.

I remember one night when Radie Harris, an intimate friend of Vivien Leigh and an insider columnist whose paper scared the hell out of everybody, gave a dinner party at Ciro's. The floor show was a breakthrough performance by dancer Kay Thompson (Judy Garland's friend who originated the "Eloise" stories) with the Williams brothers. Radie asked me to be her escort.

Up the Sunset Strip was the Mocambo, a much brighter, more glittering club. One night a gay friend and I were there for a show and drinks. It was past midnight. We lingered. The star of the evening was an animal-beautiful, startlingly sensuous Lana Turner who also stayed and danced with a young MGM stud. We all knew she had to be up at dawn for makeup and shooting a scene for a film. But Lana lingered—and danced—and shone like the star she was.

There was glamour aplenty in my young life. A youthful Elizabeth Taylor came to my Hollywood home for a party I hosted for a visiting Canadian columnist version of Louella Parsons-cum-Hedda Hopper. MGM sent a half-dozen stars, one of whom engaged in a fist fight on that rainy night on my front lawn. My party was An Event.

Charlie Chaplin, Jr., and I were buddies. He wasn't gay. He drank too much but was likeable in a boyish way. One New Year's Eve, Charlie and I'd had drinks at Ciro's and were driving to the nearby Mocambo, probably just to show off the brand new Cadillac his father had given him that day. As luck would have it, Charlie smashed it into another car in front of the Mocambo. Police and press arrived simultaneously. The media went crazy. The press was out to crucify Charlie's dad in those days for his politics. This provided a front-page story and picture that went around the world. Scandal. A drunk Chaplin in a Hollywood car crash.

Mr. Chaplin, Charlie's father, rather formally received us for breakfast at his Beverly Hills home the next morning after Charlie was sprung from jail. His dad was (as always) elegantly attired, reserved, and coolly distant. But he was furious at America for what he perceived as persecution. Soon he moved to Switzerland. Mary Pickford, who lived a couple of blocks away from Chaplin's home and was feuding with him at the time, had little or nothing to say about either the accident or the headlines. She seemed to think Malcolm (she called me Mal) was innocently engaged in a youthful indiscretion.

I learned to swim in the gorgeous Pickfair swimming pool.

From it, one looked down the hill at Rudolph Valentino's fabled home, Falcon Lair, where Doris Duke later lived. There was a marvelous stillness when I swam there—with one exception. Fred Astaire lived next door. He seemed to rehearse many hours a day and, for this purpose, drums were played. I spent many hours swimming in the Pickfair pool to the accompaniment of Astaire's drums.

In 1951, I decided to depart Mary, Pickfair, and Hollywood and enter a seminary in Berkeley to prepare for the Episcopal priesthood. I remember a decisive, telling moment one night at a glittering party at the Beverly Hills Hotel. Virtually everybody seemed to be there. I looked around the room at familiar faces of the powerful and famous, many of whom I knew. I also knew that, in ten or twenty years, I didn't want to be like them.

Instead I'd try to live a life of service to other people and discover deeper spiritual meanings. After a huge going-away party at Ciro's—when Hedda Hopper wrote that even the bartender bowed his head in prayer—I said good-bye to Hollywood.

How could I possibly know the vast and complex gay experience that would open up for me in the ensuing years? My life would be utterly changed. In fact, I'd become someone else, a person who found fulfillment and purpose. But first, I had to be able to become myself.

TWO: A PRIEST'S LIFE

IN 1978, I arrived back in Los Angeles to try to make my life. To my surprise, Mary Pickford reappeared as a character in it. She had been reclusive and bedridden at Pickfair for years. One morning, her secretary phoned me: "Miss Pickford would like to see you. Can you pay a visit?"

Mary, who looks like a skeleton, is in her bed. Greeting me, her emotion is unrestrained. She places her tiny, frail hands around my body, hugging me. She traces the lines of my face with her fingers. We call one another sweetheart and dear. Mary says her veined hands are like a monkey's, but I say my hairy ones are more so. Tears roll down her face. She points to photographs of her mother and father. "Papa died when I was four, but I love him just as much as Mama." I see the person of Mary, not the persona. I look into her face. I am in the presence of someone who was once the world's most celebrated and beautiful woman. Beauty changes; celebrity dims; applause ceases.

When I say good-bye to Mary and leave, I walk down to the swimming pool that I remember so well. It is surrounded by lush flowers. A massive pine tree looms overhead. The only sound is the wind rustling leaves. I strip off all my clothes. I enter the pool. I immerse myself in the water. It feels like a baptism.

I would not see Mary again. On May 29, 1979, she slipped into a coma and died. Meanwhile, I realized that I'd become quite a stranger in the City of Angels. While I'd been away, Los Angeles had transformed into a bustling metropolis.

In 1955, I had been ordained an Episcopal priest in the then-downtown cathedral. Later, I served parishes and college chaplaincies in Indianapolis, Detroit, and Washington, D.C. In 1961, I was a Freedom Rider in the Deep South and remained active in the civil rights movement.

My book *Are You Running with Me, Jesus?* became a best seller in 1965. It garnered critical praise as well, and in 1978, I told my coming-out story in *Take Off the Masks.*

THREE: THE LOVE OF MY LIFE

MORE THAN TWENTY-TWO YEARS AGO, I met Mark Thompson, the love of my life—a fellow writer, as well as a photographer and journalist. A man for all seasons. Being his mate and partner over the years has altogether changed my life. Mark is a real-life pioneer of the gay spiritual experience, as he's expressed in his books *Gay Spirit*, *Gay Soul*, and *Gay Body*. As we've grown together, I have learned carefully how being gay deals with the very roots of one's existence.

Mark and I didn't decide to make a serious life together until after two years of dating. During that time, we went everywhere—Cancun, Maui, Big Sur, Cabo, New York, Vancouver. On weekends I stayed at Mark's place on the west side of L.A. I recall one morning when I was reading the *Los Angeles Times* and Mark was cleaning up and taking out the garbage. I said, "Mark, can I help you?" He replied instantly, "No, Malcolm. I can handle it by myself." All right. But a few months later, when we were in a similar situation in his apartment, I was once again reading the paper. Mark said, "Malcolm, *can't you* take out the trash?" Bingo. This was the stride toward commitment. A huge sea change had just taken place. Shortly afterward, we bonded and were looking for a house that would soon become our home in Silver Lake.

We looked at dozens of houses but didn't resonate with any. We had almost given up when we walked into what was clearly our dream home. We fell in love with it. Silver Lake used to be a little-known part of the city near both downtown and Hollywood. It was bohemian, artistic, offbeat, and a bit eccentric. It's often mentioned in the same breath as West Hollywood; they are the two principal gay parts of Los Angeles, but they couldn't be more different. West Hollywood has power, money, a global reputation, and bigness. Silver Lake, on the other hand, is small, rather like a quiet village with mysterious streets and no apparent attitude. It's absolutely charming and conducive to community. Its message has been "Don't tell anybody. Let's keep it a secret." But the secret is out of the box. The world has become aware of Silver Lake. The ongoing mystery is that when people think they've found Silver Lake, it still eludes them. Maybe it's more a state of mind than a place. We often joke, when we're going to pay West Hollywood a visit, that we have to remember to carry our visas.

FOUR: GAY ELDER

TO MY SURPRISE, I discovered a brand new role for myself at a Los Angeles conference in 2003. It was called "Standing on the Bones of Our Ancestors: Exploring the Role of Gay and Lesbian Tribal Elder." Jungian psychologist and gay liberation pioneer Don Kilhefner brought us together under the auspices of the Gay Men's Medicine Circle. The conference statement read "As the post-Stonewall gay and lesbian movement enters its fourth decade, the gap between the generations has never been bigger. Different generations need each other. In fact, if tribal elders are lost, adults will be lost, and if tribal adults are lost, youth will be lost."

A full house at the L.A. Gay and Lesbian Center awaited five gay and lesbian tribal elders, including me. Tribal elder? I didn't exactly know what it meant. Anyhow, who would want to be identified as an elder in a youth-obsessed gay culture? For starters, I remembered that it was hard as hell to turn fifty. I asked: was it all over? Leaving elder aside, I could scarcely deal with the reality that I was older.

Yet now, I learned, it was important for tribal elders to carry and help expand the vision of community. So I recognized for the first time that it was essential for elders, including me, to teach and empower the next generation. Clearly, there needed to be mutual support and interdependence across the generations. The whole thing seemed to take on a ritual aspect: I had been given a new task. It was a fresh reason for staying active and involved in the community.

At the same time, some old questions continued to confront me. They concerned the evolution of love and relationship in aging. Obviously, I am aware—more than aware—that I am aging. At eighty-four, I've aged. Mark is thirty years younger. In this respect, we're like the late Christopher Isherwood and his partner Don Bachardy. My relationship with Mark is, for me, one of the wonders of the world.

I know that I am facing mortality. So are you. We're all doing that. I perceive death as a major part of living. Always we are dying; always we are living. I realize I have no control over death, so I try to let it go and accept its coming. At the same time, I realize I have no control over life either. It's hard, poetic, mysterious, tender.

While I'm still on the scene, at eighty-four, I have made a big decision to hang in there. Be. Do. Remain involved. Stay in community. Start new projects (like writing this essay). Love Mark. Listen to God, talk to God. Stay open. Forgive people. Ask them to forgive me. Embrace, rather than become isolated. Refuse to join the walking wounded. Sign off as a victim. Wake up. Try to stay authentic.

thumbnail encounters
with m. m.

jack larson

IN SPITE OF THE FACT that she snatched my first movie role away from me, I always thought Marilyn Monroe was wonderful. Fox was making a film, *Scudda-Hoo! Scudda-Hay!* in 1947, and their talent and casting departments had pegged me for the part of a boy on a bicycle who had one good scene with the film's star. Somehow the part was changed to a girl on a bicycle, and Marilyn Monroe got the role, her first. That scene didn't make her a star, but a few years later a scene in *The Asphalt Jungle* did begin her stardom.

Along with other young Hollywood actors (and some stars, including Jennifer Jones, Shelley Winters, etcetera), we each studied acting with Michael Chekhov, of the Moscow Art Theater, then a beloved exile in Beverly Hills. Mr. Chekhov adored

Marilyn M. and would talk to me about her from time to time, so I knew that besides being a rising star phenomenon and nude calendar girl, she was in his opinion seriously gifted as an actress. Fascinated by her, I saw with each of her movies how right Mr. Chekhov was and felt sorry that her studio, Fox, treated her like a dumb lucky blonde. Zanuck, the studio head, made public fun of her when she announced that her ambition (due to Mr. Chekhov) was to make a film of *The Brothers Karamazov*, playing the part of Grushenka. She would have been marvelous, but when the film was made by MGM., after she had aroused all the publicity for it, a more distinguished actress played the part.

A friend of mine, a hard-luck kid named Paul, AWOL from the Marines, was taken to the set of one of the Monroe musicals by her choreographer, Jack Cole. Paul, who often had to sleep in all-night movie theaters, was adopted for the day by Marilyn Monroe, who questioned him, fed him in her dressing room, laughed with him, and warmed him with her concern and friendliness. When he later told me how lovely she'd been to him, I knew enough about her own orphaned life to realize she had recognized him as a fellow waif and embraced him.

Michael Chekhov died in the summer of 1955 during a Los Angeles heat wave. By then I had been acting for four years and was surprised to cause so much ill will by informing the production company that they would have to "shoot around me" on the day of his funeral because I was going to be there. Marilyn Monroe possibly ran into the same studio problem because she attended the funeral too. The Russian Orthodox church where it was held was a small wooden house in old Hollywood with a cupola on the roof. We mourners were standing squeezed into a foyer off a bare former living room where the large Russian priest delivered the funeral mass with incense and dramatic motions. It was a very hot day for each of us to be given a lighted candle that our crowding forced us to hold up near our faces. I could see her face and the others glistening with sadness, and we were enveloped with incense. His death, as I later read in Monroe's own book, *My Story*, was a great loss to her. To a lot of others too.

After his death, she moved to New York City to famously study acting at the Actors Studio and then to make a series of brilliant and successful films. In my opinion, her performance in *Bus Stop* is one of the finest ever given in motion pictures.

Montgomery Clift was one of my closest friends. He loved working with Monroe in *The Misfits* and, in fact, he just loved her. Monty once told me, regarding all the bad publicity she got on *The Misfits* set during the breakup of her marriage with Arthur Miller, that "she wasn't the one in trouble, Miller was." Monty's friend Libby Holman recounted earlier how touched she and Monty had been as guests of the Millers one autumn, watching from their window as a pregnant Marilyn Monroe cleaned up a garden by carefully picking up leaves, one by one.

Once, when Monty was in Los Angeles and Monroe was living here again, he invited the writer-director Jim Bridges and me to have dinner with her at The Beachcombers, an old hangout of Monty's and mine. Monty had a drinking, problem from time to time, and when we arrived at his hotel, he was in no condition to go out. My one principle with Monty was that I wouldn't go anywhere with him if he was drinking, because he shouldn't have been seen like that. Jim and I refused to go on to dinner, but, alas, Monty had a limousine waiting with a new driver, Bill, and he went on. Ever since his terrible automobile accident in L.A., he'd refused to drive a car and always had a kindly driver, Rudy, to chauffeur him around. It turned out Monty had passed Rudy on to Marilyn Monroe, because "she needed him too." The other guest at that dinner, Monty's doctor, described the evening to me the next day. Marilyn Monroe looked gorgeous in a low-cut dress. Monty ordered a lot of appetizers which he started dipping in sauces and feeding her. She was apparently very sweet and patient about it and, as it turned out, a good sport, because when she told Monty she didn't want to be fed by hand anymore, he took off his shoes and socks and proceeded to try to feed her with his toes. When that didn't work he stuffed the appetizers by foot between her breasts. Somehow, they got through the evening, and she forgave him and continued to care about him. That, however, would have been my one dinner with Marilyn Monroe.

By the summer of 1962 she had caused some unfortunate scenes of her own without other people being as forgiving as she was of Monty. She had been fired off her last film by the Fox executives for supposedly impossible behavior and was being sued by that studio for damages. There was industry talk that she'd never work again. One morning in late July, I was walking to a bank in Brentwood when I saw Rudy in his limousine stopped at a signal across the street. He saw me and waved, but I assumed he'd drive away with some rich client when the signal changed. Instead, what looked to be a young girl in the back seat gestured for him to pull over to the curb, and Rudy beckoned me to their car. I leaned into the open window with my hand on the back of his seat as he asked me about Monty in New York. His pretty fare, with a blue silk kerchief on her head, seemed about sixteen years old. As Rudy and I talked, she would lean forward, put her hand on top of mine, then snuggle back into her seat, smiling. Suddenly, I realized that the young girl without makeup was Marilyn Monroe out for a morning drive with Rudy. When she saw that I recognized her, we said hello and she began asking me questions about Monty. I'd talked to him the night before, so I could bring her up to date and say he sounded in "wonderful shape." She seemed to want to just go on talking, but their limo was blocking traffic and as horns started honking they had to drive away with her waving back at me. Talk about wonderful shape; she looked so young, aglow, and happy, I could hardly believe it a week later when I heard she was dead.

Of all that she left behind her—her films, her photographs, her mysterious death, her romance amidst the great that seems to rival Cleopatra's—the only thing neglected is her own autobiography, *My Story*, which ends with her early fame. The book, which is copyrighted by her friend and photographer Milton Greene, is so straightforward and observed in her own voice that you don't doubt she wrote it. In the 1980s, I was at a party with Mr. Greene and asked him about the book. He told me she *didn't* write it. She had enchanted old Ben Hecht, the greatest of Hollywood screenwriters, and he wrote it for her but wouldn't take credit or royalties from it. Monroe didn't want the money, so Milton Greene took it.

Everyone got something from Marilyn Monroe, including Marilyn Monroe. She once said she "didn't want money," she "just wanted to be wonderful." She was.

a tale of two hangouts: gay and lesbian civil wars in the seventies

jeanne cordova

FROM THE CONVENT TO THE BARS, 1966–1970

I DIDN'T INTEND to live in the big city, much less Los Angeles, the city I fell in love with. As an adolescent, all I ever wanted to do with my life was to join the convent. With the help of two "medieval" Catholic parents, one Mexican and one Irish, and eleven siblings all wrapped in Catholic myth, I entered the novitiate of the Immaculate Heart of Mary nuns of Southern California after high school. Their motherhouse was on the corner of Franklin and Western in the heart of Hollywood. When the sixties, with its questioning of The Establishment and the rules governing the relevance of the clergy, swept through the seminaries and convents of California, I walked out of the convent door. I found myself in Hollywood, a young dyke in search of a life.

I spent two years having a devilishly great time as a baby butch in the gay bar scene, learning how to pick up women and the difference between butch and femme. From the bar scene softball crowd, whose games were always fueled by flirtation and sexual rivalry, I even learned how to make love.

After perfecting my butch-about-town skills, learning the lore from older 1950s-type lesbians, I was on the edge of boredom. Surely, this couldn't be all there was to being gay? My life had to amount to more than softball and sex.

My older sister worked for the *Los Angeles Times*, and one afternoon my eyes casually fell on a magazine on her coffee table. It was a copy of *The Ladder*, the infamous newsletter of the Daughters of Bilitis, the *only* national organization of lesbians in America. I pounced upon the small booklet as though it were a life raft and I were on the Titanic. I ran out the door without even stopping to ask my sister if we were also "sisters" in sexual orientation. I had to find these D.O.B. people.

On October 3, 1970, a month after picking up *The Ladder*, I arrived at my first meeting in "the movement." The butch-femme-with-ducktails women of D.O.B. were proud gay women, at least at the meetings. I wore my butch locks down around my shoulders, hippie style, but I still felt right at home in this organized group who wanted their human rights. A year later, I was the president of the Los Angeles Chapter of D.O.B., and we opened the first lesbian center in the history of my town. At the age of twenty-two, I'd found my true vocation—being an activist in the gay and lesbian fight for civil rights.

1971: GCSC, WHERE THE BOYS WERE

IN THE EARLY NINETEEN SEVENTIES, I spent a lot of hours at movement-building meetings at the Gay Community Services

Center. Los Angeles' only gay organization big enough to have a building opened in 1971 in a pair of lamely held-together Victorian houses located at 1614 Wilshire Boulevard. The Gay Community Services Center could barely afford the poor end of this world-famous street—the end closest to downtown where the homeless wandered.

Sodomy was still illegal in California, and this gave the pigs a legal excuse to harass us. It was their "civic duty" because we were criminals who broke the law. But the landlord allowed the Center's founders, Morris Kight and Don Kilhefner, to rent his property because the buildings were too shabby for proper tenants. Money was an enormous problem back then—the students and radicals who began our movement didn't even have jobs.

The hippie-style gay pad was the hub of L.A.'s gay community. The rooms in the converted houses were devoted to a wide variety of social service programs. One was full of mattresses on the floor where runaway teenagers, largely from the Midwest, found refuge. Other rooms had desks for counselors and job finders on hand seven days a week to talk to the kids and help them start new lives.

Private rooms for counseling professionals were in another section. These sessions were for men who had been busted for allegedly soliciting sex from undercover cops who entrapped them in places like Griffith Park. This group of teachers, doctors, lawyers, and accountants covered their faces with newspapers as they made the mad dash from their cars to the Center's front door. At night, almost every room at GCSC turned into a rap session facilitated by an older and wiser gay man or woman who talked about gay pride and self-love and that being a *homosexual* wasn't the worst thing that had ever happened to them.

In the first years of its existence, GCSC subsisted on private donations from wealthy gay men, virtually all of them in the closet.

Long years of work by the Center's group of founders finally bore fruit in the form of two large grants from the federal and state governments in 1974. GCSC was the first gay organization to get taxpayer funding because it had the most highly developed board of directors, studded with properly degreed psychologists and social workers. GCSC's founders were also the first in the country to find a way to access their city's financially successful, upper-middle class: closeted homosexuals who were ready to give their money, although not their names, to an out-front and proud gay organization.

The first of the two grants that would change GCSC's future was for the staggering sum of a third of a million dollars, renewable for three years! The money was from the Feds: the National Institute on Alcohol Abuse and Alcoholism. This was the first federal grant ever given to a gay organization. A national study had shown that 25 to 30 percent of homosexual women had drinking problems. The Feds had given the money to a gay agency for outreach to lesbians. The grant was groundbreaking in two ways: it was the first federal money exclusively given to rehabilitate women alcoholics, and GCSC was a largely male agency.

A second, smaller grant was received from the L.A. County Board of Supervisors to set up a women's health clinic. Herself Health Clinic, the program that brought me to GCSC as a part-time publicist, opened right next to the Center's hugely popular gay men's V.D. clinic.

The result was that, quite suddenly, the mostly male board of directors had to hire twenty-nine new lesbian employees. The very structure and direction of the fledging Gay Community Services Center was rocked by the influx of so much money and so many women.

•

THE NIGHT OF JANUARY 8, 1975 found most of the new lesbian employees of GCSC gathered in a tight pack on the second-floor landing in front of the closed door of the board of directors. Most of the women on the landing, including my friend, Pody, had, like me, managed to pick up these new "gay jobs." Every dyke in the city wanted such a job because they were safe, hassle-free employment—free from the constant worry about being found out and fired.

Suddenly there were over two-dozen salaried lesbians at GCSC. Lesbians outnumbered male employees by two to one. The inadvertent upheaval in gender balance had come as a major shock to its board of directors.

We gathered outside the boardroom to protest the director's unwillingness to let the employees select who among us would sit on the new management team. Our new belief system, feminism, taught equality of women with men. It espoused that a collective structure in which all were equal worked better than the male hierarchical method of getting things done. We also wanted to nominate lesbian feminists to the board. Most of all, we wanted to change the name of the Gay Community Services Center to include the word *lesbian*.

At midnight, after a tense, five-hour wait, the chairman of the GCSC Board, and the grand ol' man of gay liberation, Morris Kight, emerged. Waving a shock of his wispy white hair aside with his turquoise and silver ring-studded hand, he all but shoved the small body of Dr. Benjamin Teller in front of us. The frail doctor, the nominal president of the board, timidly gave the board's answer to our petition in monosyllables: no, no, and no. The board, not its lesbian employees, would appoint people to management. The board, not its staff, would select new people to join them, when and how they saw fit.

The simmering dykes, many newly minted lesbians from the radical women's movement, were not happy. I, already a veteran of several past gay civil wars, felt another battle brewing.

•

THE RAPID CHANGE also came as a shock to the lesbians. Called upon to work together in close proximity, we discovered that we were of wildly different political beliefs. These were strident, politically correct times. The first question we asked, and had to answer, on a date was "What are your politics?" If your new lover spouted the wrong answer, a true feminist was expected to turn away from bourgeois "chemistry," carnal attraction, and even friendship.

Among our sister employees we had lesbians from suburbia who called themselves "gay women" and had grown up thinking of themselves as homosexual. These women thought gay men were our brothers. Activist women from the New Left had come of age on an antiwar, down-with-the-Establishment diet. To them, being a lesbian was only the latest issue in their litany of oppressions. And finally, some of us were feminist lesbians who agreed with radical feminists that the cause of our second-class status was the patriarchy; that is, men. These latter were "lesbians-come-lately" who were sure there was little difference between straight and gay men.

I was a former "gay woman" who grew up thinking gay men were my brothers. In 1971, I had grown into being a feminist lesbian who saw all women, straight and gay, as my sisters. This meant that there was far less room in the familial tent for my gay male "brothers." But I stopped short of seeing them, as radical feminists did, as "the enemy."

MARCH 1975: THE MEANING OF "GAY"

MORRIS KIGHT SAW ME as a ringleader of the rebellious lesbian staff, and in an attempt at mollification, had his board appoint me to sit on it. He wanted to co-opt my energy and make me feel like I was on his side.

I sat at the Formica table *inside* the room on the second-floor landing, surrounded by his carefully crafted bevy of psychology and social work professionals. I, too, had professional letters after my name, MSW, a master's degree in social work from UCLA. But I was out and proud and twenty-six years old, a generation younger and living in a different world than my closet-case peers.

None of my fellow directors understood the word *lesbian* or why the women on the GCSC staff hated to be called *gay*. Looking around the boardroom, I wondered how many years I would have to sit there before new directors—lesbians who would vote for my proposal to change the name of GCSC to the Gay *AND LESBIAN* Community Services Center—would be invited to join the board? I'd put the proposal on the agenda twice. Twice it had been voted down.

Lesbians of my generation did not identify with the word *gay*. Gay wasn't us; it was men. We knew our history, our foremothers. The word *gay* evolved from the Old French word *gai*, used to define the men who played women's roles in the theater. Women who loved women took our name from the Greek island of Lesbos where Sappho taught young girls the arts of culture, letters, and sexuality.

So here I sat, a *Sapphist* among *gai* men. The only other female director, Betty Berzon, LCSW, was old enough to be my mother. She had trouble then even calling herself gay when she wasn't in this boardroom. I didn't have her vote. And I didn't have the vote of Morris Kight, who I knew was the puppet master who pulled the strings of the others. Morris didn't want a feminist revolution at *his* center.

I thought of carving my initials into the Formica table for posterity. I would have a very long wait.

MAY 1975: THE GAY CIVIL WARS

THE RINGING PHONE woke me. I sat up in bed and looked at the clock. It was Friday, May 2, and I was late to my job at the *Los Angeles Free Press*. Pulling on jeans, I let the answering machine pick up. Thank the goddess for this new invention. Not having to answer my phone two dozen times a day brought a morsel of peace to my life.

The voice of my blonde *Cubana*, butch buddy, Pody, filled the room. "Cordova? You gotta be there," the answering machine bellowed. "Pick up the phone. PLEASE!" Her voice sounded broken, as though she'd been crying.

I grabbed the receiver. "Pody," I said, gently, "I'm here. What's the matter?"

"Have you gotten your mail today?" Her breathing was hyper.

"Mail? No, it comes in the afternoon."

"Please, Cordova, go check your mailbox."

"I'm in my pajamas!"

"Please buddy! I just got something special delivery. I can't believe it. Go check yours, now!"

I scurried down the apartment stairs in my pajamas, past the carport and out to the building's metal boxes. Pody was easily excitable. This chilly excursion was probably for nothing.

A single envelope lay in my box. Pody was right. I pulled it out. Strange, no postmark. Someone must have delivered it by hand. The mailbox security locks were long since broken. Stranger still, the long, white, number-ten envelope had the Gay Community Service Center's stamped return address on it. My name and address were handwritten in pen. I turned the envelope over. Peeling open the sealed flap revealed a single sheet, three folded. I lifted it out. It felt like a Xerox. No shit, a form letter. My name was written in the after "Dear" blank space. The letter was dated April 30: yesterday. My eyes scanned. "Dear Jeanne Cordova," it read . . .

"The Center's Board of Directors has . . . made an investigation . . . the nature and effectiveness of your performance in the position of Publicist, Medical Services . . . you have been in severe breach . . . your employment is terminated, effective immediately."

Terminated? I was being fired by the Gay Community Services Center? The marine layer, L.A.'s moving blanket of heavy fog,

enshrouded the buildings around me, even the cars. Fear tight-
ened the base of my throat. "*In severe breach*"? I gagged. My own
gay brothers were terminating me. This had to be a joke. I'd always excelled at jobs. Every dyke in L.A. knew about Herself
Health Clinic. I looked around, hoping the mist made me invisible to the neighbors. Standing on the street without even a
bathrobe, I suddenly felt like a homeless person. Adrift, un-
wanted, cast out.

•

BY THE TIME I hit the cement stairs in front of 1614 Wilshire
Boulevard, I was breathing rage. My shirt was sticking half-out,
half-in and haphazardly buttoned. I'd forgotten to comb my hair.
No matter. Today would not be about fashion. Pody, and goddess
knows who else, had been fired with me. GCSC couldn't dump
employees with no warning. IBM couldn't even do that, and IBM
was 'The Establishment.'

I ran to the small reception room of Herself Health Clinic.
April, GCSC's director of medical services and my boss, sat at the
desk. She looked at me with tears in her gentle face. She held up a
single sheet of white paper.

"Christ, not you too?" I said. Other than sleeping with Brenda
Weathers, the director of the alcoholic abuse program, my boss
was a mousy, constrained, and sensible woman.

"What's going down?" she asked limply, her voice a hollow
monotone.

A spasm of panic rippled though my chest: GCSC had fired a
project director! That meant that the funding agencies would be
involved. This was bigger than I had imagined. I laid a hand gently on her shoulder.

"Get on the phones," I told April. "Call everyone. Tell them to
come here, to the clinic's office."

"Why here?"

"Because we're not leaving here. Call the others!" I barked orders as I stood next to a paralyzed April. The reception room was filling up. But luckily we could see who else approached because the open door faced a long hallway.

"Others?" April said.

"Yes, call every woman on GCSC's staff. And then call the boys who have been with us. Tell Brenda to call her top staff at the alcoholism program. Call everyone! We all need to be together."

"What a bummer," April looked at me like a wounded bird. "What if some of them are fired too? I don't want to be the one to tell them." She redirected her pleading eyes toward Pody, who had just arrived.

"Whoa . . . not me," Pody said.

"April, I'll make the calls with you." I turned around. "Pody, start packing all of our protest stuff. Take all the internal memos, the unpublished stories, the lists."

I heard sniffles and turned around. Rachel, the petite, blue-eyed coworker, was standing in the doorway. "I received this in the mail!" she cried, handing me her letter.

She looked so helpless standing there white faced with her shoulders heaving. A wave of empathy came over me. I wanted to protect her. I stepped toward her about to put my arms around her, but Pody stepped in between us and reached to hug her first.

I remained rooted at April's elbow, too stunned to speak. Why fire the woman who was the board's own candidate for the management team? She was far from being a rebel leader.

Suddenly, June Suwara's wild red bob appeared in the doorway. "What the fuck is going on here!" June demanded, brushing past Pody and Rachel. She came to a halt in front of me waving her own letter.

"It looks like D-Day. The bodies are falling," I replied.

"It's International Workers Day, that's what it is!" she shouted. "GCSC can't do this!"

"That was yesterday," I corrected. "Today is May second."

"Close enough," June fumed.

Two of the male employees, Enric and Eddy, who had been lesbian friendly, appeared in the doorway. Eddie was crying on Enric's shoulder. Enric was breathing fast. "I'm a program director! Look what I got in the mail."

Suddenly, he saw the rest of us. The office was almost full. "Not ALL of you?"

Seeing the familiar letter in Enric's hand, my shock deepened. In recent weeks a handful of the gay male employees had begun to support us as feminists demanding reform. The men called themselves *effeminists*, a word used by the radical wing of the gay men's movement, the "gay faeries." The effeminist men understood that the straight world mocked them because, as faggots, they identified with women. These guys championed feminist principles like collectivity and the eradication of patriarchy. They believed that gay men were persecuted because they openly broke gender roles and identified with women. These were usually the feminine, not the butch, gay men. They had become our natural allies.

A large frame filled the doorway. It was Colin McQueen, a bear of a white boy with a great head of reddish-brown hair that was teased into an Afro. Colin was June's assistant coordinator of the Peer Counseling program. He was new to L.A., and no one seemed to know a thing about him. Colin hollered, waving his termination letter high over his head like a battle flag, "This means war!"

MAY 1975: A WOMAN'S PLACE

THE WOMEN'S SALOON & PARLOUR was wedged into the rumpled block of 4900 Fountain Avenue in East Hollywood. Almost overnight, the restaurant had become the hangout of lesbian feminists from the beaches to the Mojave.

I strode through the front door, cocky. Walking into "women only" places—like the Woman's Building and the Westside

Women's Center—made me proud. We'd carved these safe houses out of parts of the city discarded by men and capitalism. It was one thing to work with gay men when we had to politically, but socially they had their turf and we should have ours.

The eatery was a cavernous room that looked like the offspring of a fifties diner and a hippie coffeehouse. The walls were thinly whitewashed with patches of brick and concrete poking through. A periwinkle, handpainted quote from Judy Grahn's poem, "The Common Woman" was lettered on the entrance wall: "A common woman is as common as bread . . . and will rise." Men, common or exalted, were not allowed.

The Saloon's staff was organized into a feminist collective. Theoretically, it had no boss. From chef to waiters, everyone shared in tips equally.

Colleen McKay had opened the joint on behalf of her group, the Feminist Research & Reading Society. She wrote on a side-walk advertisement board that the restaurant was "a way to invade society and create a place that reinforces what feminists believe."

The Women's Saloon was a do-it-yourself café. Customers were supposed to get their own silverware, napkins, coffee, and ice water. Tempers had flared the first couple of nights over the almost nonexistent service. It didn't hurt to bring your own sand-wich if you were hypoglycemic or had anger-management issues. Logistic competency was never the hallmark of feminism.

Waiting at the bar, I checked out the tables. Good. I had ar-rived before my new lover. Leaning back against the solid oak counter, I positioned myself so that I could see the front door. I'd pick up Rachel at the entrance. That was somewhat like a date. A tape of mixed music, now playing Janis Joplin's "Bobby McGee," was on full blast. Great! Rachel and I could dance. A good excuse to touch her.

Looking across the room, I saw Pody serving a table full of GCSC fired employees. Occasionally, I felt that my blonde-haired friend and former coworker was flirting with me. Pody was soft-butch with a smile for everyone. So it was kind of hard to tell whether her flirtations were directed at me or Rachel. It's not like butches never crossed the line and slept with one another. Feminism insinuated that butch-femme, a lesbian choreography that was decades old, was heterosexist. To be truly feminist and egalitarian, butches should sleep with butches, and femmes with femmes. I twirled the ice cubes in my Coke. What a ridiculous conclusion. No wonder everyone was having "*short* meaningful relationships."

I felt something shift in the room and pivoted toward the front door just in time to see Rachel. My chest inflated with a rush, as she strolled in confidently, clothed in a simple blue V-neck and tight-fitting black jeans. Rachel was understated, a proper lady who didn't wear her sexuality on her sleeve. I liked that, and I watched the silver of her hoop earrings catch a reflection from the ceiling's galvanized pipe. The strawberry-blonde highlights in her hair spun a halo out of my desire.

I waited, flushed with pride that it was me that she sought. Her eyes swept the room.

Finally I called out, "Rachel!"

She walked toward me, contained yet confident in her physical self. I watched her body sway loosely in her gait, knowing that in bed, the woman I was falling in love with would be all mine.

three scenes
from a hollywood life

michael kearns

"DARLING," my director said, pulling me aside for a private consultation, "you need to lose about ten pounds of baby fat before
we open."

This bit of direction, delivered by Off-Broadway wunderkind
Tom Eyen, was one of the many details that would distinguish
The Dirtiest Show in Town from previous theatrical outings. For
starters, it was the first time a director called me "darling."

With his superior intellect and severe sense of humor, Eyen
was an oddball whose sophistication was tempered by a pervasive
sweetness. "Darling," he would say, referencing a bygone time
when starlets were discovered at soda fountains, "you're my
discovery."

After a grueling rehearsal schedule that included thousands

upon thousands of sit-ups, I made my Los Angeles stage debut in the West Coast premiere of *Dirtiest Show*, written and directed by Eyen. As a writer, Eyen would go on to win an Emmy for *Mary Hartman, Mary Hartman* and a Tony for *Dreamgirls*. He died of AIDS in 1991.

The "baby fat" he referred to was bloat, the result of guzzling gallons of white wine during my first eight months in Los Angeles. In the autumn of Hollywood, 1971, Rock Hudson was starring in *McMillan and Wife*, Dick Sargent was playing Darrin Stephens opposite Elizabeth Montgomery on *Bewitched*, Robert Reed was playing the dad on *The Brady Bunch*: three gay men who were playing husbands while Raymond Burr was playing the title role in *Ironside*. Paul Lynde was camping it up on *Hollywood Squares* and Alan Sues often appeared in drag on *Rowan and Martin's Laugh-In*. Little did I realize that I would eventually meet all of them.

My connection to the entertainment capital of the world was the reluctant Best Actress-nominated Carrie Snodgress (for *Diary of a Mad Housewife*), a Goodman alumna and Tom's friend. Carrie introduced Tom to her agent, the powerful Stan Kamen of the William Morris Agency. Tom, in turn, set up a meeting for me with Kamen a few days after I arrived in L.A.

In anticipation of my meeting, the advice I received was confusing from the beginning: "Butch it up but wear tight jeans" seemed to be the general tip. I took direction well. Within minutes of meeting the handsome, no-nonsense Kamen, he was on the phone to Monique James, head of casting at Universal. During the final days of the old studio system, Universal was the only remaining studio where one could be hired as a contract player, the best possible scenario for a twenty-one-year-old fresh out of acting school.

"Monique," Kamen cooed, oozing high voltage Hollywood charm, surveying me from head to toe. "I've got an exceptionally handsome kid here who just graduated from Goodman. Can you see him?"

A few weeks later, I performed a scene for Ms. James, playing a young Will Shakespeare. She immediately sent me to Reuben Cannon who was casting a part I was "right for" on an upcoming episode of *Ironside*. The word got back to Kamen that my work was "too theatrical," but Ms. James wanted to see me do another scene. While "theatrical" was probably an accurate description, considering I'd just completed three years at a school that taught stage acting, I also think it euphemistically carried a whiff of homophobia. Monique James, a lesbian, certainly knew that being sent by Kamen was a clue to my probable gayness.

When Tom dropped me off at the Ivar Theatre in the heart of Hollywood (if Hollywood has a heart) on the opening night of *Dirtiest Show*, ten pounds lighter, I was greeted with the explosion of flashbulbs, shooting from the paparazzi's cameras. It was all at once shocking, seductive, and disconcerting. I hadn't even stepped onstage and they were clamoring to get a photo.

The opening-night audience included Cass Elliot of the Mamas and the Papas, manager extraordinaire Alan Carr, transsexual author Christine Jorgensen, poet Rod McKuen, and a host of agents, casting directors, and press people.

Carr introduced himself and insisted that we "go to lunch." He was impressed with my knowledge of Ann-Margret, his star client whose career he had resurrected.

While certainly tame by today's standards, *The Dirtiest Show* was decidedly an edgy piece of theater in 1972. Not only did the cast appear sans costumes throughout the evening, the sketch material celebrated sexuality of every stripe while condemning pollution and war. Perhaps not Brechtian in breadth, but the show had some bite.

As an actor, I had never felt so free or authentic. Forget three years of sense memory exercises and Shakespeare classes. At long last I was given permission to use myself, including my gay self, on stage. Heightening the exhilaration was the instant celebrity status the performers were awarded. The truth, of course, was that the young and sexed-up cast members were being sought as much for their fuckability as their thespian abilities.

I followed up with Carr, who did invite me to lunch at the Green Café. A magnet for industry types, many of whom were screamingly gay, the Green Café was legendary, in no small part because of Carr's largesse. Carr's flamboyance endeared him to the Hollywood community; probably because he was overweight and not conventionally attractive, his uncompromising gayness played well and he knew it. On and off the screen, queers were allowed to be court jesters as long as they never showed their balls.

Holding court, Carr introduced me to his all-male table of cohorts. "I'd like you to meet Michael Kearns," he said, in a voice that could be heard above the considerable buzz of the outdoor patio and the traffic sounds of San Vicente Boulevard. "A tall David Cassidy."

It was a reference to my mane of shoulder-length hair, something Ann-Margret herself commented on when I met her a few weeks later at Carr's birthday party, also held at the trendy Green Café. "I love your hair," the sex kitten purred. It was the beginning of an enduring friendship with a Hollywood goddess who was also a complex and caring woman.

At one point during the show's run, I injured myself and had to wear an Ace bandage on my wrist. I mentioned to Carr that I tried not to wear it when I went onstage but he had a better idea. "Wear it as long as you can," he said. "The audience immediately pays more attention to you." I took his advice.

While I was acknowledged for my onstage abilities as a performer, my offstage reputation as a hard-drinking and sexually available party boy was gaining considerably more momentum.

Nonstop parties, held in the Hollywood Hills digs of the gay, rich, and famous, inevitably led to a growing list of sexual conquests. In many instances, the real party action took place in various secret rooms, away from the main event.

At one of these orgies masquerading as a party, I found myself smoking dope with a sixties television heartthrob whose career had been derailed after more than one public sex arrest. He was wearing a bright red caftan (popularized by the zaftig Carr) which conveniently provided easy access, especially since he'd apparently left his underpants at home.

Years later, I would have a private assignation with that notoriously well-hung hunk who was one of the first "stars" (post-Burt Reynolds) to take it all off for *Playgirl*. Well, almost all. The jet-black hairpiece remained firmly attached.

Our sex date took place in an art studio on his estate. In the midst of easels and mediocre artwork, there was a cot, strategically placed below a wall adorned with the nude shots from *Playgirl*. Multiple images of his big schlong, presumably intended to reinforce the real thing, proved more comedic than erotic. This would not be the only time I'd have trouble getting it up with a Big (in more ways than one) Star.

True to his heritage, he was Greek active. While fucking me, he was looking at his images on the wall, oblivious to my degree of hardness or softness. After he came, which was punctuated by the obligatory grunts and groans of a less-than-nuanced television actor, he hopped up and headed for the bathroom.

"How was it?" he asked, cocksure, as he strode across the room.

"Uh, OK," I said, telling the truth.

I'll never forget the sight of his back stiffening, almost as if he'd been shot from behind. He couldn't wait to get me out of his "art studio."

•

I ARRIVED ON the set of *And the Band Played On*, having slept about two hours after a late night flight from Chicago. It seemed emblematic of the exhaustive journey experienced by almost everyone associated with Randy Shilts's monumental book, which, after years of behind-the-scenes wrangling, was finally being filmed for HBO.

Even before officially checking in with the assistant director, I stood on the outside steps of a classic Victorian house near downtown with Ian McKellen. It was chilly by L.A. standards, which seemed appropriate since the location was replicating San Francisco.

"Philip died November first," I told him. In my mind, I could see the two of them, drinking champagne in Ian's dressing room, backstage at the London theater where he was appearing in *King Lear*.

"Oh, darling," he said, embracing me tightly as burly grips and nondescript "atmosphere" (actors who would be seen but not heard in a party scene) brushed by us. "I'm so sorry," he said, holding me close. "You know I am."

At moments like these I wondered how the scripted material we were about to commit to celluloid could possibly be any more cinematic than real life. I half-expected to hear a voice shout, "Cut and print."

In spite of the somber subject matter (or perhaps because of it), the mood on the set was anything but sober. The first scene we shot recaptured one of those heated meetings that took place at the beginning of the plague that involved Ian as Bill Kraus, Lily Tomlin as Dr. Selma Dritz, B. D. Wong as Kico Govantes, and actors David Dukes, David Marshall Grant, and Jack Kenny. I played Cleve Jones, the founder of the NAMES Project and the AIDS Memorial Quilt, although you wouldn't necessarily know that considering the scant amount of Cleve's dialogue.

While I wished my contribution to the film could have been greater, I felt blessed to be in the company of these actors, most of whom were gay, on this rarified set. Ian took the lead in turning the tables, making gayness the norm rather than the secret no one dared acknowledge.

Instead of minimizing who we were when the cameras weren't

rolling, we maximized our queer selves, taking our cue from Ian. No matter how many times we called each other "darling" or "honey," there would be no macho grips rolling their eyes or nudging each other behind our backs.

During breaks, Ian strategized about what to say to Lily regarding her reluctance to actually come out instead of doing that dance she'd been doing—one toe in, one toe out—for decades. Being the gentleman and professional that he is, I believe he put that conversation on hold.

At lunchtime, the boys in *The Band* gathered in one trailer and carried on like high school girls at a slumber party, sharing juicy gossip and squealing with laughter. Free at last.

I had never felt such a degree of comfort on a Hollywood movie set. The queers were the majority for a change and behaved accordingly. It had been an arduous fight but a sweet victory. While never losing sight of the film's profoundly sad storyline, it was a day of triumph with an undercurrent of tragedy.

●

IDENTIFYING THE RIGHT PRESCHOOL for your kid carries with it the emotional involvement, not to mention the financial consideration, that used to accompany a search for the right college.

In L.A., this quest is marked by a variety of philosophies, all containing a veritable language of its own. Diversity is the battle cry of almost all of Los Angeles preschools, so Tia and I would ostensibly be able to fill more than one quota. The very qualities that were potentially poison in the adoption scenario transformed into gold when it came to finding a preschool and, subsequently, a K–8 school.

But no matter the degree of our desirability on paper, there would be a mandatory personal visit to the perspective school as well as a slew of probing questions along the line of, "Is she potty trained or not?"

The director of one well-respected preschool chose for us to participate in a Mommy and Me session so that she could observe Tia in that setting. Daddy and Me didn't exist.

Tia was herself—loud, aggressive, oppositional, and a bit confrontational. She was also accessible, funny, playful, and verbal.

At the end of the session, where Tia was the only black girl and I was the only male mommy, we formed a circle and the children were asked to sing their favorite songs.

Little Susie sang, "It's a small world, after all . . ." Then adorable Billy half-sang, half-whispered, "Twinkle, twinkle, little star . . ."

After several more darling renditions of familiar kiddie ditties, Tia let loose with, "R-E-S-P-E-C-T, find out what it means to me. Sock it to me, sock it to me, sock it to me . . ." There was a collective gasp from the mommies (and me's) as they glimpsed a soul sister unleashed.

I spoke to the director, whose observations about Tia were largely negative, delivered in a condescending tone that often seems to be the norm when a self-described authority speaks to a single man who is raising a child.

This was not the school for our particular panoply of diversity.

We wound up enrolling at L.A. Family School, where we were embraced in spite of our improbable family unit.

From the moment Tia began school, there was a heightened shift in my sense of self. This almost always occurs with those of us who are hands-on parents; in fact, we begin identifying ourselves by using our child's name. I became "Tia's Daddy" instead of "Michael" practically overnight. Now, even when I call parents whom I've known for several years, I introduce myself as "Tia's Daddy." It is indicative of how we perceive ourselves, stripped of our own personality in deference to our child.

While I enjoyed being "Tia's Daddy," I was determined not to forfeit other aspects of myself, including the daddy persona I'd cultivated in the sexual marketplace. Sex provided a respite from my fatherly duties; some of my partners may have called me "daddy," but I didn't fix them macaroni and cheese or read them a fairy tale after our liaisons.

"I'm really a dad," I told the unsuspecting boy (in gay parlance, that's thirtysomething) as he put on the baggy shorts (no underpants) and an oversized T-shirt designed to deliberately emphasize his pulchritude.

"I know that, dude," he said, grinning, like someone who could almost, but not quite, be cast in a daytime soap opera. This was an afternoon delight while Tia was at school, learning her ABCs.

"No, really," I said.

"Does he live with your ex-wife?"

Accustomed to these assumptions, I answered, "No wife. And she is six years old."

"She lives with you?" he asked, incredulously, like I was talking about a pet kangaroo or something.

"Has since she was five months old."

"Cool," he said, not comprehending any of it.

Oblivious to the photos of Tia and me on the bedroom walls in various father-daughter configurations, my date had riveted on his own image reflected back at him from the mirror above the headboard of my bed.

my space highways

tim miller

WHEN I WAS ABOUT TEN, my dad and I built an amazing tree house high in the branches of an old Chinese elm in my suburban L.A. backyard. This was a time before kids commissioned six-figure architects to design their tree houses, so instead we just cobbled together two enormous wooden boxes, cast off from someone's console RCA color TV that we had found in an alley, and made a glamour-filled, split-level duplex tree house. I was able to create a whole world, a complete space for myself up there in the Chinese elm. Decorated with seventies throw rugs and a pubic-hair-revealing poster of David Cassidy, it was my own private queer boy Utopia. I'd invite my little friends into my treetop lair, pull up the rope ladder, and try to convince them that we should cover ourselves in Mazola corn oil and play naked Twister. Sometimes they agreed! This tree house was the prototype for Highways Performance Space, near the end of the old Route 66 that wends its way through West Hollywood as Santa Monica Boulevard until it terminates by the sea by the statue of Saint Monica.

I had always been looking for an urban queer tree house in L.A. For years I thought it might be in Griffith Park. I am *definitely* not the only gay man to have looked for it there! I often think about my history with the park growing up here in L.A. County. I remember numerous family trips to gloriously tacky train museum Travel Town to soothe my little-kid's love for locomotives. I remember going to work with my traveling salesman dad, picking up a Tommy's Burger by his office at Beverly and Alvarado and going up to Griffith Park to look at the city as we ate. I remember a school field trip to the Observatory where I was frightened and exhilarated by the Foucault's Pendulum as it did its scary Vincent Price swing a few feet from where Sal Mineo's blood flowed at the end of *Rebel Without a Cause*. I remember making out with my first boyfriend near Dante's View as a high school kid. I remember numerous trips to the Greek Theater and Hollywood Bowl to get major doses of art and culture. I remember the two years I lived in Silver Lake near Sunset Boulevard and would ride my bike through the rich folks' neighborhoods to find my way into the park and sniff around the other gay boys. From Travel Town for a train-obsessed little boy to Dante's View for a boy-obsessed (and nature-loving!) teenage male, Griffith Park offered invitation and possibility of one kind of tree house, a safe and charged place where queer art, politics, and sex could collide. However, this desire for a queer tree house space really reached fruition—since after all this would be a "fruit-bearing" tree house—with the opening of Highways Performance Space.

When Linda Burnham and I cofounded Highways Performance Space in 1989, we saw the space as a fierce crossroads, a gathering spot for artists and diverse communities to come together and chart new futures amid a very difficult time. Our venture was fueled by nine years of Reagan-Bush horrors, the AIDS crisis, the looming Culture Wars, numerous dirty wars in El Salvador and Nicaragua, and the emerging Queer Nation. Highways became a cross between an emergency room triage center and a kind of tree house headquarters for artists looking our time square in the eyes.

After moving to New York City as a teenager and spending almost ten years toiling in the East Village salt mines of career-obsessed artists, what really pulled me and Doug Sadownick, my partner during those years, back to my L.A. hometown in the late eighties was that performance in L.A. was much more fiercely connected with social context, personal identity, and political praxis. New performance work was coming from cultural communities: Asian or Latino or lesbian or gay or homeless or disabled or whatever. A new model of the artist as citizen was taking shape, the artist who is also a social visionary, a social worker, and a social activist. That's what attracted me to coming back to L.A.: to be able to have colleagues like John Malpede and the Los Angeles Poverty Department exploring homelessness, Rachel Rosenthal and her eco-feminist visions, Michael Kearns's ground-breaking solo and ensemble performances confronting HIV-AIDS, Luis Alfaro and Eric Gutierrez's narratives of a queer Chicano kids, David Schweizer and his stylish queer theater spectacles all joined with Keith Antar Mason, Elia Arce, Guillermo Gómez-Pena, and many others to make L.A. the capital of the art-as-social-change world that I wanted to belong to. What I loved about all these artists' work was its intimate connection to the world.

We pause now for a bit of historical context: there had been an explosion of feminist and lesbian feminist performance work in L.A. in the seventies and early eighties constellated around the Woman's Building in downtown L.A. This remarkable period of artistic ferment, beautifully documented in the books *The Amazing Decade* and Terry Wolverton's memoir *Insurgent Muses*, had a huge impact on queer art in L.A. The work coming out of the Woman's Building opened up a tremendous amount of space for lesbian and gay artists in Southern California. L.A. became the steaming cauldron of autobiographical personal narrative and a return to story and text which transformed creative practice in the United States and set the stage for an identity-based multicultur-alism of the eighties and nineties. As artists started to tell stories and put value on what happens in our personal spaces, autobiog-raphy suddenly opened up the world to the incredible vitality and specificity of everyone's lives and how that connects us directly back to social challenges. This grassroots movement was on fire.

And, of course, the gasoline that accelerated those flames at Highways was the Reagan-Bush inaction on the AIDS crisis. Highways origins and growth pains do a tango with the early pe-riod of ACT UP. The ACT UP model had a huge impact on gay artists at the very end of the eighties and into the nineties. High-ways was created side by side with ACT UP in many ways. Many performance artists put forth great effort as part of ACT UP, either in L.A. or in New York or Chicago. ACT UP trained a whole generation of queer artists how to take over the streets, how to shift public policy, how to get millions of public dollars re-leased, how to get buildings built, to learn if there's a certain kind of social practice you can put into play to change the world.

In *Stretch Marks*, the first performance I premiered at High-ways in 1989, I used a section of a piece I made for a demonstra-tion in front of County Hospital in East L.A. A demonstration is every bit as good a reason to make a performance as creating it for opening night. I was deeply involved in work to pressure the County of Los Angeles to provide an AIDS ward in the biggest hospital in the world; my political work for a year and a half was primarily around that issue. The AIDS ward soon was opened. I was arrested twice—and beaten up once—by the police, trying to make it happen, but after a couple of years of our creative and activist exertions in this county of ten million people, there was an AIDS ward. That doesn't mean the world had changed, but there was a specific goal in my work and in my political life:

improved health care in the County of Los Angeles, where I was born and where I live. The struggle continues, but the results were tangible. This would not exist without thousands of hours of protest people put forward to embarrass one of the most corrupt and undemocratic bodies in the country, the L.A. County Board of Supervisors, to get off their butts and shell out. This performance was somehow birthed in that psychic tree house. Indeed, the full-evening piece at Highways built toward a melancholic climax there in Griffith Park at the haunted train museum of Travel Town.

•

BUT ENOUGH ABOUT political praxis! This was all damned sexy! Just as the erotic heat of ACT UP was fueled by the existential fever of the plague, so was Highways buzzing with sexy chi! I was leading huge, free gay men's performance art workshops funded by the California Arts Council. Fierce performances around sexuality, race, and gender were drawing packed houses and stirring the dating pool and activist ranks. Highways and ACT UP collaborated on several huge parties, wild kinky raves in an empty warehouse awaiting renovation on the property, where many hundreds would gather for politics, performance, and priapism!

July 13, 1991
Last night big party called TROUBLE at Highways in the old warehouse building. Big benefit for ACT UP and Highways. About two thousand queers. Lots of energy. Hundred people or so were having sex in what will soon be Doug and my house in that building. A good christening, I think. I wandered through what will soon be my study. My dick out of my pants. All these sweaty bodies. Mostly men. A few cute leather lesbians. Even some boys and girls fucking. It felt like a good way to begin to define the space of

my next home. A special vitamin shot of life energy. I keep saving room on my dance card for that energy. I ran into an old friend from NYC who I had sex with a few times on a roof of a building on St. Mark's Place. Who knows what he was thinking of me as several cute Highway boys draped themselves over me, one of them pinching my nipples. The evening ended with Keith Antar Mason and me watching a dwarf woman and a very humpy guy dance naked on a platform with his hard dick painted florescent green and glowing in the black light as it twirled and ricocheted, the clear winner in my personal baton twirling contest.

I realize it is crucial not to get all nostalgic for a summer-of-love, early nineties, Queer Nation world of art and activism of which Highways was perhaps the flagship. It was not all Felliniesque platoons of queer boys on our scooters racing through nighttime L.A. streets on our way to a demo or a sex club. It was a hugely embattled time for Highways, the prime target of the radical right as the most attacked arts organization in the United States by the right-wing culture wars. This was in no small part my fault as the heat-seeking missiles sought me out as one of the queer artist poster kids of the so-called NEA 4 crisis. In 1990, I, a wandering queer performance artist, had been awarded a National Endowment for the Arts Solo Performer Fellowship, which was promptly overturned under slimy political pressure from the Bush White House because of the lush, wall-to-wall homo themes of my creative work. We "NEA 4"—me, Karen Finley, John Fleck, Holly Hughes—then successfully sued the federal government with the help of the ACLU (if you're not a card-carrying member, become one!) for violation of our First Amendment rights. We won a settlement where the government paid us the amount of the defunded grants and all court costs. The last little driblet of my case was the "decency" clause governing funding for the arts that went all the way to the Supreme Court!

The time was also haunted by the loss of friends from AIDS, their ashes pouring through our fingers after the numerous memorials that happened there. Those ashes of friends dead from AIDS mixed into the garden soil surrounding Highways. This is not a metaphor; I speak quite literally here. I can remember my dear friend playwright James Carroll Pickett's ashes slipping between my fingers onto the roots of a Highways rose bush. My space Highways was clearly also a gathering place to mourn our losses, a reliquary for the sorry knell of that time.

This montage of some of the sorrows of that very alive time that was also haunted by death keeps the nostalgia at bay. And who needs nostalgia when you have our dynamic and juicy present! When I opened the Highways calendar of performances in the mail yesterday and took in all the amazing programming—the wild new generation of queer performers, drag warriors, and choreographers who continue the tradition by baton-twirling dildos and finding new art-society cocktail mixers—I saw once again how crucial Highways continues to be and how completely Artistic Director Leo Garcia honors where Highways comes from but also keeps creating new sparks and connectivity to our time right now!

•

I HAVE BEEN THINKING a lot of late about what "space" is, and more importantly what "my space" is. When I ran Highways, I knew what that phrase meant. My space was a useful tree house in Santa Monica for queer visions and nightmares and web-spinning dreams of the diversity-rich future. But since I stepped down as artistic director of Highways several years ago, those two little words "my space" have become more complicated. Chase Korte, an actor I worked with during an intensive performance workshop I led in 2004 at the University of Minnesota, died in 2007 in a car accident. After finishing at the university, he had

moved to L.A. to seek his fortune and begin his adventure as a
performer and actor. After shooting a role in an independent film,
Chase died driving back to L.A. somewhere in the nighttime
desert. His page on MySpace.com has become on ongoing memorial for his close friends to remember him, to speak to him, to
ask him to look after a dog that recently died, and for him to be
sorely missed. His version of "MySpace" is now an ongoing, sor-
row-drenched space of a young life cut short.

Such musings led me to recall my favorite story by Tolstoy.
The title is usually translated as "How Much Land Does a Man
Need?" but I have always done my own translation and replaced
the word "Land" with "Space." In Tolstoy's tale, there is some
kind of existential contest in which however much land you run
around in a single day will belong to you. One greedy contestant
wants so much land that he runs all day long and keels over in a
heart attack when he tries to run too far. Cheery Tolstoy lets us
know that how much space the man needs is only the six feet of
his grave. This is true, yet it doesn't do justice to these charged
spaces of Internet mourning or queer performance space building
that fuel and feed juicy communities of people at certain times
when they need it, as Highways Performance Space has done now
for almost twenty years of gay performers in L.A. How much
space does a man need? Maybe just enough to climb up the rope
ladder at a tree house like Highways, claim his spot in the light,
and tell his queer story.

writing not wronging—
the lgbt "community" in l.a.

rosalyne blumenstein

(T)HE JOURNEY: NO PASSPORT REQUIRED

ALTHOUGH I DIDN'T need my passport to relocate, moving from New York City to L.A. was like moving to a foreign country. My journey to Los Angeles was not a well-thought-out three- or five-year strategic plan. It came from an impulsive heart and a spirit that needed a drastic change. It came out of a place of desperation. It came from a desire for something different, for the unknown. It was initiated by a breakdown that could only be healed and managed through change, transformation, risk, and growth. I wasn't so much moving toward something—I was moving from, and leaving behind the community I was part of within the so-called "inclusive" LGBT movement.

Thus far, my experience of L.A. is not so much about the "wronging" but, I hope, about the "writing." I didn't realize that there was more "wrong" than "right/write" within the movement. Los Angeles seemed to be ten years behind the East Coast, and I didn't feel that I was willing to take on another fight. This view is not only my personal and professional judgment of the socio-political challenges of the queer movement. It is also intimately related to my journey and experience of that which is grand about the L.A. experience: the gifts, the indulgences, the solitude, as well as the isolation.

Back to the "righting/writing of the wronging." Los Angeles seems to have many more trans-identified social service programs, yet there is in no way a real community. As I traveled from East Coast to West, I wasn't even sure what I was looking for professionally, let alone personally or spiritually. With patience, tolerance, and the ability to trust, I was hoping it would all fall into place. However, I did not find a place within the trans-oriented nonprofit social services sector. I have been able to counsel, coach, and therapeutically intervene with trans people one on one in the private arena.

Within the social services arena, I have met many people of trans experience that I believe in. And I have been able to support their work, their abilities, their determination, and their courage. However, I have not been impressed by the politics of the larger organizations they are affiliated with. For instance, L.A. has an amazing institution that does great work for the LGBT community, but it is still called the L.A. Gay and Lesbian Center. That's a problem! As a woman with a transsexual history who identifies predominantly as straight, I have worked tirelessly for the rights of all trans people within the LGBT movement no matter what their sexual orientation or gender identity. And within that work, it was imperative to assist those who identified as straight or bisexual with an opportunity to celebrate and own their sexual orientation as well as have it known within the agency that was serving them.

THE POWER OF LANGUAGE

TRANSGENDER IS A TERM much celebrated and utilized in Los Angeles and nationally. It is a term I helped coin as a professional in the early nineties to name a high-risk category within HIV/AIDS prevention work. But it is not a term I ever use to identify my personal experience, which seemed problematic in terms of trans work in L.A. When I attempted to introduce myself to the various organizations and their leaders, my expertise was not utilized. (Maybe part of the problem was my loud-mouth, tell-it-like-it-is, sometimes obnoxiously overbearing presence.) In any case, my real desire was to reinvent myself within the social work profession and not be on the front lines fighting the trans battle or be a poster child for the increasingly visible TG/TS movement.

Throughout my academic and professional career in New York, I tried to educate the populace about the power of language. I felt there should be a discussion about the terms *MTF* and *FTM* used to identify women and men of trans experience. I personally coined the terms *woman of trans experience* and *man of trans experience*. These terms acknowledge the person first as their core gender (male or female) and also celebrate the cultural heritage of the trans experience. This did not go over well here in L.A. Many of the trans folk working in the field, as well as those within trans communities, utilized the terms MTF, FTM, or transgender as their personal choice of language. They seemed offended that I did not use this language to self-identify. In addition, the gay and lesbian folks I would run into would casually use those acronyms to describe someone they knew or were serving. For me, the language is problematic on many levels.

In my view, if a woman of trans experience is consistently identified as MTF (male to female), her femaleness is never fully accepted as a legitimate identity. Likewise for men of trans experience. And what of those folk who don't buy into total gender constriction and want to celebrate the fluidity of gender? Many people of trans experience are no longer "on the road"; they have arrived within their core gender identity, but the terms MTF and FTM do not let them be there. My own trans journey began when I was three years old. I took it to another level when I was sixteen. When do I get to just own that which is me: woman, female, not MTF! This discussion seemed to be silenced in L.A.

COMMUNITY/CONFLICT

GEOGRAPHY IS A PROBLEM here: Is it really possible for Los Angeles to have community when it is so spread out anyway? Isn't that why West Hollywood is supposed to play a pivotal role within the queer community? West Hollywood is supposed to be the place where queer folk get to celebrate queer identity and live fulfilled existences. However, the queer folk who get to celebrate identity and establish a life with a roof over their heads are the gay white men of privilege who can afford housing. WeHo is not a diversified queer community but much more vanilla.

Standing back from the front lines has afforded me an opportunity to be more objective about LGBT. And this is how I have seen it over the five or so years I have been a resident of L.A. I think we have gone backward, just like the larger society. There seems to be a parallel process going on with the way in which government is running things and the way in which our social movements are following.

Here's the deal and my take on it: I believe all should be able to live the way they want, to experience some semblance of freedom, to love and be loved, to feel fulfilled, to dream, and to be on a journey. Too much of the gay agenda, from where I stand, is all about mimicking a Christian, heterosexist mentality. I believe that the sexual minority movement should be about many different kinds of loves, not just the sanctity of marriage. It's about not buying into just the "white picket fence and the 2.3 kids." And, while I'm at it, let me say that the sexual minority movement should not just be about those who want to appear "normal" in the rest of the world's eyes. After all, the sexual minority movement is not *just* about same-sex love, desire, or freedom. What it should be about is resisting a system that is gender constricted, that insists there is only one way to be. Bisexual or pansexual people are some of the most amazing people in the world, and their voices are not heard within the L.A. queer movement.

The gay agenda has become about wanting the same things everybody else wants, which is not wholly a bad thing, but it has become the voice of the whole queer movement—and it isn't. In fact, most voices that are silenced within the L.A. movement are those

- getting their asses kicked on the streets because they don't blend.
- with little power within the political system.
- queer folk housed in boxes in downtown Los Angeles.

West Hollywood and the rest of L.A. make believe they are all inclusive, but they aren't really. You hear leaders talk about gay pride/LGBT pride, but then they go on to discuss gay and lesbian issues without reflecting on bi and trans issues. You will hear folks in WeHo City Hall utilize the words *transgender* and *bisexuality*; they even have a transgender task force that produces many positive events for the trans communities. But many still fail to see the complexity, the diversity, and the various sexual orientations that embody the trans experience. Sitting in meetings and focus groups would remind me how much I miss being a part of the New York discussions. But I do not miss the fight within the fight—here or there. Or the annoyance I would feel as I heard things that reminded me that "these gay and lesbian folk just don't get it."

Given all of this, I think B and T folk within the L.A. gay movement have the opportunity to participate within the movement. In the larger scheme of things, to be *gay* in L.A. is really about gay and lesbian issues, trans folk who identify as gay or lesbian, and bisexuals who are in gay or lesbian relationships. Unfortunately, this leaves out all those whose sexual orientation is hetero or bi. With this reality, the message is this: if you are attracted to someone with a trans history, then you must be gay. Which makes it even harder for a woman or man of trans experience to have a loving, intimate relationship with another human being. In L.A.—where so many of us buy into the youth-oriented, perfectly reconstructed body presentation—it can be almost impossible for someone who has a trans history to get involved in a loving intimate relationship, especially if they identify as heterosexual.

MY (HUMBLE) SOLUTION

BELIEVE IT OR NOT, I am really happy about my journey here in L.A. Los Angeles has afforded me the opportunity to change internally, to process, to review, and to reorganize my thoughts as well as my actions. The beauty that is L.A.—the solitude, the weather, and the slower pace—has made me realize many things. The best way to explain my journey is with the St. Francis prayer:

Lord, make me a channel of thy peace;
that where there is hatred, I may bring love;
that where there is wrong, I may bring the spirit
    of forgiveness;
that where there is discord, I may bring harmony;
that where there is error, I may bring truth;
that where there is doubt, I may bring faith;
that where there is despair, I may bring hope;
that where there are shadows, I may bring light;
that where there is sadness, I may bring joy.
Lord, grant that I may seek rather to comfort than
    to be comforted;
to understand, than to be understood;

to love, than to be loved.
For it is by self-forgetting that one finds.
It is by forgiving that one is forgiven.
It is by dying that one awakens to eternal life.
Amen.

I've spent many years in my personal journey wishing people would get me, understand me, give to me, support me—me me me me! Coming to L.A., I have had to reestablish myself within the professional arena as well as reevaluate my belief system to move forward. I have not reached, nor do I wish to reach, the finish line. I am grateful to L.A. for the opportunity to review my id and my ego, to reestablish myself, and to take a backseat within the movement and privately support new LGBT leaders by helping them to set their goals, work through some past trauma, get clean and sober, and live their dreams.

Usually one thinks of coming to L.A. to be in the spotlight, but I have experienced the opposite. Maybe I have developed away from self-seeking behaviors to a less self-absorbed stage that is more affiliated with nurturing others. Or maybe it's because the aging process has told me I need to stay out of such harsh lighting!

Seriously, I've had to come to a deeper place of self-acceptance which on many levels has been the most challenging for me. I live in Hollywood where all the (outwardly) beautiful people are, and I moved here in my forties. I have always been "a striking looker," and moving here has made me look even deeper than the shell—since the shell is wrinkling up as we speak. I am on many levels surrounded by a loving twelve-step community and loving friends. I have belief in myself as well in a power greater than myself. I am still alone—grateful, but alone. I have adopted two cats, and I am officially middle-aged. I never freakin' wanted to be middle-aged. Yet, it turns out that being middle-aged in Hollywood is not that bad. Sometimes it seems to be more peaceful, and I am humbled.

leaving los angeles

viet le

For Li-wen

> Where are you
> in the cities in which I love you,
> the cities daily risen to work and to money,
> to the magnificent miles and the gold coasts?
> —Li-Young Lee, *The City in Which I Love You*

I AM LEAVING LOS ANGELES for Saigon and Hanoi. On the eve of my departure, I am writing to remember. Loved ones I associate with L.A. have moved, one by one over the years, diminishing echoes in the hills of this city. Ariel suddenly left for Florida after the end of a relationship, another beginning. Driving at night by the Dodger Stadium sign on Sunset, I can smell her kitchen—empanadas, muffins, rice; its walls the tart color of the lemon cakes we'd bake. Now her one-bedroom apartment on a steep ravine is inhabited by strangers. They will never hear the poems we wrote and read to each other, our laughter echoing in the black-and-white checkered linoleum kitchen.

Let me begin again.

At fifteen, I was determined to be a hustler in Los Angeles. Or at least meet them. Skipping class, I took the closest bus from Villa Park High School in Orange County to downtown Los Angeles. Strip malls and suburban homes blurred and swerved; the freeway journey a gray memory of exhaust and cumulus clouds. Waste and want. Escape was an hour away.

Using John Rechy's *City of Night* as a guide, I followed the echoes of his footsteps: Pershing Square, Griffith Park, West Hollywood, endless boulevards. *Where are you?* I didn't realize the Los Angeles of the seventies and its geographies of desire had shifted. In Pershing Square at noon, there was none of the bustling activity I'd read about. I walked the perimeters, mainly empty—a homeless person warming himself in the sun, a commuter scurrying to catch the next train. I stayed for an hour or two, then moved on past City Hall, the parade of postmodern edifices. Sunshine and noir. Now I realize I was looking for community, communion, distraction, refuge. I was lost.

I would often skip class and go to South Coast Plaza, Westminster Mall—spend part of the day cruising. In bathrooms, I learned the choreography of lust. Strangers at urinals, half-erect. The foot tap in the next stall, hushed breathing, smell of chlorine, touch of skin. Hand scrawls on the wall, different scripts: J/O AT NOON. 3869870. HERE MW 3-4P. MACY'S SECOND FLOOR. YOUNG AND HUNG 3698796. FRIDAY AFTERNOONS. TIME/DATE? The familiar choreography reenacted in other malls, beaches, campuses. Mid-mornings turn into afternoons.

Crowded in a bathroom stall with a stranger, faucets dripping, our ears trained for incoming footsteps echoing down the hall, opening doors. The urgency of fear and desire: shirts slid up, bare torso brushing torso, hand on cock. We would never kiss.

Once, somewhere between Los Angeles and Orange County, I met a trick. Sweltering midday strip-mall parking lot, I stooped into his dilapidated two-seater:

"What's your name?" I ask as I buckle up.

Brian Foster: early thirties, vague Larry Bird resemblance.

"Fifty bucks OK?"

Upstairs in his bare flat—eyeing his limp-hanging vines, *I Love Lucy* video collection, oppressive floor-length curtains—I wondered if this was what Jeffrey Dahmer's apartment looked like. I felt for my Boy Scout pocketknife, insignificant in my tight black jeans. He filled up his bathtub with water. I told him I needed something to drink, asked him to stop by the nearby liquor store for condoms and vodka; I'd wait there. Hearing his car leave, I bolted out the door, the sunlight blinding me.

•

I AM WRITING TO REMEMBER. But I have already forgotten so much about the city in which I was born, Saigon, and the country memorialized in North American popular consciousness as a war, a wound, a mistake, a lesson to be learned. Waste and want, refuse and refuge, refusal and refugees. *Apocalypse Now*. But Saigon now is unrecognizable, a metropolis. I feel out of place, out of time yet at home there. In a way, it reminds me of Los Angeles but is nothing like it. Displacement. Saigon's constant high-rise construction—dreams of magnificent miles—willfully obliterates recent memories of halting poverty and dirt, powerlessness and desperation. What happened before, after, in between?

•

EVERY TIME I TRAVEL I try to find home, or to find a way to make myself feel at home, a way to locate myself between the coordinates of despair and desire. In cities in Canada, the United States,

Korea, Australia, France, and so on, always at the same places, I try to find myself, others like myself: gay bars, Chinatowns and Little Saigons, art institutions. I first developed this habit in Los Angeles, feeling simultaneously at home and out of place. *Where are you?* I wanted to feel at home with the community of artists there, on the sidewalks lit by the glow of gallery windows and cigarettes embers. Weekend after weekend. I sought refuge in the writing and performance workshops, the readings and rehearsals; under the strobe lights of "gameboi" at Rage or at Akbar, the heavy bass through my body; on the torn vinyl seats of the mom-and-pop restaurant, *phô* steaming up my glasses; in my car on the freeway, in limbo. And sometimes, before, after, in between, I was home.

Home is the first and last destination: departure and arrival—where one leaves from and comes back to. Los Angeles was home to my many first artistic attempts. The failure of art and language. My first performance workshop was with Denise Uyehara. I was a grad art student at UC–Irvine; she was a visiting artist. I associate her warm, freckled grin with Los Angeles, although she has since moved to dry, high Arizona. A certain cast of summer light reminds me of afternoons spent gesturing through light slivers in an oak-floored Venice Beach dance studio—ten performers holding hands, an undulating human ribbon, a silly and serious exercise. The echoes of tumbling bodies, voices in the rafters; the ocean breeze; the room aglow, golden.

One of my first gallery exhibitions was at *deep river* on the outskirts of Little Tokyo, near Al's Bar, a dank, dive bar with wall-to-wall graffiti, ageless patina of smoke and grime. Neither place exists anymore. The area was the heart of a jazz district in the twenties. Now the "arts district" is being redeveloped with high-end lofts. The musical screeches and thumping from Al's Bar combined with the din of chatter from the gallery on opening nights has been replaced by the clink of glasses and ambient music from the new brewery across the street. Walking through that area alone at night, I get disoriented amidst the construction, save for a few spots: here is the brick toy building, its battered chain-link fence; here is Bruce's old loft, with its faded Mondrianesque, primary-colored façade; here is the hunched street lamp near the vanished gallery casting abstract shadows on the yellow sidewalk.

•

IN HANOI, I often eat on the sidewalk, at makeshift street vendors where a bowl of steaming *phô* or *chao* could be had for fifty cents. One humid evening, after visiting a gallery in the crowded, narrow Old Quarter filled with tourist shops, it starts to pour. Hungry, I stop by a sidewalk vendor selling *com binh dan* ("peasant" food) and order rice, grilled fish, and smoked pork with cabbage. Sitting on a bright-red plastic chair eating my dinner, a skinny young male joins me—this table is one of the few dry ones. He looks about thirteen, and, judging from the grime on his clothes, face, hands, he is a manual worker. He eats only shrimp soup, about fifteen cents; my meal costs two dollars. He asks me about my life. I find out that he is twenty, has only finished fifth grade, and recently moved from a rural province to deliver coal door to door by bike in Hanoi. He wanted more freedom.

"I know every corner of this city," he beams. "I love walking aimlessly."

I think of my adolescence, scouring the streets of Los Angeles and Orange County, willfully lost. He seems lonely and is happy for the slow-paced conversation. And I am too. It seems like he wants to take a stroll after dinner.

"Are you a student? Where do you live?" he asks. Each question makes me realize the gaps that exist between our worlds and that I can't do anything about it. I do not tell him that I am a doctoral student doing research on art and that I am living in a hotel paid for by my language program. I just tell him that I am a student and the vicinity where I live. I offer to buy his dinner, which he politely declines. After we both finish, he waves goodbye, rides off into the dark drizzle. The vendor woman tells me that in the morning he lost all of the day's coal when his bike toppled over.

I don't want this story to be a tale of pity. I was ashamed that so many things came between me and the coal seller. Of course, in all of my other interactions in Viet Nam with vendors, artists, government officials, curators, other expats, my subject position is foregrounded, as perhaps it always is anywhere in the world. Depending on how I am read in Viet Nam—as an average local, Northerner/Saigonese, *Viet Kieu* (Vietnamese from abroad), academic, tourist, Chinese (I am a quarter Chinese), organizer, student—I get treated vastly differently. I often wonder, had my parents stayed in Viet Nam after the fall of Saigon, *who would I be?* As my parents were part of the old regime, I would not have access to higher education and would perhaps be carving out a living among the many street vendors I see in the city. Before my cousins left Viet Nam in the late eighties, they sold goods on the black market in open-air stalls. My mother and I left in dire conditions, not expecting to come back. But when I and other *Viet Kieu* return, the irony of the situation and the underlying resentment of the locals for the economic disparity between them and nonlocals hangs heavily, suffocating like the humid summer air.

Walking along Ho Hoan Kim, the central lake in Hanoi, I am cruised by some young male hustlers who target tourists and *Viet Kieu* like myself. I feign ignorance but know certain areas are notorious; the sex trade is rampant here. Who would I be? Vendor? Rent boy? House boy? Exploited laborer? Artist? Perhaps I would be lucky and part of the emergent middle class. Again and again I search for myself in the city. *Where are you?* In a way, I'm also searching for other spectral traces. Brothers, sisters, cousins. Viet Nam is still largely agrarian—80 percent is rural. Daily, thousands flock to the polluted cities in search of a life, dreams of modernity. Refuse and refuge. In Hanoi, luxury and poverty fester side by side, like the green mold growing on the ornate, mustard-yellow colonial-era buildings crumbling throughout the garden city.

> What makes Argia different from other cities is that it has earth instead of air. The streets are completely filled with dirt, clay packs the rooms to the ceiling, on every stair another stairway is set in negative, over the roofs of the houses hang layers of rocky terrain like skies with clouds. We do not know if the inhabitants can move about the city, widening the worm tunnels and the crevices where roots twist: the dampness destroys people's bodies, and they have scant strength; everyone is better off remaining still, prone; anyway, it is dark.
>
> From up here, nothing of Argia can be seen; some say "It's down below there," and we can only believe them. The place is deserted. At night, putting your ear to the ground, you can sometimes hear a door slam.
>
> Italo Calvino, *Invisible Cities*

Calvino's Argia reminds me of the infamous Cu' Chi Tunnels, near Saigon, a seventy-five mile labyrinth of tunnels that was used in guerilla warfare against U.S. soldiers during the Viet Nam War, or the American War, as it is referred to in Viet Nam. Today it is a tourist destination; vendors hawk reproduction Zippo lighters with slogans from the war: I KNOW I'M GOING TO HEAVEN BECAUSE I'VE ALREADY BEEN TO HELL: VIETNAM. Nostalgia and necrophilia.

The passage also reminds me of the processes of memory and forgetting, slow sedimentation. Memories are buried, memories are unearthed, exhumed. Archeological. I am ending with another beginning. A few weeks after I came back from my research trip to Viet Nam last summer, before going to sleep, out of the blue, I broke down crying desperately. I can't explain it. I couldn't pinpoint my sorrow, my sense of impotence, helplessness. My rage at being unable to effect change. Poverty and dirt. Corruption. Amnesia. Garden cities, sidewalk vendors, slums, constant construction, cities daily risen to work and money, invisible cities. Waste and want. There were so many profound interactions, fleeting images, intimacies I wanted to share and capture. I was too emotionally and psychically overwhelmed with things to process. Before, after, in between. But I felt utterly unable to. The failure of art and language.

Let me begin again.

Los Angeles.

I will return to this city of echoes.

Where are you in the city in which I love you? Waste and want, refuse and refuge, refusal and refugees. What has happened before, after, in between?

I am writing to remember. But I have already forgotten . . .

house on fire

mark thompson

THE SOFT THUDDING of bare feet on raw wooden floorboards was a comforting sound, like splashes in a puddle or steps at the front door when coming home late at night. Why I was there, I really didn't know. The place was a miserable maze of grimy corridors and head-banging overhangs. Grease on the walls was so thick that even the slightest brush left a queasy stain. It was not a nice place to go during one of the first nights I spent in Los Angeles. But who ever said comfort food was supposed to be all that good for you?

Gay bathhouses—and this was one of the Southland's most notorious—have always been instructional places for me. Being born in the repressed fifties meant little sex education. Coming out in the early seventies was announced with a big bang but with little finesse. Where else was a young gay man supposed to learn the finer points of loving other than in these lusty temples built from hormonal discharge and communal dispatch?

I had spent my early adulthood in San Francisco during the disco decade. What a rollicking place to be, and at just the right time. There was a bathhouse on every corner, or so it seemed, some as plain as the nose on your face, others as fancy as the imagination could let free. Decorated with Minoan friezes, jungle gyms as seen only on the best playgrounds, and even, in one case, a French chandelier, these queer-hallowed grounds served not only private but public needs.

Sure, they were meant for sex with a wink and a nod, yet their larger purpose was just as vital, if not always so recognized. It gave an entire generation barely out of the closet a place to see and be seen in a social sense; to share news and gossip, foment community spirit. Both kinds of nakedness were not only necessary but also liberating in many ways.

So here I was again, new boy in town, too lonely and dazed to actually want sex but needing connection beyond the usual voyeur-exhibitionist thrill games such hot spots provided. Besides, hell, there was a plague coming on! It was either this or another tedious night at the Hollywood Bowl. And truth be told, the parking was much less of a hassle here. Funny how that was my first important lesson about living in L.A.—where and how to park it.

My second important lesson, as depressingly deduced in those sleazy hallways, was that San Francisco is not Los Angeles. Not by a long shot. The region of my birth and upbringing was naturally beloved. I was now one sorry transplant, kicking and screaming all the way down, 385 miles down to be exact. It was impossible not to contrast and compare.

The latter city just had to lose. But as I fled away that night (more likely slid out on greased skids) little could I know that the one thing that had mysteriously eluded me in the North—true love—was waiting just around the corner in the South. Maybe this heated land of manufactured fantasies was not as fake as I projected it to be.

Not long after my desultory visit, the rattrap I'd visited was totally consumed in a raging fire. The bathhouse was on the second floor of a block-long building occupied below with modest businesses—taco joints, discount shoe stores, and the like. Located on the east end of Santa Monica Boulevard across the street from a dilapidated Sears, the structure immediately set off a dark, forbidding plume of smoke that could be seen for miles around. One grease fire supreme, marking an otherwise routine Saturday afternoon. Goodbye and good riddance to ManSpace. Word soon spread all over town that the blaze had been deliberately set for insurance reasons. A convenient endgame at the dawning of the Age of AIDS.

The incident was duly noted, but my attentions were already drawn elsewhere; from secular temples to Episcopal churches. My life partner-to-be was a priest in one, as fine and decent a man as I'd ever met. It was an improbable union in the eyes of most, given our differences in background and age. But the little voice inside that was always telling me to seek and find whatever was just around the corner had become a commanding boom to submit to the treasure at last.

My courtship with Malcolm was as proper and measured as to be found in any Jane Austen novel. She could not have dictated it better, for the relationship was meant to be. There was no headlong rush to love here. Instead, a tacit understanding that durability is built from a well-considered accretion of common knowing, trust, and belief in each other. I took him home for quiet walks on native beaches. Never had the Big Sur headlands appeared so romantic.

He took me to the Cock 'n' Bull, a legendary Hollywood hangout, among other touchstones of his youthful heyday. The faux-Tudor tavern invented the famous Moscow Mule cocktail in 1947 during the advent of the Red Scare. People ordered the drink joking that J. Edgar Hoover would now surely know they were Commies too. Given his penchant for the high life, the FBI chief was probably in the next booth knocking one down with boyfriend Clyde. Sincerity has never been a virtue of Hollywood's denizens. But apparently one person in town was—Mary Pick-ford. The silent screen star had been an intimate friend of Mal-colm's. I had seen many of her movies in film school. Well, it was something to start with. A slight but not inconsiderable building block in a life soon to be shared together, one where mutual posi-tive regard is the solid foundation.

Any problems were not so much with us but with the town we had decided to stay in. If anything, my ambivalence about Los Angeles was growing as fast as my affections for my future spouse. I wrestled mightily with staying here. To me, this was not the City of Angels, but rather of cheesy demons. I just couldn't shake the unrest. Oddly enough, it was the sight of another fire, a much greater one this time, that finally put things into perspective.

I'd arrived in Los Angeles in the spring of 1984. Two years later, we went shopping for a home together and found one, a cozy Spanish-style nest in the hills of Silver Lake, a hilly bohemian en-clave in the historic heart of a city being rapidly gentrified. I im-mediately surrounded the place with thick shrubs and fencing, an intuitive move on my part to keep the perceived changes at bay. It remains to this day a magical island of calm in a neighborhood of rapid flux.

One night, however, that veil of protection proved as ephemeral as any studio set when the entire city itself seemed to be engulfed in flames. It was by now spring of 1992, and four white policemen had savagely beaten a black man whose only crime was speeding. A trial was called, the verdict for the cops was acquittal, and despite the best pleas for peace by the victim, Rod-ney King, the long-suffering underclass of a town mainly known for glitter threw the gauntlet down.

Goodbye to all of that: the glamour and fake poses, the ersatz pieties for social justice that had as much substantial reality as the tinseled fabrications this dream factory routinely churned out. For tonight, it was all burning. No more pretense shadows and light, just the bald naked truth at last set free in one terrible conflagration.

I drove through the curfew lines with a pass in hand to my place of work, an internationally known gay publishing firm whose headquarters were located on the tenth floor of an imposing high-rise on Hollywood Boulevard, just across the street from famed Grauman's Chinese Theater. Hardly anyone was there. Only the most skeletal of staff required to get out another edition of *The Advocate*, which was published like clockwork every two weeks. We completed the work but our hearts weren't in it. How could anyone not be distracted and dismayed by the raging spectacle unfolding at our feet?

From our black-granite tower perched on the slopes of the Hollywood Hills, we could see over the entire Los Angeles basin: from downtown to the east all the way westward to the Pacific Ocean and the long distance south to the harbor at San Pedro. A sweeping panorama encompassing hundreds of square miles. It was the end of the day, the vast horizon marked with dusty glints from a setting sun. But there were other illuminations casting rosy hues in the sky as well: fires, hundreds of them, dotting the landscape in every direction.

As we stood and watched with dumbfounded horror, we could see the fires spread as quickly as any runaway cancer. Angry protestors had overwhelmed the riot's epicenter, a South Central neighborhood ghetto, and were now fanning out across the city, throwing lit bottles of gasoline out of speeding cars into store windows all along the major streets. Within a mere five minutes, we counted dozens of new fires shoot up in steady order, eerie pinpricks of light against the darkening map of L.A.

It was time to go home now, as these lengthening arteries of smoke and flame were coming closer to us. I made it back to Silver

Lake just in time: a nearby Radio Shack was ablaze and live cinders and gray ash were falling into the yard. Our telephone rang. It was friends from Seattle checking in after seeing the grim scene on the 6 o'clock news. With garden hose in one hand and a mobile phone in the other, I stood outside watering down the yard while describing this curious rain. There was no trepidation or dread in the tone of my voice, a lack of affect they quickly commented on. I said I didn't know why, somehow the situation seemed almost normal in a land of roiling quakes and other big natural disasters. It was only then that I realized I'd at last made my peace with being an Angeleno.

The riots were over in a few days: fifty-two people dead and hundreds of millions of dollars in property damage. But the aftermath did not seem to linger long, as if the powerful Santa Ana winds that sweep down from the San Gabriel Mountains ringing the city had blown memory along with ash out to the sea.

There is little substantial architecture here. These dry, endless plains are filled instead with tract after tract of stucco huts. Whether modest or grandiose, they uniformly stand without any pretense of real presence. It all came upon the land so soon and can just as rapidly be taken away. Why think about tomorrow when all we've got is today and the weekend's box office grosses?

In retrospect, however, 1992 was a signal year in quite a different way. It marked the end of one gay generation, spiritually burnt out or physically dead from the previous decade's ravishment of AIDS, and the rise of a new young queer breed, more cautious and afraid. I was among the many of my era to have found that they now, too, carried the virus. This discovery and its consequences would bring my professional career to a halt within the next few years. The memorial services for friends and lovers came with such regularity that one almost ashamedly lost count.

By mid-decade, exciting breakthroughs in medical science began to offer some hopeful treatment options. Where before there had been nothing but a guarantee of death, now there was promise of life. The afflicted could at long last raise their heads out of deep trenches of depression and despair, look around, and take in fresh gulps of optimism. Maybe there was a tomorrow after all. It sounded so easy, but was it? On the surface the scenery seemed the same, but underneath, Los Angeles was poised on the brink of another cataclysmic upheaval.

Like most everyone here, the city's gay citizenry has little if no collective memory. Hard-won achievements for civil rights in the recent past are rarely perceived as the monumental benchmarks they were, but more as part of a routinely accepted entitlement package. National gay strategists have long acknowledged Los Angeles as the movement's ATM, endlessly producing a ready stream of cash. There's a lot of queer money in these glitzy hills, home to semicloseted movie moguls and other celebrity figures. A trigger of guilt, further tripped by the panic of AIDS, kept those big bucks coming in over the years.

But as the nineties came to a close and AIDS began to increasingly appear as yesterday's news and somebody else's problem, a new mindset started to take hold. The party was on again, only this swing around there was less reasoning for defiance, either childish or caustic, only the need for fun in the sun. No excuses now for germy backrooms and other dark subterfuges: we were out and about everywhere. Hey, even Ellen herself said she was a lesbian. Our will, our grace, had never shined so bright.

It was all good. The new century came and with it boom times—and not just for us. The city was growing upward and inward fast. New bones in the form of tall modern buildings and hundreds of thousands of fresh immigrants filled in the blank spots everywhere. The only thing that remained the same was finding a decent parking spot. Weedy old Red Car trolley tracks, long unused, were paved over in West Hollywood, and the place renowned for its slumming was now positively chic. And downtown L.A., a once-thriving province gone to seed, was being transformed almost overnight into a haven of urban living. All good, or so it looked.

Over two decades have passed since I made my reluctant entrance, not long in the life of a city with a timeline as brief as this one. Like a starlet with a single-track mind, Los Angeles has never come to know itself very well. It's a destination without a purpose. A nice place to be, convenient for making fame and fortune, but not necessarily a life with meaning. Everything is so available, yet unattached to rootedness or cause. Lucky me, to have found enduring love. But the constant din for it as expressed from every billboard, chat room, and newsprint rag is as restless a force as any violent wind.

I'll never forget the day Griffith Park exploded into flames. Over eight hundred acres of the nation's largest urban park burned out of control in the spring of 2007, the city's driest year on record. No rain for us, just more ash. The underbrush in the park hadn't been cleared in decades, so all that accumulated fuel ignited with a roar.

I ran down our front steps and up the street to the nearest intersection so I could have a clearer view of the five-story fireballs erupting from the neighboring ridgetops, less than a mile from our house. The shrill cacophony of sirens and helicopters overhead was deafening. Gusty Santa Ana's were really fanning the flames by late afternoon. I could feel the white heat on my face even standing many blocks away. It was a frightening sight to behold. For the first time since living here, I was truly scared.

I raced back home to once again shield against flying embers and acrid smoke, passing the big picture window of the gay gym across the street. I could see the fire reflected in the glass. But whether the people inside could see the advancing blaze—or even if it mattered if they could—was not evident in the attitude of anyone there.

How curious, yet comforting in its way. Ah, yes, comfort, such an easy commodity to come by in this town, or so it would appear.

Where once such a place would have been buried from view, here it was now open to the world, busy and crowded as ever with handsome men. Ogling one another, talking on their cell phones, all the while cycling on their exercise bikes. Furiously pumping, over and over. Going nowhere in the inferno's red glow.

head shots

patricia nell warren

IN 1982, when I first set foot on the streets of West Hollywood, it wasn't a city yet. Over the following years, as my own life wove deeper into WeHo, I would meet some amazing people. They became a gallery of living head shots, each with a richly detailed background of a growing *urbs* (as the ancient Romans called a city). From its beginnings, West Hollywood had the arts, media, and film industries densely imaged in its daily life. The people I met were images of that history.

That year, 1982, after twenty-five years in New York state, I moved to northern California. While still unpacking boxes, I got a phone call from independent film producer Jerry Wheeler. Jerry's story is one among many independents since the indie film movement surged in the late 1970s. He had just bought *The Front Runner* film rights from another indie producer, Howard Rosenman. He wanted me to come down to L.A. so he could tell me about his own plans for this controversial film, which previous owners of the rights had failed to make.

Jerry put me up at the Beverly Hills Hotel. For my spare time, he gave me instructions on how to get acquainted with a quaint nearby neighborhood he called "WeHo." He explained that this was an unincorporated part of L.A. County, outside the city limits of Los Angeles, where gay people had always hid their then-illegal activities from the prying eyes of LAPD. So I explored into West Hollywood . . . and there I had my own first brush with L.A. law. Accustomed to New York City permissiveness on jaywalking, I found myself being cited by a frowning cop when I crossed Santa Monica Boulevard in the wrong place.

Jerry loved the Sunset and Santa Monica strips, and we spent a couple of evenings there, cruising along in his car as he pointed out Whisky a Go-Go, Studio One, and other famous nightspots that I had heard about back East. I don't remember Jerry mentioning the rent-control uproars that, two years later, would rouse West Hollywoodians to incorporate into their own city.

Jerry wanted me to write the screenplay for *The Front Runner*, but I was consumed with a huge historical novel that Random House had contracted me to write. So Jerry hired other writers. As the eighties passed, his production struggled. No stars wanted to play the two gay male leads in my story. His casting director scoured WeHo and L.A. for young actors who might be more courageous.

By the late 1980s, Jerry himself was visibly struggling. In 1990, he died of AIDS.

•

LOS ANGELES MEDIA specialist Tyler St. Mark was another WeHo media habitué, whom I met through Harold Fairbanks, veteran WeHo reporter for *Update*. After West Hollywood launched itself into independent citydom in 1984, Tyler became the city's first media coordinator, as an associate of the city's PR firm, The Communication Works.

Naturally, a publicist's career abounds in stories. The year 1984 saw that historic flurry around removal of the FAGOTS STAY OUT sign at Barney's Beanery. As mayor-elect Valerie Terrigno tried to ceremoniously remove the sign herself, she stripped the vintage screws. So it was Tyler who actually wrenched the sign off the wall. He hurried it out through a crowd of hostile, glaring patrons to the press conference on the sidewalk.

That same year, Tyler became the first publicist to undertake a perilous task of AIDS education for a hostile American public. "The Works" was contracted by APLA in consortium with the GLCSC to create Los Angeles County's first AIDS-awareness campaign. Tyler's brainchild was the Mother Cares campaign, featuring actress Zelda Rubenstein as the gay community's non-judgmental "Mother." Barely four feet tall, Zelda had a non-threatening posture as well as a unique perspective on prejudice.

Tyler and Zelda toured many a West Hollywood bar and club. There, the diminutive actress forged boldly through the crowd wearing her calico apron and lovingly shaking her wooden cooking spoon at her "sons at risk." The idea was to dialogue with men in a warm and nonconfrontational manner. But it was hard work. The gay and bi male community was still hostile to any suggestion that its freewheeling sex life could put its members at risk.

"Don't forget your rubbers," Zelda would remind them earnestly, and "don't play with strangers."

•

IN 1991, with my historical novel *One Is the Sun* now published by Random House, I moved to the Los Angeles area and started writing *Harlan's Race*, a sequel to *The Front Runner*. This was how

I got to know Rosewood Avenue, that quaintest of WeHo streets. It became a character in that novel of mine, as well as in the next sequel, *Billy's Boy*.

"Rosewood Avenue is one of the best-kept secrets in Los Angeles," resident Philip Labhart told me. "We like to keep it that way."

Philip was a blithe and breezy Texan in his mid-thirties, a well-known producer of TV advertising who won every award in his specialty. His ads and infomercials got recognition because of his gift for telling powerful human stories in them. Now Philip wanted to produce two-hour stories—feature films. His Labhart Production Group operated out of a sound studio on Sunset Boulevard. He and his partner, Richard, lived in a little Spanish Revival house just west of Robertson, with a guesthouse in the back where they put me up for a while.

Philip would have loved to produce *The Front Runner*, but the film rights were still tied up in the Wheeler estate, so he settled for launching development of *One Is the Sun*. He had found the book at his favorite bookstore, Unicorn. Philip gave me an office at Labhart, and we had a lot of fun working on the project.

In April 1992, when the L.A. riots broke out, it was to Philip and Richard's house that his staff evacuated. The studio was in a stretch of Sunset targeted by looting. With the city under a dark pall of smoke and fires burning everywhere, we all lived through extreme anxiety wondering if the rioting would spread into West Hollywood.

This talented man's story came to a sudden end in 1993 when Philip died of AIDS-related lymphoma.

•

AIDS WAS PUTTING a tragic end to stories of other WeHo residents I got to know. Celebrated male model Gene Momberger had been one of the most beautiful *GQ* cover men of his generation. When I met him through Tyler, Gene was living alone in a tiny courtyard apartment off Poinsettia, now so thin that little was left but his amazing eyes. He was one of those in whom the fight for life prompted a huge growth of spiritual power. While Gene was still able to drive his baby-blue Cadillac convertible, he loved to take us down Sunset to his favorite café or club. From there he receded to a hospital bed, still fighting spiritually, and finally died in 1994 with a few of us around him.

Another casualty was Scott Forbes. I first met him on the evening that happened to be his last at Studio One.

The famed club had finally been sold, and Scott was alone in the echoing building, puttering around his office, packing up business records and mementos. We kicked back for a while with coffee, and he talked feelingly about the changes he'd seen. Scott was a walking library of stories about the disco era. We encouraged him to put them together in a book, with photos from his huge archive—a task that never got done. There was that now-familiar sadness around Scott, of an HIV-positive man whose friends and colleagues were mostly dead of AIDS.

Scott would soon join them, dying of complications of a post-operative infection.

•

AFTER JERRY WHEELER PASSED on in 1990, the people who had worked on his production arced back to their own careers. One was noted publicist Kim Garfield. She was typical of the charismatic women who seemed to abound in WeHo's arts world. Kim Garfield and I stayed in touch over the years, and she did some PR work for my own company later on. She was a joy to be around, with her big grin and Tallulah Bankhead voice. Kim's story, and her all-time love, was the theater. So she focused on publicity for productions all across the Southland—notably *Garbo* at WeHo's Court Theatre in 2003.

A typical American city has its stories of churches being established. For WeHo, "typical" meant the coming of the Metropolitan Community Church, and the MCC had the charismatic Rev. Nancy Wilson. Nancy's enthusiasm for LGBT people's right to a spiritual life was infectious. I was asked to speak at MCC, and remember a Sunday service where her congregation got so worked up with her preaching and the gospel singing that a *Los Angeles Times* reporter who attended with me forgot all about the need to maintain journalistic neutrality—he joined the dancing and clapping throng.

•

BY 1993, TYLER ST. MARK had become my own publicist, and we were hatching plans to retrieve *The Front Runner* film rights and start an independent publishing company, Wildcat Press. Through Tyler I met other West Hollywood figures, friends or clients of his.

Among them was veteran screen actor Robert Arthur, once a hot teen talent from the post-World War II era. By the 1960s, Bobby's movie career crashed because of alcoholism and closet angst, and he spent some time on skid row before joining AA and getting his life back. In the 1970s, after coming out, Bobby became a pioneering gay activist.

When I met him, Bobby held forth in a tiny downtown apartment in the Figueroa Arms, one of L.A.'s first condos. Tyler and I often went there to visit him amidst his clutter of movie mementos. Bobby was the first to fill me in on WeHo's past as a haven for Hollywood's under-the-counter sex life. He had partied with the best, and knew who had carried on with whom in which weekend bungalow—in many cases with himself—and he had a thousand and one stories. One of his best was about how Greta Garbo swept him off to keep her company during a secluded New Year's weekend at her courtyard apartment in Villa Celia. She was still living in WeHo during the 1940s, before moving into her famous end-of-life seclusion in New York City.

Today, Bobby lives in his home town in Washington state.

●

IN 1994, I found myself teaching school in West Hollywood. The city had always thought of itself as a haven for young people fleeing discrimination; now it was challenged to show concern for growing numbers of disenfranchised and homeless LGBT youth. An LAUSD drop-out program called EAGLES Center had located in a small building on the corner of Santa Monica and Hilldale. My visit to the school led the director to invite me to teach history and writing skills. With its shortage of certified teachers, LAUSD allowed volunteer teaching.

The forty-two students were age fourteen to twenty-two, mostly male, black and Latino. Many lived in homeless shelters. The stories they told, of what they'd been through, were heartbreaking. At the 1994 graduation ceremony in Plummer Park, six happy seniors in caps and gowns finally got their high school diplomas, thanks to this program.

Daily exposure to their issues was a searing experience. "Community support for our youth" still had a way to go to be real. Most WeHo restaurants and cafés didn't like to see the students showing up—they sat there too long and didn't spend enough money. One of the few places that kids were welcome was the now-vanished Six Gallery. When EAGLES produced its 1994 yearbook, the kids went out to sell ads in it—and found local businesses slamming the door in their faces. The yearbook had to be funded by donations.

More inspiring was the first gay and lesbian high school prom in LAUSD history, which EAGLES helped organize. It was held at the downtown Hilton that year. Filmmaker Charley Lang, who lived a few blocks from the school and was one of my fellow volunteers, produced and directed a wonderful documentary about the prom, called *Live to Tell*, released in 1995.

After teaching for a semester, I continued in LAUSD as a commissioner of education for several years.

•

ON THE OTHER SIDE of the age spectrum, searing problems also faced seniors in a city so historically biased towards youth and beauty.

This fact hit me in 1995 when I was helping a local PAC canvass in West Hollywood to help Jeff Horton get reelected to the L.A. Board of Education. As I later wrote in a magazine piece titled "Elephant Graveyards," I found myself face to face with some elderly citizens who were living isolated in crannies. On canes and walkers, they came haltingly to the doors of their tiny apartments to listen to my spiel for the candidate. From their comments, it was clear that they'd voted with their feet and left "community life" many years ago because they felt so ignored.

Morris Kight was one powerful senior resident I got to know who refused to be pushed into isolation. Stories about Morris tend to intersect with hundreds of other stories—for example, he and MCC sparked one of the first protests at Barney's Beanery. After I met Morris, I supported some of his activist crusades, and always looked forward to the colorful Thanksgiving dinner that he threw for friends at the Yukon. He cared intensely about the city, taking it on himself to tidy the garden at the Matthew Shepard Triangle. The magnolia tree planted there in Morris's memory is a fit symbol for a life story that goes on inspiring.

Another unstoppable senior is Rita Norton, whom I met during my 2007 campaign for West Hollywood city council. As one of the founders of The Friends of the West Hollywood Library over thirty years ago, and librarian at this institution for over twenty years, Rita has whole shelves full of stories about WeHo arts, culture, politics, and personalities. As a member of the West Hollywood Senior Advisory Board, Rita is also working hard on the unfinished story of what the city needs to do for elder residents. Rita loves to hold forth at her table in the Silver Spoon with daughter Marcy, another charismatic woman, who is a former U.S. prosecutor and chair of the Women's Advisory Board.

•

IF GARBO COULD STEP out of her own immortal head shot and come back, she would look around in vain for the quiet village-like haven that she enjoyed. Today, amid growing political controversy, WeHo's graceful period architecture is steadily being eroded by blocks of condos and businesses. The city is writing a new chapter in its own history as a progressive yet problematical urbs—with cutting-edge human rights policies in place, yet with some of the highest rents, nastiest parking problems, and most densely populated neighborhoods in the country.

It remains to be seen how West Hollywood will recolor its own head shot, its collective picture of thirty-seven thousand residents by day, eighty thousand by night, as the city moves deeper into the latest millennium.

art(i)choke

x. alexander

NOT LONG AGO, I possessed something valuable. Something men would go to great lengths to acquire. I was fresh, ripe, and untouched.

Everybody wanted a piece of me. And that's what I gave them . . .

1. CUT THE STEM

THE HEAT BEATS DOWN on a sunshine world. Palm trees line the streets, privilege and beauty abound . . . even the freeways are exhilarating in that unique metropolitan way. I've arrived in Los Angeles.

From the moment I step out of the car, the campus hums with nervous energy, the sound of a thousand lives changing all at the very same time. Wherever I go, my fellow freshmen smile and say hello, and when I respond, they don't gawk or ignore me. *They must think I'm normal*, I realize, and then: *Maybe I am*. I still wake up drenched in sweat some nights, recalling the excruciating years when I'd open my mouth and nothing but a strangled squeak emerged. It took two years to find a proper diagnosis. It was psychological—my voice *had* changed—my brain just didn't get puberty's memo. By that point, though, I'd already spent those crucial teen hell years with the freak stigma—"that boy who talks funny." I was afraid it would follow me here, too, but when I meet the guys in my dorm, my voice sounds just like theirs.

I am just like them.

Outside, the sun sinks beneath a promising horizon, casting a shadow I don't recognize. The shape before me is impossibly tall, not the profile of an inconspicuous boy from the Pacific Northwest, but of someone with greater things in store. I wave to prove the shape is mine—and when the shadow waves back, I'm overjoyed to make his acquaintance. Then I feel it: the weight of the future, in the distance but drawing nearer. If I wasn't before, I'm certain now: *this* is where it'll find me.

I can't let inexperience squelch this golden opportunity, so I make a pact with the powers that be: I will go places I'm afraid to go. I will tear down my defenses. I will stand and fight. I may be bruised and bloodied . . .

But I will never be beaten.

I will come out alive. I will speak and be heard. I will experience *everything*. From here on, my life is devoted to telling tales of my survival. I don't mind suffering, because one way or another, I always will. My only condition is that, when all's said and done, it makes for a damn good story.

After sixteen years in purgatory and another two in hell, I'm finally free to start over in this City of Angels. This world of possibility. I intend to make myself known here . . .

And this time, it'll be the real me.

(Production office. West Hollywood.)

I sit in front of his desk.

I have nothing to say.

I try to think of something.

"Are you OK?" he asks. Phones wail and printers murmur, but I don't speak. The ability momentarily escapes me, like some foreign practice I'm aware of but unaccustomed to. Better to do nothing than make the wrong move.

"You don't seem like yourself today," he adds. I detect rare traces of concern in his eyes; I see myself through them . . . the competent college graduate, fresh out of film school . . . smart, but too timid to make an impression . . . slight, uncertain, directionless. Just a lowly assistant.

How strange, that someone who barely knows me tells me I don't seem like myself. If he knew me, he'd realize that not seeming like myself is actually *a lot* like myself, especially in the office. Self-preservation was the first art I mastered, long before I dreamed of filmmaking. I learned to guard my words like precious cargo, carefully scrutinized before release, because back then each came at a price: that humiliating look one gets when he's not quite Normal. That's how I honed my powers of observation, the tools of my trade. When the outside world ignored me, I'd simply fold inward—my interior life subbing for the absence of the exterior. Now checking my personality at the door is part of my morning routine, because nobody wants to deal with *me*—I'm a human being with needs of my own. What they want is a do-it-right/get-it-done automaton, capable on the outside. Inside? Nothing.

But I'm not wired to excel in the fine art of fast platitudes. I choke—which happens often—and the awkward ambient sound I know so well blasts at full volume. If my life had a soundtrack, it would be this:

silence.

The truth is, I'm just bored. I live the same day over and over: calling the same people, leaving the same message. I resent wasting time that'd be better spent on creative endeavors, suppressing what I really feel because truth won't pay the bills. This may be a "stepping stone," but where is it taking me? The more I stumble down this trail, the more convinced I am that my path is unwinding elsewhere, without me.

So my response is this:

"No, this *isn't* me. I have more potential than you care to know. I'm not mindless or complacent, or even remotely happy. I would never subscribe to your condition of my own irrelevance, so you're lucky it isn't me you're dealing with. How could I possibly be myself amidst this futile flurry, in this system that's designed to grind the self right out of you?"

The words echo in my skull, pending brain's approval—and that's where they'll stay, unspoken. This machine is bigger than I am—I, the expendable cog—and it will churn on no matter how I feel. Speaking up would only reveal my childish refusal to accept that the real world's made of equal parts waste and disappointment.

So I shrug and say, "I'm fine." The boss seems satisfied. And it's back to business.

2. CLIP THE THORNS

BACK IN THE SUBURBS, I was that weird kid with black lines at the top and bottom of the TV screen, the first on the block with a DVD player. Here, film is everywhere. We play "the movie game" while our professor drones on about the zoetrope. Steven Spielberg comes to class one day. My screenwriting instructor accuses me of not paying attention, but when we turn in our scripts, I'm told mine is the best.

But I'm not content being just another film geek. The guys in my dorm play Stratego on weekends, spouting off rapid-fire Simpsons *quotes that must be funny in context. An hour passes during which I say nothing, so nobody notices when I bid my tacit adieu— inexplicably headed for fraternity row.*

I have no business here: Rush is a dog-'n'-pony show guys like me don't place in. I was too timid to even sign up! But walking this street of houses labeled in a foreign alphabet, my incapacitating fear of rejection is overpowered by a tourist's fascination: though the letters differ, each house is the same—hip-hop blasting from the balcony while guys in polos and flip-flops guzzle from red plastic cups. From out here, it's like some kind of paradise, an oasis of booze, babes, and brotherhood (all things I've never known). I curse the series of events that rendered me bland and bookish, a goody two-shoes by default (while the bad boy within itched for liberation). Yet I can't lower my guard without invitation. I walk up and down, drinking it in, hoping . . . but Rush Week's almost over, and with it, my chance at trading up for the paradigm of college living: joining the proud ranks of the male elite.

Then I pass the second to last house, and like the others, there's a polo-clad guy on the lawn, holding a red cup. The difference between him and everybody else is, he looks *at me and says, "Hey, man . . . you wanna come in for a beer?"*

I've never had a beer before, but I say "Sure" and follow him inside. By the end of the night, I'm pledging Kappa Sigma.

(Thai restaurant. Beverly Hills.)

I sit at the table.
I have nothing to say.
I try to think of something.
A bottle of Fiji rests between us, and even though I've out-grown my H2O elitism, it's a handy conversation piece. He works for Fiji corporate, so he tells me all the juicy inside info about the world's premier fresh water source, and I ask burning questions like, is it *really* from Fiji? I don't discuss my work, because that means whining or bragging. Unfortunately, I have little else to talk about, so when the conversational wells of Fiji run dry, it's

awkward. I get that "floating away" feeling again, where I wish someone would reach out and pull me back to earth—but he doesn't know how, and I can't tell him. I polish off the last of the bottle. We split the check.

Four days later, he returns my call. After a vaguely condescending preamble about how he doesn't want to be "that guy" who doesn't call back, he explains, "I find myself struggling to think of things to say to you." I know where this is headed.

I want to put up a fight, and say, "Fuck you! I'm actually a really interesting person!" That, in the past, I've been guilty of revealing *too* much, coming across as *too* interesting, and chasing people off *that* way. But it won't make a difference. His mind's made up—easier to nip it in the bud now than waste more time getting to know me.

So I respond contritely, "OK. Thanks for letting me know." And it's over. I've only known him for a few days, so I don't care that I'll never see him again, but losing yet another one is distressing (and my lack of surprise, even more so). I'm dying to drown my sorrows—but when I open the fridge, all I see is Sparklett's. How pedestrian.

An hour later, I'm at a lounge in Beverly Hills, trying to pinpoint the exact moment I lost my touch. I'm stunned by the answer to an increasingly relevant question: *Is this the best I can do?* The vodka summons an important conclusion. If I accept defeat this easily, he's right. I really am boring.

Unwilling to forfeit this round, I compose a text message to see if we can hang out again, as friends, and prove that I'm socially functional on *some* level:

"i'm not that quiet. it just takes time 2 get 2 know me."

Immediately I'm empowered—and, OK, tipsy—but nevertheless proud of my indomitable spirit, my readiness to put myself out there no matter how often I'm discarded. It's one of my best qualities—it's what makes me *me*—one of many reasons he'd be lucky to have me.

After a quick check for typos, I push "send" with a smile.

I never get a response.

3. BRING TO A BOIL

DAYS PASS IN A BLUR, all of them sunny. The best thing about moving to a place where no one knows you is that your history is whatever you want it to be. You're only a virgin if you say you are; otherwise, who's the wiser?

Still, I can't shake a bleary air of discontentment. Fraternity life is everything it should be, a haze of shameless strippers and marijuana-fueled road trips to Berkeley and Vegas. But I'm like a stowaway. These "brothers" didn't grow up with me; their acceptance was instantaneous (and unearned). One wrong move and they'll discover me—that freak from high school hidden in the back berth, hitching a ride to a better life. And I'll be cast out again. I miss the cinema floor's twenty-four-hour film competition thanks to Greek Hell Week, but I barely know the guys in my dorm anyway. If it's true that friends from film school are the people you work with later in life, I'm fucked.

Then in freshman writing class, I meet a girl named Jenny, and even though I hardly know her, I see myself marrying her someday. It's ridiculous. I don't plan to settle down until I'm a middle-aged, flourishing filmmaker with his star-fucking days in the past, but Jenny's sweet. It fits somehow. I walk her to lunch after class, but my tongue ties when we reach the cafeteria. Girls never like me like that, or if they do, I'm oblivious—I'm never called cool or sexy or anything better than "nice" and "smart." Someday there'll be a cute story about how we met freshman year and I knew instantly she was the one, but couldn't make my move 'til I had the fame and fortune to impress her. 'Til then, I wait.

In the meantime, some friends ask if I want to go to a rave called "California Love" on 4/20 . . . and if so, do I want some Ecstasy? I say, "Sure," figuring if I can't achieve happiness the natural way, buying some for twenty bucks isn't a half-bad deal. Then the night comes—I'm nervous because I don't know what this pill will do to me, but I pop it anyway. A half-hour later, life zooms by at twice its normal pace, and even though I know better, I am both alarmed and beguiled by the possibility that it'll never stop.

(Coffee shop. Los Feliz.)

I sit at my laptop.
I have nothing to say.
I try to think of something.
On weeknights the café overflows with fledgling writers competing for electrical outlets, camped out for hours, but on Fridays traffic moves quickly. Customers pop in for a preclub pick-me-up or a nightcap after dinner, and they're gone just as quickly.

Once upon a time, I'd be just stopping in, too, on my way somewhere better. These days, I'm more consumed by the pesky necessity of survival. Maybe I spent too much time in my head and didn't notice my alienation until too late; or, more likely, my isolation is innate. Either way, the primal force driving me now is desolation. Like drinking alone or excessive masturbation, writing has become an unhealthy fallback plan, a masochistic habit. A few friends have said they'll call if they go out, but I know better than to wait at home. My phone remains dark and silent.

My iBook, on the other hand, emits a misleadingly optimistic glow, ever hopeful that This Is It!—success, that elusive panacea. But I'm useless when my heart's not in it. When I look over what I've written, every line reads: Shouldn't you be having fun tonight? My work has followed suit with my personal life, poisoned by desperation.

I glance up for the millionth time. A trio of gossipy girls giggles in unison . . . a fortysomething duo canoodles on the sofa . . . only I am alone, except for the guy my age now retreating to a lonely corner with his cappuccino. When he looks my way, I realize I know him: he's a writer on a hit TV show, an acquaintance's acquaintance. We spoke only briefly, but I remember having a lot in common. He opens his PowerBook, fingers hovering the keys fitfully—but he, like me, seems distracted: constantly checking his cell, surveying our surroundings. I surmise we share something else: a mutual desire to be elsewhere, and the lingering if improbable hope that by the end of the night, we will be.

I smile, comforted by the affirmation: I got it right. Success *is* about sacrifice. He's alone, I'm alone . . . two well-liked guys who have *chosen* to spend this Friday night writing. Loneliness comes with the territory—but it couldn't hurt to say hello, right? Bond over our secret connection before returning to the dreaded grindstone? Now's my chance to salvage something from the evening.

I'm about to get up when his eyes catch someone else's: a blonde, all dolled up in her Friday best, breezing toward him. They kiss hello. She apologizes for the wait. He asks if they're on the List.

"Yeah, you ready?"

He packs up his laptop, takes a swig from the telltale "to go" cup (a detail I hadn't picked up on). Our eyes meet on his way to the door—then his glaze over me and move on, with no trace of recognition. Once again the only lone wolf, I stare after him long after he's gone. New patrons surround me, and like always, I notice something about each—what they drink, how they talk, who they're with. I watch everybody, but who's watching me? If I melted into the floor, they'd only wonder, "Who left their laptop here?"

A vibration against wood jolts me out of my self-pity. I snatch up my phone, now more than ever craving the sirens' call. YOUR VERIZON WIRELESS BILL IS READY! the incoming message informs me.

It's after eleven. No hope for rescue tonight. I tuck my phone away and turn back to the blank screen, doomed to another night in frantic pursuit of progression. I must look awfully committed . . .

But tonight, like many other nights, I'm here only because there's nowhere else I belong anymore.

4. BON APPETIT

TWO WEEKS LATER, I can still hear—*feel*—the music pulsing, vividly recall the sounds and colors of California Love. "You're so cute!" One friend's ecstatic proclamation reverberates through my mind like a mantra: words to live by. I'm still reeling from the comedown.

It can't be withdrawal, can it?—but rather, the fallout of everything else. As Finals Week rolls around, everybody's preoccupied with exams, studying—saying good-bye. That's why, when the prospect arises, it's easy to slink off to where the lights are down and the music's bumping. Even in a campus apartment, it's almost like being back in that Land of Shadows . . . where everyone's a silhouette.

As the party heats up, I get the sense I don't belong here. But I'm used to that by now. I get drunk. Things get louder. Then it's easy to feel warm and welcome. Nobody knows me, but everyone wants to. I'm sur-rounded—no, enveloped—by the crowd, eyes and hands all over. I've never been the center of attention; even I'm surprised how witty and en-gaging I can be when I know I have the floor. In fact, the only one not watching me is the one I came with. He doesn't know what to make of me . . . because I don't know what to make of myself.

He asked me to dance at the rave. I wouldn't. He touched me, but I pulled away. Even with sight and sound assaulting me in disorienting hyperspeed, I held distressingly tight to self-control, and not because I was afraid or ashamed or even confused. I swallowed that pill fully pre-pared for ecstasy, eager to indulge whims and abandon inhibitions—and discover who I was without them. But to my surprise, I was the same person. I longed for nothing in that kaleidoscopic wonderland, but some-thing just out of reach, as always. With my friends off god knows where, I was alone in fluorescent darkness, my pulse pumping twice as fast (or was my mind the only thing racing?) "I think my heart's gonna ex-plode," I told him, without a clue how right I was. He stayed with me all night, though I couldn't figure out why.

But something in me needs to know.

The crowd thins. The music changes. Finally, I catch his eye, he smiles . . . and it's time to make a choice. In just a few days, I must give up my paradise for the summer and return to a frayed family, forgotten friends, and the outdated freak version of me I left home to escape from. I'm a film student and frat boy now, I've lived so much more this year than I ever did in the eighteen prior, but have I really become anything, or is it all tentative? My brave new world is being erased all around me. Soon I'll wake up in my old bed and it'll be like this was only a perfect dream. Like it never happened. I panic, desperate to cling onto anything that will make me not me anymore, so I don't have to go back as the same boy, empty-handed.

"I'm so drunk," I tell him, and he says, "You're welcome to stay if you want . . ."

So I choose—not that it's much of a decision. For years, I watched everybody else live and imagined a day when I would too, and then I moved to L.A. and it happened. It happened because I made it happen, by exposing myself to the whole damn city. I want to belong here and I want to belong everywhere else—that's why I never belong anywhere. No matter what I do, half of me is screaming. So why not dive right in?

Do I know I'm changing my life forever? Yes. Do I realize that, if this is a mistake, I may never turn back? Absolutely. But that's the beauty of it. With every new experience comes a high unlike any other, as innocuous outer layers are plucked away to make room for a fresh imprint—and the revelation of what's underneath. It's shattering; it's intoxicating; it's a godsend; it's hellfire. Only this time I'm not shedding them; they're being stripped off me one by one because *they* want a piece. I am finally wanted. Already I'm addicted to the feel of the unpeel, determined to replicate this mix of agony and rapture at any cost. The rush of being cracked wide open.

This is why I'm here. To show what my insides look like.

A gaping black hole looms ahead, but now I have something to look forward to. I may be leaving, but I'll be back. And when I am, I'll finally do, see, have, and be everything I wanted.

(College campus. Los Angeles.)

    I gave what I had to give.

    The rest has been stripped away.

    Technically, I got what I came for: there's no part of me that resembles what once was. Even my core, the only constant, has turned inside out on me. All the world sees now is the solitary dreamer within, once hidden by thorny outer layers—the disparate facets of my persona that used to keep 'em guessing who I was *deep down*. Now they know: just this. A struggling artist too eager to throw himself to the wolves for the sake of a good story . . . who limped off to die once mauled. No one's very interested in tales of my survival. Funny, I used to think my art would be the instrument that allowed me to speak to the world; instead, it sucked me out of it.

    The last evening classes let out as I arrive. Students whiz past on bikes and skateboards. With my messenger bag slung over my shoulder, I could almost be one of them—a freshman on his way back to the dorms after a night lecture on postmodern cinema—except I'm not wearing sandals or a college sweatshirt. I look more accomplished somehow, like I've discovered my place in the world. And maybe I have, but it's not the one I asked for.

    I get coffee and open my laptop, but my twelve-hour workday has drained me. No writing tonight. A voice in the darkness beckons, so I wander, and as I walk, slip into a trance. I still know this place better than any other; it's the only place that's ever been home to me. My other life—the dead-end jobs, scores of would-be romances, a writer's frustration—melts away like a bad dream from a stranger's life. I'm back here, where the future's brighter, reliving my glory days. There's almost no chance I'll run into anybody who knows I'm not supposed to be here; I don't get a second look from anyone.

My destination remains unknown 'til I'm already there—the spot I went to disappear on rough nights. I could cry here—and often did—and nobody ever found me. The tears fall before I remember why I've come.

I don't know anything anymore. I reached the pinnacle of my potential. I lived an amazing life. But it ended as soon as I left this place. I don't understand how everyone just deals and moves on when life out there is so harsh and senseless. I'm twenty-four, and already I've figured out that aging is just one prolonged disappearing act . . . the excitement of young love, the daring to face new adversaries, the hope that we'll transcend our crippling limitations . . . all the best things fade away. They're already all but gone. Six years later, I'm right back where I started: a ghost, ethereal and overlooked. Damned by silence.

I'll always love this city for what it gave me, but I can't ever forgive it for snatching it back so quickly. There are pieces of me scattered throughout Los Angeles; some belong to people who've forgotten they have them. But if I close my eyes, I can still remember what it was like to stand here for the very first time, with so much to offer . . .

There's a hum on the horizon. My entire life is out there, unknown. A weight pushes toward me, into me, through me . . . drawing me forward. I'm whole again; I feel just the very beginnings of being pulled apart. There's so much I want to do, and everyone knows it. They're grabbing at me from all sides—I can barely keep up with the rate at which they try to devour me. But I'm not concerned.

The world and I have a deal. If I live up to my potential, this city will keep its promise, too—and I will always live a life that is mine, full of passion and adventure and danger. I don't ever want to leave this place.

But I don't have a choice.

I dry my tears and look around, reluctantly dragging myself back to reality. My surroundings are silent and motionless, but I notice with a stab of panic that someone has spotted me—a boy's figure splayed out in the grass.

He's looking *right at me*. For once, *I'm* being watched.

Moments pass. He doesn't move. I squint in the dark.

His eyes are glassy, unblinking: *he's a sculpture*. A damn creepy one, at that. There's an open book in front of him, his shoes are kicked off carelessly. The expression on his face implies that he's about to just about to cross that line between innocence and experience. On a bright afternoon, he must look right at home, but at midnight there's something profoundly sad about his presence, still lying in the grass with his nose in a book long after everyone else has gone home.

He'll be here forever, won't he? Other students move around him, passing him in the exact same spot day in and day out as they carry on with their lives; they'll graduate and get married and find places in the world, but he'll always be right here in front of the cinema school . . . not knowing what it's like to look back instead of forward . . . never knowing that the bitter flavors of disenchantment and failure await the moment he leaves.

He's frozen—in what looks like the best moment he'll ever have.

Lucky bastard.

•

ARTICHOKE [AHR-TI-CHOHK]: A vegetable comprised of tasty buds that are peeled away to reveal the inedible center ("choke") and edible base ("heart"). If undisturbed by man, the artichoke will blossom into a vivid violet-blue flower.

Nearly all artichokes cultivated for commercial purposes grow in California.

a west hollywood fairy tale

ty lieberman

MANY FACTORS INFLUENCE a good night in West Hollywood: whom you go out with, whom you go home with, and whether your liver functions correctly in between. But the overture for the evening always takes place alone, in your car, searching valiantly for the only thing scarcer in WeHo than a working actor: a free parking space.

My deepest, darkest dream is to create the seminal *Parking Guide to Los Angeles*, an A to Z tome of every free, restricted, pay, and illegal-but-no-one's-really-watching parking spot in the metro L.A. area. I think I'm sitting on a goldmine. Perhaps I'll start an online service—for $9.99 a month, you're always in the know with real-time parking updates. If people are willing to shell out fifteen dollars to valet their Volvo every night, I bet they'd pay ten dollars for my little service.

But I'm not going to write that book. At least not yet. Remarkably, I've found some measure of success doing what I moved to
Hollywood to do: writing films. My first feature, *Kiss the Bride*,
came out early 2008. My advice to any young writer is as follows:
keep writing scripts, and then find people who happen to want to
make the exact film that you wrote. I know, I know, that's not very
practical advice—but this a fairy tale, so practicality goes right out
the window.

Assuming, of course, you can find that parking space.

•

I ARRIVED on the West Coast in September, 2004. I stood a few
hours in the Aspiring Screenwriter line, they studied my astrolog-
ical charts, took my head shot, forced me to drink soy, and I was
initiated. I was home.

The first month I was here, parking was never a problem. I
stayed out in Glendora, living with my uncle, aunt, and three-
year-old cousin. My first week here, the family makes sure to take
me to all the key touristy areas—Hollywood Boulevard, Santa
Monica pier, In-n-Out, and of course, Disneyland. But while we
innocently drive down Santa Monica Boulevard for the first time,
I entered the *real* magic kingdom: West Hollywood. One hundred
hot, tan, shirtless guys . . . and the ten thousand others who lust
after them. Rainbow flags hanging from every light post: my little
cousin had never heard the word "rainbow" before, so I made her
memorize all the colors (and still quiz her on them every time I
see her. One day, she'll understand).

Contrary to popular belief, they are *not* handing out jobs underneath the Hollywood sign, so I started temping at various entertainment and nonentertainment jobs. The longest-tenured job
I had was at Creative Artists Agency—I temped in the mailroom
for six whole weeks. My duties consisted of opening fan letters,
(looking for money, and then throwing away the rest), alphabetiz-

ing incoming mail, and organizing Julia Roberts's baby gifts. It was a fun experience, but it didn't really open any doors for me. The next job I had was temping at a mental hospital in the Valley—apparently six weeks at CAA were all the qualifications I needed. Six months after that, I was off selling magazines outside of Glendale. I didn't *exactly* have my pulse on the entertainment industry, but there was one thing I never stopped doing . . .

Writing. I don't consider myself a particularly great writer (which you're probably discovering as you read along), but if you churn out five hundred pages of *anything*, you're bound to wind up with twenty or thirty good ones. Put twenty to thirty good pages in a hundred-page script, and you're not doing too poorly. Besides, no one really fails in Hollywood—they just give up too soon. So I kept writing. I should have been generating new material, and new ideas, but I kept getting drawn back to a story I started as a student . . .

While in college, I was invited to the wedding of someone I had . . . well, we had . . . let's just say, it was a bit of *surprise* to hear about his pending nuptials. To a woman. Not a Santa Monica-and-Highland kinda girl either—this was the real thing. My initial thought for a wedding gift was an electric razor—I was gonna attach a little note that said, "lose the beard." I thought that little joke might fly over his head, not to mention it's never wise to provide potential closet cases with sharp objects. Instead, I splurged on a gift card to Blockbuster. On the envelope, I wrote something to the effect of, "I'm moving to Hollywood this fall, maybe you can rent one of my movies one day." That night I went home, downed a couple ~~shots~~ bottles of vodka, and started jotting down notes for a new screenplay . . .

It was always called *Kiss the Bride*. From the first draft I wrote the summer before I moved out West, there were maybe two scenes and ten lines of dialogue that made it through the entire process, but the title never changed. I was very confident in the script, sending it to as many people as I could sucker into reading it. And there were two basic schools of thought on the material:

a. No thank you;

b. We like the script, too bad it's about gays. What else do you have?

Anytime I got "b," I would hurriedly send off one of my other scripts. These other scripts were treated to only one school of thought:

a. No thank you.

I've been out here six months. Some of my friends are heading home already. And though my background-acting career is just taking off (*Charmed* and *The O.C.* in the same week? Sweet!), I was less than satisfied with my writing career. So I did what any red-blooded American gay does when looking for a quick fix—whored myself out online. I looked at every contest, workshop, and seminar Google could throw at me—but it wasn't until I searched for "gay screenwriting" I found what I sought.

Outfest. The oldest and largest LGBTQ film festival in the country. At this point, I really didn't know what made something a "gay film" (actually, I'm still not 100 percent sure). All I know is we didn't really have much of a queer cinema selection in my hometown of three thousand people—in fact, the "gay district" was pretty much confined to the perimeter of my bedroom. I went to college in Ann Arbor, and there it was a little better—one through-and-through gay bar, one club that turned gay two nights a week, and of course, one of the largest fraternity systems in America.

But still, not a lot of queer *films. Whatever,* I thought. *I've got one gay character, a gayish theme—that should qualify.* I submitted the first ten pages to this festival, then they asked to read the entire script, and by that summer I got my first-ever response "c":

c. Congratulations, and welcome to the Outfest Screenwriting Lab.

The Outfest Screenwriting Lab is an offshoot of the festival itself—five mentors, five writers, five screenplays, and three days at the luxurious Chateau Marmont. The purpose of the lab is to workshop LGBTQ-themed screenplays—nurture them as if they were our own children, and then beat them mercilessly into the ground as if they were stepchildren. As of 2005, there were zero films that had made it through the lab and into production. I announced my intentions to change that. The Lab was a fantastic experience—not just for learning craft and the amazing feedback, but for bonding with *actual* writers. I met some truly great people in the Lab, including the fabulous Pat Reznick (who later introduced me to my agent) and *Latter Days* director C. Jay Cox.

They gave me a coveted all-access festival pass, allowing me to attend swanky Hollywood Hills pool parties, pre- and post-screening receptions at theaters around town, and a free, unending supply of Absolut vodka and Tylenol PM. I spent the entire two-week festival making contacts and working whatever room I stumbled into. It almost made the scabies worth it. In all, I garnered a list of two-dozen people eager to read the new draft. For a month solid, I carefully rewrote, retooled, and realigned *Kiss the Bride*, pouring my blood, sweat, and other bodily fluids into its pages. I finished it August 19, the day of my twenty-third birthday, and grandly sent it via e-mail to all the people whom I was convinced were salivating over the chance to read the next Ty Lieberman magnum opus.

The response was overwhelming:

No thank you.

•

APPARENTLY, it's possible to sell magazines fifty hours a week, cater sixteen hours a week, and still find time to keep churning out screenplays. I know because for about four months, this was my life. The current incarnation of myself, which sleeps until ~~ten noon~~ whenever-my-trick-kicks-me-out-of-bed cannot believe I used to have that schedule, but you do what you must when desperate. And believing the only two-dozen people who would ever want to adopt my child, in fact, *don't*—yeah, you start picking up extra catering shifts to ease the pain.

Flash forward to Christmas 2005. It's the last Friday before the holiday, and I'm venturing out in West Hollywood. The parking hunt is on . . . *sigh, the Pacific Design Center meters are full. Let's try Melrose . . . Damn . . . Come on, Doheny, you owe me . . . hell yeah! Doheny meters, I love you* . . . I was heading to The Abbey, which is my favorite place in all of West Hollywood, but also a bit of a vortex. No matter where I begin, somehow I always seem to get sucked into The Abbey by the end of the evening.

I was only there because of my friend Karen. She was in town from New York just for the evening and didn't fly across country just to sit in my Valley apartment all night. Based on my three seconds of screen time in *The O.C.*, Karen was convinced I was a big-time celebrity. I told her the odds *anyone* at the bar would recognize me were slim to none, and Slim just closed out his tab. Three steps into The Abbey, and I hear my name being shouted. A gracious gentleman remembered my face from Outfest and wanted to know whatever happened to that wedding script that I had. Now if I had written down twenty-four names during the festival, then this guy must have been number twenty-five. How could he not have been on the list? Smelling blood, I excitedly rattled off all the changes I'd made to the script, and he volunteered to read it over the holidays. This is how I met Bob Schuck, producer of *Kiss the Bride*.

Two weeks later, Bob calls me and says he loves the script and wants to send it to his friend C. Jay Cox. I think, *Hey! I know that guy!*—Hollywood is the biggest small town on Earth, and West Hollywood's even more so. C. Jay reread the script and saw the potential: limited scene locations, "talky" exchanges, serious gay themes . . . all the things that were "wrong" with the film suddenly became why it was selling. Funny how that works out. Two months, four meetings, and multiple cocktails later, I optioned the script to the production company founded by Bob, C. Jay, and their partner Richard Santilena. It was their first film venture, and so when they opened up their production account they called it KisstheBride, LLC. This led to much amusement for me, as I got to cash a series of checks literally underwritten by the title of the film.

•

I'M BACK IN BUSINESS. I estimate the odds of the film actually getting made at about 25 percent. Judging by the reactions of others, I am grandly overestimating those chances. Because films *don't just get made in Hollywood,* especially from first-time writers who can get by shaving once a month. The only thing I had in my corner were three producers who truly believed in the material—and by extension, yours truly. All we needed was the money . . .

Ah, the money. The reason nine billion unproduced screenplays are floating around Hollywood has nothing to do with attaching stars, fixing structural problems, or punching up dialogue. Give me fifty million dollars, and I think I can find a way to make your film. All we were asking for was five hundred thousand. The next six months basically consisted of five rotating events:

I would rewrite pages;

I would be "encouraged" to rewrite the pages again;

We would be very close to getting the money we needed;

We would not get any of the money we needed;

I would cry into my margarita at Fiesta Cantina.

The words "delay" and "dilemma" also surfaced a few more times than I would have hoped. Outfest 2006 came and went—I didn't have my all-access pass anymore. When I covered up the year on the badge, I could still sneak into a few events here and there, but it wasn't the same.

Then came that fateful September day. Driving home from my magazine enterprise, I got the phone call I'll never forget: "How do you feel about Tori Spelling as the bride?"

The answer was: Amazing! First, I knew she would nail the role. Second, with Tori on board, I was utterly certain there *would* be a role to nail. As much as I'd like to think people want to invest in a "Ty Lieberman script," attaching Tori to the film made it a more popular investment. We were ready to roll.

Well, almost. I had some unfinished business to take care of first. My magazine job, I was actually sad to leave. The people were nice, the donuts were free, and I could sneak away to work on my script during down time. My catering gig—not so much. I'd been catering for five years, including sixteen months in L.A. Outside the venue, they kept a bonfire in the parking lot, to keep the valets warm and supposedly add to the "rustic hunting lodge" motif. As a final gesture to years of catering disservice, I triumphantly announced my retirement, promptly took off my vest, and heaved it into the fire. I was expecting wrath, but my boss merely said, "Man, I've always wanted to do that." I threw in my work shirt just for good measure, and walked off into the night, shirtless, having shed the skin of my past food service imprisonment.

We started filming October 30, 2006. The second day of shooting, I scraped the entire left side of my car trying to squeeze into a "parking spot" near the set. I didn't care—I had a film to make! Or *watch* getting made. Basically, my on-set duties involved guarding the craft services, taste-testing the craft services, blocking traffic, rolling fake joints, and walking Joanna Cassidy's dog. I never did any more rewrites, but since C. Jay Cox is genuinely a sweetheart, he'd let me sit in the director's chair by the monitor, and I would mouth "action" as if I was directing the film. Yes, I felt like a ten-year-old in a candy store. Or a Catholic priest in a store of ten-year-olds.

During the last week of shooting, the behind-the-scenes cameras were on set filming vignettes for the DVD. One of the producers said (*on camera*) this film had "the power to change lives." I filled with pride: here was little old me, from a tiny hamlet in northern Michigan, storming into Los Angeles, and writing a magnificent screenplay that now had "the power to change lives."

That night, we were up until sunrise, filming a scene in a strip club where the characters fondled and disparaged women, swore incessantly, smoked weed, and derogatorily used the words *fag* and *retarded* multiple times. I guess if you think about it, an earthquake has "the power to change lives" too.

Kiss the Bride was the closing-night film at the Outfest Film Festival in 2007. It was indeed the first film from the Screenwriting Lab to be completed, and I hope the first of many from the Lab. At the last minute, I was asked to stand in front of the sold-out crowd at the Orpheum Theatre—eighteen hundred people. Forgoing the chance to say something poignant, I pretended to read scenes that were cut from the film, which generated a lot of laughs. I immediately shot myself in the foot by joking that I was actually younger than the festival itself (by six weeks). The queens were not amused. It's just not right for writers to be in front of microphones—we're not used to any kind of spotlight. We belong behind our keyboards, mumbling into our cereal and checking out our StarMeters on IMDB. I'm also still floored that *The Advocate* wanted to do an article about me. How many writers get phone calls that begin, "Here are the details of your photo shoot"?

I'm lucky. I'm very lucky. I've been told more than a few times *this isn't just supposed to happen*. When you look at the big picture, Hollywood breeds failure. Taking all my scripts into account, I've heard almost four hundred no's from people. If I'm lucky, I hope to get to four thousand by the end of the decade.

But it only takes one "yes."

It only takes one parking space.

And fairy tale endings can come true.

about the editors

chris freeman and james j. berg are editors of *The Isher-wood Century*, which won the Lambda Literary Award for Gay Studies, and *Conversations with Christopher Isherwood*.

Freeman gave up tenure at St. John's University in Minnesota because he was in love with Los Angeles. Since relocating, he has edited John Carlyle's *Under the Rainbow: An Intimate Memoir of Judy Garland, Rock Hudson, & My Life in Old Hollywood*, has written for *Variety*, *GLR*, and *The Advocate*, and has taught at the University of Southern California. He lives in West Hollywood, at last.

Berg has worked at colleges in Maine and Minnesota. He is the editor of *Isherwood on Writing: Christopher Isherwood's Lectures in California*. He is the former senior editor of *The Evergreen Chronicles*, a journal of GLBT literature. Berg is dean of social sciences and arts at College of the Desert, in Palm Desert, California. He lives in Palm Springs.

about the contributors

East L.A. native **pat alderete** writes about varrio life, rendering the complex inner worlds and strict social hierarchies of a community too seldom observed in literature. Her short stories are published in *Joteria* and *PEN Center Journal* and have been anthologized in *Hers 2* and *3*; *Los Angeles Gay and Lesbian Latino Arts Anthology 1988–2000*; and *A Geography of Rage*. She has written two one-act plays, *Ghost and the Spirit* and *Love and Fire*. Her one-woman performance, *Tina Gets Married*, was produced in 1999. Alderete is at work on a book of short fiction about Chicana/o life in East L.A.

x. alexander graduated from the University of Southern California in 2005 with a BFA in screenwriting. He has known he wanted to be a filmmaker ever since he was banned from games of make-believe for telling the other kids where to stand and what to say. After writing a film column for *INsite Boston* magazine for two years, he is sporadically engaged in rewriting other people's screenplays and developing his own material. He is unemployed, single, and writing in coffee shops. He's never actually eaten an artichoke.

terry l. allison (PhD, UCSD) is dean of arts and letters at California State University Los Angeles. He loves to write mostly unpublished editorials on the sad state of political sense in the United States but did manage to publish an anthology, *States of Rage*, with Renée Curry. He is working with Caroline Symons on a history of the Pink Flamingo Relay and still mourns his lost connection to the rhythm and flow of aquatic sport.

Author of *Branded T*, **rosalyne blumenstein** is a licensed clinical social worker in the state of California and an LMSW in the state of New York, specializing in addiction and recovery issues, using harm reduction as well as abstinence-based models. Rosalyne has worked on trauma-related issues; PTSD; core identity exploration; LGBT issues; death, dying, and bereavement; serving the HIV/AIDS population; sex and body workers; and cultural sensitivity. Rosalyne can be contacted at Rosalyneb@sbc-global.net.

The Reverend **malcolm boyd** is author of twenty-nine books (including the gay classic *Take Off the Masks* and the international bestseller *Are You Running with Me, Jesus?*) and editor of five others. He is an Episcopal priest and poet/writer-in-residence at Los Angeles' Cathedral Center of St. Paul. A civil rights, peace, and gay activist, he served three terms as president of PEN Center USA West.

sean church is the pseudonym of a somewhat well-respected figure in the Hollywood motion picture studio community. He feels the use of his real name in telling this particular story would likely shock the still homophobic powers-that-be in the studio world. "Despite some stories that you might hear in the media," says Mr. Church, "homophobia is still a major problem in this town." Mr. Church is considering moving back to New York, but in case he has to continue to live and work in Hollywood, he feels the need to remain an anonymous chronicler of his bathhouse days.

jeanne cordova is the former publisher and founder of *The Lesbian Tide*, the gay and lesbian telephone book of Southern California, the *Community Yellow Pages*, and the queer magazine the *Square Peg*. Cordova has lived in Los Angeles since orange groves covered the Valley. Her work has been published in *Lesbian Nuns: Breaking the Silence*, *Persistent Desire: A Butch-Femme Reader*, and elsewhere. She's working on a second memoir, *When We Were Outlaws: Love & Revolution in the 1970s*, which should be in bookstores in 2009.

teresa decrescenzo is the founding executive director of GLASS, the Gay and Lesbian Adolescent Social Services, the oldest, largest organization in the country providing services to minor GLBTQ youth and their families. She is also the only woman ever to serve as president of the Los Angeles Gay and Lesbian Center's board of directors. In addition to her work at GLASS, Terry is an adjunct faculty at Cal State Northridge, where she teaches social policy, social work practice, and the sociology of the LGBT community. She lives in Studio City with two perfectly horrid little Yorkies.

ghalib shiraz dhalla is the author of the critically acclaimed *Ode to Lata*, the first gay South Asian novel to be excerpted by *Genre* magazine and to be featured in the *Los Angeles Times*. Dhalla scripted and associate-produced the film adaptation (*The Ode*). A passionate activist, he cofounded the South Asian program at the

Asian Pacific AIDS Intervention Team and is one of the founding members of Satrang, a support group for questioning/out South Asians. His second novel, *The Two Krishnas*, is forthcoming. His Web site is www.GhalibDhalla.com.

dalton fronterhouse is an eighteen-year-old queer white male—and proud of it! He is currently transitioning out of the foster care system into his own apartment. His latest work was performed at Plummer Park, in a spoken word performance, under the directorship of Ms. Joyce Lee.

greta gaard's publications include *Ecofeminism: Women, Animals, Nature* (1993); *Ecological Politics* (1998); *Ecofeminist Literary Criticism* (1998); and a volume of environmental creative nonfiction, *The Nature of Home: Taking Root in a Place* (2007). Currently at work on a murder mystery, she teaches environmental literature and writing at the University of Wisconsin, River Falls.

eric gutierrez has written cultural criticism for the *Los Angeles Times*, *Newsday*, *Latina*, *Tu Ciudad*, and *The Advocate*, among others. His essays and fiction have appeared several collections, including the Lambda Award-winning *The Man I Might Become*. He was a Burton Fellow at Harvard Divinity School where he earned a Master of Divinity. His book *Disciples of the Street: The Promise of a Hip Hop Church* (Seabury Books) was published in 2008.

eloise klein healy is poet-in-residence at the Idyllwild Summer Poetry Festival. She was founding chair of Antioch University's MFA in Creative Writing Program, cofounder of ECO-ARTS, an eco-tourism/arts venture, and founding editor of ARKTOI, an imprint of Red Hen Press. Her latest collection is *The Islands Project: Poems For Sappho*.

daniel hurewitz is a professor and historian and, most recently, a parent. His latest book, *Bohemian Los Angeles and the Making of Modern Politics* (2007), discusses the cultural roots of American gay politics. He has also written a book about New York's gay history and is currently living in that city, where he teaches at Hunter College.

For more than a quarter of a century, award-winning artist/activist michael kearns has been a force in the world of art and politics. "Three Scenes From a Hollywood Life" is excerpted from his memoir-in-progress, *Drawing Blood*.

Actor/writer/producer jack larson started his career as a young actor at Warner Brothers. He became famous in the 1950s as "Jimmy Olsen" on TV's *Superman*. He wrote the libretto for Virgil Thompson's opera *Lord Byron*. He and his longtime partner, writer-director James Bridges, collaborated on many films, including *Paper Chase*, *Urban Cowboy*, and *China Syndrome*. The L.A. native lives in Brentwood in a beautiful hilltop Frank Lloyd Wright house with "Dewy," his beloved white German shepherd.

viet le (MFA, University of California-Irvine) is an artist, writer, and curator whose artwork has been exhibited nationally and internationally. He has received fellowships from the Fulbright Foundation and PEN Center USA. A doctoral candidate at the University of Southern California, Le recently curated the performance event *Miss Saigon with the Wind* at Highways Performance Space in Santa Monica; the visual art shows *humor us* at Los Angeles Municipal Art Gallery; and *Charlie Don't Surf!* at Centre A in Vancouver. He's currently cocurating the internationally traveling exhibition transPOP: Korea Viet Nam Remix.

ty lieberman lives in Sherman Oaks, California. He's still writing screenplays, looking for another needle in his ~~gaystack~~ haystack. And he still hates paying for parking.

dan luckenbill is retired from the UCLA Library's Department of Special Collections. A UCLA graduate, he was commissioned as an artillery officer in the U.S. Army and served a year-and-a-half in Viet Nam. He studied writing with Christopher Isherwood, John Rechy, Elisabeth Nonas, and Terry Wolverton. His first fiction was published in *Gay Sunshine* and *Gay Literature* and was anthologized in the first men's "gay liberation" anthology, *On the Line*. His recent fiction has appeared in volumes edited by Alex Buchman, *A Night in the Barracks*, *Barracks Bad Boys*, and *Battle Buddies*.

Hailed for its humor and passion, tim miller's solo performance work has delighted and emboldened audiences all over the world. He is the author of the books *Shirts & Skin* and *Body Blows*. His *1001 Beds*, an anthology of his performances and essays, won the 2007 Lambda Literary Award. He is the cofounder of Performance Space 122 in New York City and Highways Performance Space in Santa Monica. He can be reached at http://hometown.aol.com/millertale/ or www.myspace.com/timmillerqueerperformer.

karen marie christa minns is a Gemini lesbian working artist and educator, with GLASS, Inc.—and proud of it! Between novels, she does social work with disenfranchised youth. Her latest novel is *Bloodsong*.

brad taylor negron's early success came in stand-up comedy, which quickly led to an appearance on the *Tonight Show* and an HBO special. Many motion picture roles have followed, including *Punchline* with Sally Field and Tom Hanks and the Disney classics *Angels in the Outfield* and *Stuart Little*, though he's most recognizable as the Pizza Man in *Fast Times at Ridgemont High*. Taylor's essays can be found on Hilary Carlip's freshyarn.com as well as Arianna Huffington's news outlet 236.com, where he writes a humor column. His Web site is www.taylornegron.com.

torie osborn is author of *Coming Home to America*, and former executive director of the Los Angeles Gay and Lesbian Center, the National Gay and Lesbian Task Force, and the Liberty Hill Foundation. She serves as senior advisor to Los Angeles Mayor Antonio R. Villaraigosa.

ed pierce received his BA in French literature from Yale, his MAT in English from Brown, and his JD degree from Harvard. Upon receiving his law degree, Ed moved to Los Angeles, where he practiced business law for twenty years. From 1997 to 1999, he was vice president of legal affairs and general counsel for GeoCities. He serves on the national board of directors of the Gay, Lesbian and Straight Education Network (GLSEN) and on the board of advisors of the David Bohnett Foundation. He lives in Los Angeles with his longtime partner, Rob Saltzman.

robin podolsky is a writer, scholar, and political flak who lives and works in Los Angeles.

christopher angel ramírez is a Latino digital artist with an MFA in digital arts and new media. As an artist, he is invested in creating spaces of social belonging where others witness a multiplicity of voices. Christopher engages his time and energy with a life-work project involving queer Latino men, "Color Bonita." His next project deals with women and incarceration. Christopher has been featured at three consecutive Outfests. He works in the writing program at the University of California, Merced. Connect with him at www.colorbonita.com.

daryl keith roach's acting credits include *The Bacchae*, for which he was a 2007 Ovation Award nominee; the title role in *Hercules on Normandy*; and *Master Harold and the Boys* at South Coast Rep, for which he was awarded the Dramalogue Award for

Best Actor. He's been on *Seinfeld, Cheers,* and *The Practice,* among many other television shows, and he appeared in such films as *Pee-wee's Big Adventure* and *Crocodile Dundee in L.A.* In 2004, he developed a nonprofit organization called "*MUSICaids. . . . . life thru music,*" which provides funds for HIV/AIDS research. Through concert events and workshops, *MUSICaids* combines the healing power of music and strength of community to produce results through edu-tainment. The Web site is www.musicaids.org.

eva s. is a fifteen-year-old, mixed-race lesbian who is out and proud and wants to make all queer teens safe. Eva is leaving foster care to begin a new life in an adopted family. Her latest work was produced in West Hollywood, at Plummer Park, in a spoken word performance, under the directorship of Ms. Joyce Lee.

mark thompson spent twenty years as a journalist and senior editor at *The Advocate.* He is the author of five books and many essays on gay history and culture, including the widely acclaimed trilogy *Gay Spirit, Gay Soul,* and *Gay Body.* His reflection on coming out during the 1970s in San Francisco was included in *Love, Castro Street.* Most recently, Mark has been touring an exhibition of his photographs of noted gay artists and spiritual leaders, "Fellow Travelers: Liberation Portraits." He lives in Los Angeles with his life partner, Malcolm Boyd.

"'Black Opera Gloves' is a memoir based in fact, but a few names and details have been changed," says stuart timmons, who writes fiction as well as history and journalism, most often about Los Angeles and gay politics. A UCLA graduate in film, he wrote *The Trouble With Harry Hay: Founder of the Modern Gay Movement,* a biography of one of the city's most influential radicals. More recently he wrote (with Lillian Faderman) *Gay L.A.: A History of*

Sexual Outlaws, Power Politics and Lipstick Lesbians, which covers local gay life from 1880 to 2005 and won two Lambda Literary Awards. He was also awarded the Monette–Horwitz Award for his LGBT scholarship.

patricia nell warren is the author of the best-selling gay novel *The Front Runner*. Her most recent book is nonfiction, *The Lavender Locker Room*, about the history of GLBT athletes. Warren has been involved in women's rights battles, as well as Internet free speech cases that went to the U.S. Supreme Court. In recent years she has become active in politics, assisting with Democratic Party fund-raising and serving as commissioner of education in the Los Angeles Unified School District. Many prestigious awards have come her way, including the Barry Goldwater Award, the New York City Public Advocate Award, and the Independent Publisher Gold Medal. Wildcat Press is her own independent publishing imprint, with its Web site at www.wildcatpress.com. Her personal page, with posted editorials and articles, is www.patricianellwarren.com.

winston wilde is a sexologist and psychotherapist in private practice in Beverly Hills. He is the surviving lover of gay American writer Paul Monette.

john morgan wilson is a veteran journalist, author, and TV documentary writer. He's perhaps best known for his Benjamin Justice mystery novels, which have won the Edgar Award from Mystery Writers of America and three Lambda Literary Awards. He lives in West Hollywood.

terry wolverton is author of six books: *Embers*, a novel-in-poems; *Insurgent Muse: Life and Art at the Woman's Building*, a memoir; *Bailey's Beads*, a novel; and three collections of poetry:

Black Slip, *Mystery Bruise*, and *Shadow and Praise*. She has also edited fourteen literary anthologies, including (with Robert Drake) the award-winning series *His* and *Hers*. She is the founder of Writers at Work, a creative writing center in Los Angeles, where she teaches fiction, creative nonfiction, and poetry.